Andrew Stuart Bergerson, K. Scott Baker,
Clancy Martin, Steve Ostovich

The Happy Burden of History

Interdisciplinary German Cultural Studies

Edited by
Scott Denham · Irene Kacandes
Jonathan Petropoulos

Volume 9

De Gruyter

Andrew Stuart Bergerson, K. Scott Baker,
Clancy Martin, Steve Ostovich

The Happy Burden of History

From Sovereign Impunity
to Responsible Selfhood

De Gruyter

ISBN 978-3-11-048597-4
e-ISBN 978-3-11-024637-7
ISSN 1861-8030

Library of Congress Cataloging-in-Publication Data

The happy burden of history : from sovereign impunity to responsible selfhood /
by Andrew Stuart Bergerson ... [et al.].
    p. cm. -- (Interdisciplinary German cultural studies ; 9)
Includes bibliographical references.
ISBN 978-3-11-024636-0 (acid-free paper)
1. Germany--History--1933-1945--Historiography. 2. National socialism-
-Historiography. 3. Germany--History--1933-1945--Biography. 4. Germany-
-Moral conditions--History--20th century. 5. Genocide--Germany--History-
-20th century. 6. Impunity--Germany--History--20th century. 7. Collective
memory--Germany. 8. Self--Social aspects--Germany. 9. Responsibility--Social
aspects--Germany. 10. Social change--Germany. I. Bergerson, Andrew Stuart.
DD256.48.H37 2011
943.086072--dc22

                                                                    2010050344

Bibliographic information published by the Deutsche Nationalbibliothek
The Deutsche Nationalbibliothek lists this publication in the Deutsche Nationalbibliografie;
detailed bibliographic data are available in the Internet at http://dnb.d-nb.de.

Cover image: L. Mikelle Standbridge, *Sisyphus*, 2008. www.standbridge.net

Printing: Hubert & Co. GmbH & Co. KG, Göttingen

∞ Printed on acid-free paper

Printed in Germany

www.degruyter.com

Contents

List of Illustrations

About This Book

We should admit to some things up front. This book is unruly. The "introduction" and "conclusion" break with generic expectations for an academic monograph. The analysis also transgresses the conventions of our disciplines. Like most academics we have been trained to exclude those questions from the scope of our investigations that do not fit our disciplinary paradigms. It is precisely the questions that fall between the cracks, however, that concern us in this book. This kind of work is often described as *interdisciplinary*, but it would be better to describe this book as *integrative* as we have tried to develop a coherent approach to a problem—responsible selfhood—that is inherently incoherent. We justify this epistemological juggling act because it fits how we operate in everyday life.

You may be interested in knowing who we mean by "we." Often we are referring to the four authors of this book. It would be rather hypocritical of us if we were to write a book about historical responsibility and ignore our own. We also play the role of ethnographers at times and participate in our own study. So we should tell you a little more about us. For the most part, we have lived a privileged life. Our families immigrated from Europe in the late nineteenth and early twentieth centuries. Steve was born in the 1950s in Wisconsin. Clancy, Drew, and Scott were born in the 1960s in Ontario, New York, and Oregon. We are all now professors with tenure. Steve currently holds a position at the College of St. Scholastica in Duluth, Minnesota; the rest of us are at the University of Missouri-Kansas City.

Politically we are inclined more or less to the Left and philosophically towards existentialism. Drew comes to these postures through Judaism; the others more or less through Christianity. Steve even toyed for a while with a career in the clergy. We are all men and heterosexual for the most part; we are all currently married with children, though not all for the first time. We share a similar kind of intelligence, which made writing this book easier. We identify with liminality and try to act as allies for those who are less fortunate.

At times, we use "we" in the much broader terms of philosophers and theologians, who tend to speak in terms of human beings in general. And yet this universal "we" is never far removed from the particular contexts of the Third Reich. We are not saying that our German informants are representative in a statistical sense of all of humanity. We are also not trying to suggest that Germans are unique or uniquely prone to historical irresponsibility.

Rather we are saying that there is something to be learned about selfhood and responsibility from the extreme nature of the historical situation in which Germans found themselves during the Third Reich. This case is also useful to us as academics because the debate on historical responsibility in Germany has already developed to sophistication.

Yet that claim does not really clarify the situation either, insofar as we four authors actually inhabit an ambiguous position inside and outside of our study group. We have spent many years in Germany and have established lasting relationships there. This book stands in a long tradition of vibrant transatlantic dialogue regarding German culture and history. It would be a mistake to ignore our deep appreciation for Germany as well as the contributions we have made to German Studies just because we were not born into German citizenship or families. One of our points about selfhood is that we are a *bricolage*.

So please do not read this book as yet another accusation by Americans of how the Germans have failed to come to terms with the Nazi past—what the Germans call *Vergangenheitsbewältigung*. If we are not quite Germans, we are still Germanists, which means that we must look critically at ourselves. We do so in this book in terms of our academic traditions because it is the world in which we are most intimately involved, but we could easily have focused on other aspects of our past and present. Even as North Americans, however, the Third Reich is very much about who we are too. The Nazi past challenges our notions of responsible selfhood no matter who "we" are.

In the end, we come to this project as German scholars who have devoted the bulk of our lives to seeking answers to German questions. These are the sources and the setting in which we live. So for instance, Drew has spent many years conducting research into the history of everyday life in Hildesheim, a mid-sized provincial town in north-central Germany. A detailed description of his oral history research method can be found in his 1998 dissertation, "A History of Neighborliness," and 2004 book, *Ordinary Germans in Extraordinary Times*. From the larger set of 38 interview partners, Drew chose ten to serve as informants for our study. Their pseudonyms are: Theodora Algermissen, Ruth Busche, Jürgen Ludewig, Sarah Meyer, Gerhard Mock, Reinhard Oetteling, Martha Paul, Günther Seidner, Hartmut Teufel, and Thilly Tappe. Drew selected them because of the ways in which their particular life stories raise interesting questions about selfhood or responsibility. If you pushed us to identify a protagonist to our story, it would probably be Theodora. Drew's first interview partner from Hildesheim, she stands out because of the way she raised the issue of responsible selfhood herself.

Hans F., who appears in the chapter on Lies, is neither a pseudonym nor a Hildesheimer. Hans taught with Drew's mother at a private school in New York; Drew interviewed him in 1989. As the reader will discover, however, the interview process did not end in 1989, or in the case of the Hildesheimers, with Drew's return to the States in December 1994. Ethnographic research involves returning to the material, the place, and the people repeatedly over time. This book is the latest stage in that long-term process of critical engagement.

Clancy, Scott, and Steve decided which German philosophers, playwrights, and political theologians respectively should be included in this study based on the degree to which these literati addressed our concerns about responsible selfhood. Like Bertolt Brecht, Friedrich Nietzsche, or Johann Baptist Metz, their biographies or reception were often intertwined with the Third Reich, which allowed us to bridge the gap between theory and practice. In other cases, like Albert Camus and Simone de Beauvoir, we included people who were not German *per se* but whose lives and letters were so implicated in the Third Reich that they, too, must be counted as participants in this German question.

We know that there are many other examples that we could, and perhaps should, have addressed in this study. Ours is ultimately a rather small sample. Encouraging you, our readers, to apply insights gained from these cases more widely is the whole point of this exercise. We look forward to your responses.

The reader may also be interested in how four people did the actual work of co-authoring a monograph. Drew brought us together gradually through a series of conference panels and attempted articles. He met Steve in December 1998 at a workshop hosted by Alon Confino and Peter Fritzsche on "The Work of Memory" at the University of Illinois at Urbana-Champaign. He met Clancy in 2003 at UMKC when Clancy first joined the Philosophy Faculty. Clancy, Drew, and Steve began their work with the problem of self-deception. Drew invited Scott to participate in a panel for the German Studies Association in 2006 in the context of expanding the project to irony. It was at this point that we first outlined the larger book project including chapters on Non-Conformity and Myths. We now suspect that we should have included a chapter on humor as well, but the book seems long enough as it is.

As we presented our individual papers at academic conferences and workshops, we discovered many similar patterns in the lives and letters of ordinary and intellectual Germans. The process of integrating these themes into coherent chapters involved clarifying terms which held specific meanings in different disciplines; moving evidence to follow the line of argumentation rather than disciplinary focus; adapting arguments gleaned from one author to draw out new insights from the evidence of the others; and many rounds of revisions guided by the detailed advice from the series editors at de Gruyter, led by Irene Kacandes.

The plot of our argument emerged first in the chapter on Lies. While compiling Irony, Drew noticed that it began to fall into roughly the same logic. Steve drafted Non-Conformity with this interpretive structure in mind.

We discovered the overarching themes of responsible selfhood and sovereign impunity relatively late in the game. Much of this criticism can be found in the chapter on Myths and in The Finish. These chapters were drafted in a more traditional way by Drew and revised by the team thereafter.

We accrued many debts in writing this book. Drew's interviews were funded by the Friedrich Weinhagen Stiftung in Hildesheim. At the University of Missouri-Kansas City, support was provided by the Bernardin Haskell Fund, the University of Missouri Research Board, the Dean of the College of Arts & Sciences, the Faculty Center for Excellence in Teaching, the Office of Research, the School of Graduate Studies as well as the Departments of History, Philosophy, and Foreign Languages & Literatures. At the College of St. Scholastica, financial support was provided by the Philosophy Department, the School of Arts and Letters, its Dean, and the Faculty Development Committee. Additional funding was provided by Cornell University.

Much of the material discussed here has been presented as lectures at Kansas State University, St. John's University in Collegeville, Santa Monica College, and the University of Michigan; at annual conferences of the Association for Integrative Studies, the German Studies Association, the Midwest Modern Language Association, the New Directions in the Humanities Conference, and the Trans-Missouri German Studies Symposium; and in our courses.

Elements from or versions of these chapters have appeared in print. Some of the material from Non-Conformity and Irony appeared in Bergerson, "Eigensinn, Ethik und das nationalsozialistische *Reformatio vitae," Sehnsucht nach Nähe: Interpersonale Kommunikation in Deutschland seit dem 19. Jahrhundert*, hrsg. Moritz Föllmer, 127-56 (Stuttgart: Franz Steiner Verlag, 2004) and in Baker, "Bertolt Brecht and the Insufficiency of Irony," *Brecht Yearbook* 34 (2009): 206-24. Material about Hamann and Nietzsche have appeared in Martin, "Hamann on Reason, Self-Knowledge, and Irony," *Socrates: Reason or Unreason as the Foundation of European Identity*, ed. Ann Ward (Cambridge: Cambridge Scholars Press, 2007) and *"Mundus Vult Decipi*, or, The Pleasure of Being Duped," *International Studies in Philosophy* 39/3 (2009).

We would like to thank Mikelle Standbridge and Todd Wade for their photographs; James Bell for his early collaboration on the idea; Katrin Dalitz for her help with the interviews; Broadway Cafe in Kansas City for their hospitality; Joanne Brownstein for her sage advice; Kevin Baker, Dustin Stalnaker, and Manuel Vaulont for their help with copyediting; and Drew's interview partners for sharing their stories.

The manuscript benefitted greatly from the suggestions of friends and colleagues: Alan Berkowitz, Jacques Cukierkorn, Susan Feagin, Sven Felix Kellerhoff, Elissa Mailänder Koslov, Alf Lüdtke, Maria Mitchell, Sandra Ott, Larson Powell, and Paul Steege. We are deeply indebted to Scott Denham,

Irene Kacandes, and Jonathan Petropoulos, the series editors at de Gruyter, for their close critical readings of our manuscript. Above all we would like to thank our wives and children for supporting us over the many years. In so many ways they made this project possible. We dedicate this book to them—in love.

August 2010   Kansas City/Duluth

Myths

It is during that return, that pause, that Sisyphus interests me.
— Albert Camus, *The Myth of Sisyphus*, 1942

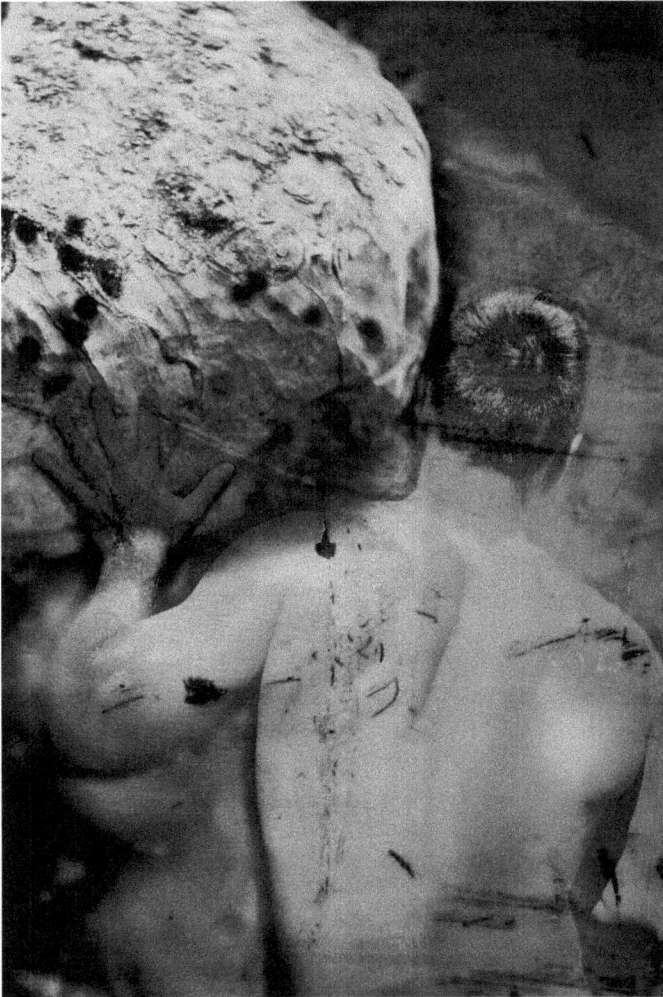

Figure 1. L. Mikelle Standbridge, *Sisyphus*, 2008.

Selfhood and Responsibility

Do you remember Sisyphus? He was the poor guy in Greek mythology whose fate was to push a boulder up a hill only to watch it roll down and then to have to push it up again—over and over, condemned to do so for *eternity*. He is a symbol of meaninglessness in our culture. But what more can be said about him? What more is his story telling us? And how was it that he ended up in this condition anyway?

Ambiguity characterizes the life story of Sisyphus. He was the king of Corinth, but it is unclear whether he founded the city or received it as a gift. He proved with clever creativity that Autolycus was a cattle thief, but used the commotion of the confrontation between the victims and the thief to seduce Autolycus's daughter. When the Oracle told Sisyphus that his offspring by a niece would aid him in his fight with his brother, Sisyphus seduced and impregnated her. When she learned why he had seduced her, she killed their children—and he killed her in turn. Contemporary Greek sources lauded him for promoting commerce and sea travel but also claimed that he was fraudulent, greedy, and disreputable. Yet none of these actions earned him his boulder.[1]

In his classic essay, "The Myth of Sisyphus,"[2] Albert Camus, the twentieth-century French existentialist, offers a reading of Sisyphus that we find helpful to make sense of these ambiguities. To Camus, Sisyphus demonstrated "a certain levity in regards to the gods." More specifically, "he stole their secrets." Camus tells the story like this: Aegina was the daughter of Aesophus, a god. When she was carried off by none other than Jupiter, Aesophus was shocked, and complained to Sisyphus. Sisyphus, who knew of the abduction, "offered to tell about it on condition that Aesophus would give water to the citadel of Corinth."[3] In other words, Sisyphus tried to leverage a god.

At first, the gods gave Sisyphus a relatively mild sentence for his hubris, and they were quick to parole him when asked; they allowed him to return from the underworld to life. After all, his underlying motive seemed to be humane in that he used his ingenuity to try to improve the lives of the people of Corinth. Another explanation is that he once again tricked the gods into allowing his release.[4] Camus identifies the seeming contradictions in Sisyphus's character. "If one believes Homer," Camus writes, "Sisyphus was the wisest and most prudent of mortals. According to another tradition," Camus

---

1   Robert Graves, *Greek Mythology*, vol. 1 (New York: Penguin Books, 1960), 216-220.
2   Albert Camus, "The Myth of Sisyphus," in *The Myth of Sisyphus and Other Essays* (New York: Vintage International Ed., 1991), 88-91.
3   Camus, "Myth," 88.
4   Graves, "Sisyphus," 217-218.

continues, "he was disposed to practice the profession of highwayman. I see no contradiction in this."[5]

Neither do we. In fact we see in it a rather productive way to think about selfhood and responsibility—the subject of this book. The challenges of everyday life can require the creative solutions of the bandit. Ordinary people often develop a sophisticated set of strategies to negotiate the contradictions and demands of modern living. Being clever does not in itself discourage responsibility; there is a certain wisdom in piracy.

Still, viewing the life of Sisyphus from both a divine and human perspective can raise some disruptive questions. On the one hand, making demands of a god does not seem to us to be a sober or circumspect act. On the other hand, if banditry is wise, it is a short step to begin to wonder if the gods made the right decision in condemning Sisyphus at all. Do the gods have the right to pass judgment on human behavior? In thinking about Sisyphus, we find ourselves wondering if the gods can ever fully appreciate the nature of our responsibilities as human beings to ourselves and others.

This humanism is arguably Camus's point of departure. He uses irony to get us to identify with Sisyphus as the protagonist of this story: even the ancient Greeks understood his name to mean "very wise."[6] As a philosopher, Camus wants us to begin to think for ourselves—and to do so in existential terms. Sisyphus anticipates the wisdom that Camus wants us to discover in this fable: that responsibility is best measured on a human scale and investigated through human stories.

This book concerns responsible selfhood in complicated human situations. It is an effort to understand how we act in everyday life to become who we are and the impact of those strategies of *self-cultivation* on ourselves and others. Myths are useful as a way to ground our investigation of selfhood because myths inform our histories and biographies—that is, the way we tell the stories of our "selves." Like Camus, we discover our responsibility while moving between the way we tell the stories of our lives and how we live them.

Sovereign Impunity

If we are more like Sisyphus than we like to admit, then we should take care to figure out what he got wrong and what he got right. Sisyphus, the philosopher thief, claimed that he was thinking first and foremost of how he could help others. His behavior suggests the exact opposite: that he was asserting what we call *sovereign impunity*.

---

5   Camus, "Myth," 88.
6   Graves, "Sisyphus," 219.

At its most basic, *sovereignty* is a claim to individual autonomy. For German princes after the Treaties of Westphalia that ended the Thirty Years War in 1648, being recognized as sovereign meant that they could sign treaties with and fight wars against other princes, the Holy Roman Emperor, or even the Pope. In modern international law, the sovereignty of states places governments on an equal footing with one another as autonomous legal entities.

Sovereign immunity, by contrast, refers to a particular perk that sets the government apart from the ordinary citizen—the legal nicety that the Crown cannot be sued for grievances.[7] Heads of state are often *de facto* insulated from criminal prosecution insofar as the laws they obey are the laws they have written. To be sure, many modern democracies build into their constitutions the ability to remove a sovereign who is caught breaking the law—for instance, through impeachment. Yet removal from office does not always lead to criminal prosecution thanks to the vagaries of politics.

Sovereignty sets princes equal to one another but in positions of autonomous mastery over their subjects. Popular parlance tells us a lot about how we think about these privileges of sovereignty. When individuals kill, they are tried for murder; but when states kill, we call it politics. Whether by divine right or simply inheritance, princes assert the right of command over their subjects. Through such tools of state as armies, police, law, and religion, they can determine life and death for ordinary people.

In republican forms of government, sovereign power is supposed to derive not from the gods but from the people. Citizenship promises us that ultimate authority is in our hands by the fact that we can remove our leaders from office. Even in modern democracies, however, we often presume that our government has to have the authority to act while it is still in office if it is to be effective. So for us moderns too, violent claims to mastery seem to be required for the defense of autonomy.

We give our rulers this considerable degree of freedom from everyday ethical obligations on the assumption that they are acting in our interests. Yet experience tells us otherwise. As a framework of *Realpolitik*, or the pursuit of power in the name of state interest, the luxury of being above the law as head of state all too often becomes an excuse for external aggression and internal oppression. Political philosophers and scientists have long debated the problem of how to constrain state authority when heads of state use their power against their own citizens and then use their office to insulate themselves from accountability.[8]

---

7   Richard Falk, "Revisiting Westphalia, Discovering Post-Westphalia," *The Journal of Ethics* 6/4 (2002): 311-352; Don Mayer, "Sovereign Immunity and the Moral Community," *Business Ethics Quarterly* 2/4 (October, 1992): 411-434.
8   E.g., "Algeria: Truth and Justice Obscured by the Shadow of Impunity," *Amnesty Inter-*

Modern genocides put these principles into question because the presumed immunity of the head of state from prosecution seems to leave open the door for the exercise of violence with impunity even against non-combatants. This loophole was one of the reasons why the antifascist coalition that defeated Adolf Hitler in 1945 put the political leaders of the Third Reich on trial for crimes against peace, war crimes, and crimes against humanity. They wanted to set a precedent, however fragile, for holding heads of state accountable to written international laws and universal codes of ethical behavior.[9]

Modern individualism shares many of the same attributes of sovereignty. We presume that we are most responsible when we are capable of autonomous action. Modern political theorists like Thomas Hobbes, John Locke, and Jean-Jacques Rousseau even argued that the sovereignty of the state flows from the sovereignty that individuals exercise over their own lives.[10] Also like the early modern prince, the modern individual is defined in terms of its domination over its conditions of existence such as the natural world, everyday life, and other human beings. We tend to recognize "who we are" in terms of the things we make, earn, or buy; the mountains we climb and storms we weather; and the position of status and power we presume we deserve by our merit. Modern society legitimizes this ordinary kind of sovereign impunity in the way we imagine and cultivate a self.

So our play on words has a substantive point. More than just *immunity* from legal consequences, sovereign *impunity* presumes an arrogant disregard for any form of accountability for the violence involved in becoming who we are. In our everyday lives we find ourselves asserting the right not just to cultivate a self immune to all constraints, divine or human, but doing so without concern for the people who get hurt in the process. Here lies a paradox of modern selfhood. Grounding responsibility in autonomous selfhood enables the very sovereign impunity we find irresponsible.

Self-Cultivation

Did Sisyphus act responsibly? No doubt, had we asked him, he would have said that he was acting in the interests of the people of Corinth—for instance when he negotiated water for the city in exchange for tattling on Jupiter. We

---

national, 8 November 2000, <http://www.amnesty.org/en/library/info/MDE28/014/2000/en>, downloaded November 2008.

9   Michael Marrus, *The Nuremberg War Crimes Trial, 1945-1946: A Documentary History* (Boston: St. Martin's Press, 1997).

10 Thomas Hobbes, *Leviathan*, introd. Herbert W. Schneider (Indianapolis: The Liberal Arts Press, 1958); John Locke, *Second Treatise of Government*, ed. C. B. Macpherson (Indianapolis: Hackett, 1980); Jean-Jacques Rousseau, *The Social Contract*, trans. Maurice Cranston (London: Penguin Books, 1968).

suspect that he was using these kinds of situations to cultivate an image of himself as capable of standing up to the gods. He clearly liked to imagine that he could mock Olympus with impunity.

To us his heroic persona betrays considerable selfishness. Sisyphus seemed only superficially concerned in the fate of Aegina and the suffering of her father; he took an interest in this crime solely as an opportunity for self-assertion. Similarly absent from his consideration seemed to be whether the people of Corinth wanted Sisyphus to appeal to the gods on their behalf. Might the gods have responded to his hubris by punishing the Corinthians too? Sisyphus is silent on this matter. We doubt if he thought at all about the possible consequences of his actions for others.

It is important to Camus's reading of this myth that, for most of his tale, Sisyphus remained woefully unreflective about his own self-deceptions. Sisyphus even thought he could master death itself. Trying to avoid his own punishment, Sisyphus put Death in chains. Unfortunately for everyone else, his hubris left the dead walking among the living, unable to find their proper place in the underworld. Pluto had to free Hades from his jailor just to put things back in order.[11]

Camus also depicts Sisyphus as a bit of a macho. Just before death he tested his wife's love. "He ordered her to cast his unburied body into the middle of the public square."[12] When he woke up in perdition he felt betrayed, as if *his* fate had been sealed by *her*.[13] In the hell of divine condemnation, Sisyphus, like many unreformed criminals, continued to deceive himself that he was the wronged victim of his story rather than its tragic protagonist. Here we see the full depths of his addiction to sovereign impunity. He acted as if he were accountable to no one for the consequences of his own behavior.

In other words, Sisyphus spent most of his earthly life as an impunity junkie. He insisted that he was above the law, and his stubborn disobedience only got worse with every new crime. His posturing remained rather consistent throughout his life. It was this continuity in his self-cultivation that allowed him to imagine that he was a coherent, autonomous, heroic individual, standing up to the gods in the name of human needs and human freedom.

By *self-cultivation* we mean the many behaviors that contribute to identity, the responses to situations that shape the kind of person we become, and the stories we tell about this development of selfhood. We chose Sisyphus as the main figure of this chapter because he is the archetype of a person who cultivated a self with impunity. Even when there were good outcomes,

---

11 Camus, "Myth," 88; Graves, "Sisyphus," 217.
12 Camus, "Myth," 88.
13 Graves describes it as a trick by Sisyphus to circumvent death ("Sisyphus," 217-218). It makes sense to us that he was doing a little of both.

Sisyphus was acting irresponsibly. The only way he was able to ignore the contradictions between what he claimed he was doing and the consequences of his actions was to deceive himself, emphatically, that he was immune from the judgment of higher authorities as well as obligations to his fellow human beings.

We also tell the story of the life of Sisyphus here for the same reason they retold it in ancient Greece. It is only in the human framework of everyday life that we can discover the nature of responsibility. What the history of Sisyphus shows is that human beings are the progenitors of their own myths. To commit even his small act of hubris with Aesophus required that Sisyphus ignore how both the Olympians and the Corinthians might react to his deeds. The lies, the myth making, and the storytelling began the moment that Sisyphus convinced himself that he was clever enough to get away with it.

Historical Responsibility

In this book we investigate everyday strategies of self-cultivation in order to discover how to apply them responsibly. Following Camus, we are convinced that developing an adequate answer to this question is necessary to living a good human life. Also like Camus, we believe that identifying the criteria of responsibility cannot be accomplished in abstraction from our historical condition.

Unfortunately we have been encouraged in the Western cultural tradition since Plato to try to understand our condition in the world by taking ourselves out of our changing circumstances, and moving to a level of abstract thought where we can pin things down "at last." Modern reason is even more concerned with mastering our concepts, and through them the world in which we live, including ourselves. Rene Descartes took a crucial first step in his famous dictum, "I think therefore I am." It authorized human beings not only to master the natural world through thinking but to ground truth in thought. He reinforced a tendency towards impunity when he further qualified "methodological" thinking in terms of skepticism, limiting ourselves to those ideas that we have—i. e. he has—determined to be "clear and distinct."[14] Our conviction is very different: that we are historical beings who exist under particular, concrete conditions.[15] To us responsibility is not a matter of abstracting ourselves from history in a quest for control. It depends instead on how we respond to our ever-changing conditions.

---

14 Rene Descartes, *Discourse on Method and Meditations on First Philosophy*, trans. Donald A. Cress, 4th ed. (Indianapolis: Hackett, 1998).

15 See Hannah Arendt, *The Human Condition*, 2nd ed. (Chicago: University of Chicago Press, 1998).

The guiding question of this book might be framed as: *what does it mean to be responsible in history?* Our responses are, of course, informed in part by intellectual traditions, cultural norms, and many other inherited factors. Historical contingencies are one reason why philosophers like to remove themselves from everyday conditions which seem to undermine our ability to derive universal principles. By contrast, we situate ourselves as philosophers in the ambiguous position within history precisely because acting responsibly requires attention to the conceptual, ethical, and even physical frameworks of the situations confronting us. By saying that these inherited ideas impact our behavior is not to prioritize or authorize them to continue to do so; it is to recognize the role that they play in our lives so that we can make well considered choices for what we wish to do with them.

The four of us share an interest in modern Germany that makes our inquiry both specific and complicated. For us, the question of historical responsibility always leads us back to the issue: *what does it mean to be responsible for Nazi crimes?* This question has plagued and inspired decades of German scholarship. Nazi crimes, especially the Holocaust, were so monstrous a set of events as to defy human understanding—they make German history into *an unmasterable past*, in the phrase of Charles Maier.[16]

Historians have troubled over how to relate the Third Reich to the rest of modern German history. If, because of its moral enormity, we insist on the abnormality of genocide, are we not making it inexplicable as the product of human deeds? If, however, we make genocide into simply another event in German history, are we really taking seriously its moral enormity?[17] Legal categories and methods for determining responsibility fail. Even the lines demarcating perpetrators, victims, and witnesses break down in this context. This situation is exacerbated as the generation of those who experienced the Third Reich passes away and as a third postwar generation begins to question whether they too should bear the burden of the Nazi past.

The meaning of responsibility in light of the Third Reich is neither a purely academic question nor a question for Germans only. The Holocaust is the paradigmatic case of a system of mass destruction that absurdly drew victims, resisters, and perpetrators into its deadly logic of irresponsibility.[18]

---

16 Charles Maier, *The Unmasterable Past: History, Holocaust and German National Identity* (Cambridge: Harvard University Press, 1988); s. a. Saul Friedlander, *Probing the Limits of Representation: Nazism and the "Final Solution"* (Cambridge: Harvard University Press, 1992).

17 For a discussion of these issues by a liberal defender of the Enlightenment, see Jürgen Habermas, *The New Conservatism: Cultural Criticism and the Historians' Debate*, trans. Shierry Weber Nicholsen (Cambridge: The MIT Press, 1989); and Habermas, *A Berlin Republic: Writings on Germany*, trans. Steven Rendall (Lincoln: University of Nebraska Press, 1997).

18 Zygmunt Bauman, *Modernity and The Holocaust* (Ithaca: Cornell University Press 1989);

For historians, this book may offer new insight into the "ontological" origins of this problem, in that we link dynamics in genocidal societies to analogous ones within the operation of selfhood. Modern German histories, as well as the histories of many other modern societies, are filled with examples of such dynamics. We can neither escape nor let go of the Holocaust because these potentialities are still with us.

This persistence challenges our sense of responsibility. Genocide, starvation, oppression, exploitation, prejudice, dehumanization—we want no part in them ourselves and want to find ways to prevent them from happening to others. If our conversations with our students and the wider public are any measure, you share these intentions. There are spoilers, of course, who actually prefer to use violence to solve problems;[19] they are obviously not our audience for a book on historical responsibility. The problem is that most of us struggle to figure out what we can do in order *not* to get drawn into these systems of violence, and we often find ourselves lacking adequate answers.

Exercising responsibility in history is a seemingly overwhelming task, as any German could attest. It is as if we are caught in a condition where being responsible in the present requires us to take responsibility for the past as well. But how can we do this? Unable to restore life to those killed by terror or genocide, how can we ever render justice to them? This situation makes us doubt that their demands can ever be satisfied. If, however, we cannot take responsibility for the past, how can we ever hope to act responsibly in the present? What can any one of us actually do to stop the violence?

Our Approach

Greek myths present us with two different models for thinking through the problem of responsible selfhood. On the one hand, we have Prometheus whose crime of hubris leaves him passive: chained to a rock, a victim of buzzards who daily peck out his liver. On the other hand, we have Sisyphus who was condemned to spend eternity rolling a boulder up a hill. We are drawn to Sisyphus because his rock is his task and not just his condition.

The labor of Sisyphus involves not only struggling to move the rock up the slope but also to watch it roll back down and have to begin his work over and over again. His tale reminds us that our rock of responsibility is always waiting for us. It cannot be avoided. Neither can we delude ourselves that we will ever succeed in keeping it in its place—that is, in the past.

Lawrence L. Langer, *Versions of Survival: The Holocaust and the Human Spirit* (Albany: State University of New York Press, 1982).

19 Stephen John Stedman, "Spoiler Problems in Peace Processes," *International Security* 22/2 (1997): 5-53.

The labors of Sisyphus capture the Germans' struggle to deal with the Nazi past, or *Vergangenheitsbewältigung*. We use the German Sisyphus as a figure for our work to understand the nature of historical responsibility. Camus tells us:

> The gods had condemned Sisyphus to ceaselessly rolling a rock to the top of a mountain, whence the stone would fall back of its own weight. They had thought with some reason that there is no more dreadful punishment than futile and hopeless labor.

Dealing with the Nazi past can certainly feel like a futile and hopeless labor. And yet Camus finishes his essay ironically. He demands of the reader: "One must imagine Sisyphus happy."[20] How was this possible for Camus's Sisyphus? How could it be possible for the German Sisyphus? And what can it possibly mean for us as a model for cultivating a historically responsible self?

Before we go any further in exploring these questions, a word of warning from Camus. "Myths are made for the imagination to breathe life into them."[21] Myths encourage subversive reinterpretations by the reader. So it is only fitting that a chapter on myths has its own non-conformist logic. It is not your typical introduction; but then again Germans probably did not top your list of successful models of historical responsibility either. The Third Reich has cast its pall over Germany and German Studies for decades; it is next to impossible to laud successes in light of so many failures. This chapter is more akin to a political fairy tale. In it, we read historical facts through a mythic text to winnow out of the complex history of German memory a model for an on-going engagement with the Nazi past. The pay-off, we hope, will be a better understanding of how to cultivate a responsible self.

Our approach is existential. Academic readers tend to expect analyses that emphasize the beginnings and endings of stories. Scholars are trained to use introductory and concluding chapters to abstract truth claims out of everyday details. A chapter about myths has to be more self-critical. We offer you no Archimedean point before, above, or beyond everyday life from which to observe it in safety. We need to provide you with some background to the events in our story that you may or may not already know. We do so, however, in the recognition that we are all embedded in a story already in progress.

---

20 Camus, "Myth," 88, 91.
21 Camus, "Myth," 89.

Myths of the Self

We have inherited from the Enlightenment and Romanticism mythic constructions of the self as a *heroic individual*. Built into our respective academic disciplines of historical, literary, philosophical, and theological criticism, the tropes of the historical subject are not simply *master narratives*: that is, overarching tropes that frame the ways in which individual stories are told, based on the perspective of the powerful.[22] They are also *narratives of mastery*. To be a historical subject is to exercise the authority of a heroic individual over oneself, others, and one's circumstances.

These narratives of mastery contributed to the political tragedies of the twentieth century by legitimizing particularly violent modes of being, behaving, and believing. Here we are criticizing the specific case of the Aryan *Übermensch*, or superior type of human being, who served as the protagonist in both the Nazi revolution and its genocidal war to conquer *Lebensraum*, or living space. We also see the cultivation of mastery operating across the political spectrum in much of modern German lives and letters.

In many respects, we are reasserting a familiar postmodern critique of modern reason. This critique perceives reason to be infected by violence thanks to the way it seeks to eliminate difference.[23] To be rationally responsible is to master a situation in a quest for a kind of control that seeks to eradicate whatever resists mastering in its stubborn otherness. In the story we will now tell, we want to draw your attention to how the violence of mastery is built into the way we understand what it means to do history and live historically.

Progress

The nineteenth century was characterized by attempts to render history as an academic discipline "scientific."[24] This professionalization was accomplished in two major ways. In the *historicist* approach, history was defined as an empirical science reliant on a critical method to uncover the facts of the past the way it "actually was." The historian was responsible for integrating these facts into coherent, meaningful, and allegedly objective narratives. In the *hermeneutic*

22　Konrad H. Jarausch and Michael Geyer, *Shattered Past: Reconstructing German Histories* (Princeton: Princeton University Press, 2002).

23　Herculine Barbin, *Being the Recently Discovered Memoirs of a Nineteenth-Century French Hermaphrodite*, introd. Michel Foucault, trans. Richard McDougall (New York: Pantheon Books, 1980); Foucault, *Discipline and Punish: The Birth of the Prison*, trans. Alan Sheridan (New York: Vintage Books, 1977); Foucault, *Madness and Civilization: A History of Insanity in the Age of Reason* (New York: Vintage Books, 1988).

24　Joyce Appleby, Lynn Hunt, and Margaret Jacob, *Telling the Truth about History* (New York: W. W. Norton, 1995).

approach, the historian was charged with interpreting the past, but in terms of an underlying purpose accomplished through supra-historical forces at work in events. In the German context, the former is associated with the school of Leopold von Ranke; the latter with G. W. F. Hegel.

On either basis the work of history shared the characteristic faith of all nineteenth-century science—a belief in progress.[25] Human action in history took on meaning as it contributed to this progress either directly or through (self-)sacrifice for a higher goal. One was encouraged to take the long view of events, abstracting from what had happened and was happening, in order to locate the purpose of history in its endings.

You might wonder where this belief in historical progress and direction came from. The answer to this question is delayed rather than clarified by pointing to the history of science. Karl Löwith, more helpfully, identified the belief in historical progress as a secularized form of *eschatology*, the end expectation characteristic of Western religions.[26] What historical rationality does—and it shares this trait with many aspects of modern reason—is place a religious belief under rational control.

Notice the violence associated with this hope. Apocalyptic literature reveals the world as a battleground in the cosmic conflict between good/light and evil/darkness. Believers hold onto their faith at all costs in order to see the end of this conflict in the coming of the reign of God. On Judgment Day, evil will be eliminated and only the good will remain. Eschatological hope is violent not just in its adoration of this cosmic conflict as the means to a better end but also by holding out the historical end of history as an elimination of difference so that only the same—the saved—remain. History itself testifies to this violence as numerous millenarian movements sought, and continue to seek, to institute their vision of utopia in history and bring about the exclusive reign of their god.

Modern philosophers have tried to deal with this violence in the same way they have dealt with other aspects of religious beliefs: by bringing them under the control of reason. Hope in this interpretation is not really about millenarian violence or utopian intervention, but has been tamed by being tied to progress, a concept that can be measured empirically or at least rationally assessed somehow. Though framed in terms of reason, the violence inherent in this utopianism has neither been eliminated nor even brought under control, as actual events in the last two centuries have shown. The violence has at best gone underground in our telling of history. We use progress

---

25   Friedrich Nietzsche, *On the Genealogy of Morals* in *On the Genealogy of Morals and Ecce Homo*, trans. Walter Kaufmann and R. J. Hollingdale, ed. Kaufmann (NY: Vintage Books, 1989), 148-159.

26   Karl Löwith, *Meaning in History* (Chicago: University of Chicago Press, 1949).

towards the envisioned goal of history not only to make sense of historical existence but also to justify the violent sacrifice of some for the future benefit of others. The myths of historical progress incubate and legitimate our claims to sovereign impunity.[27]

The disturbing part here is that it is not just something that happens to us: we also do it to ourselves. Self-cultivation is intimately related to self-disciplining. Are we not willing to make sacrifices even up to and including our own lives for the benefit of those who come after us? Do we not presume that these kinds of sacrifices are a good thing? Yet what happens to those we sacrifice for these goals? And what happens to us in the process?

Modern rationality allows the belief that what is good in me or for me is also good for all others. Many of the examples we will examine in this book demonstrate our willingness to degrade others in order to rationalize sacrificing them for a higher goal. How do we know when we have crossed a line and abandoned our humanity, our common decency, our responsibility?

In our scientific rendering of history, we have a tendency to ignore these questions so that we can concentrate our attention on progress. Belief in progress becomes our justification for violent sacrifice in the moment. In retrospect this belief further encourages us to forget the dead, to forget those who have been or must be sacrificed in the name of progress towards a blessed future. In this way, history writing itself becomes less about remembering and more of an exercise in violent forgetting.

Systems of Violence

Responsibility begins with the recognition of violence. We are not referring to the random kind of violence that is part and parcel of any human society. We are talking first of all about systems of violence: where the power to do harm in one instance is vastly multiplied by the relatedness of this act to analogous acts at other times and places. A good example would be ritualized forms of antisemitic violence.[28]

We are also referring to those kinds of systems of violence that solicit our aid, as perpetrators and victims, in those processes of destruction. Think, for instance, of the head of the Jewish council who agreed to ship trainloads of Jews to Auschwitz to try to save the rest.[29] Is he a victim, a collaborator, or a perpetrator? Is the conscience of the resistance fighter any cleaner? The

---

27 E. g., see Stefan Berger, *The Search for Normality: National Identity and Historical Consciousness in Germany since 1800* (New York: Berghahn Books, 2007), ch. 2, esp. 26-32.

28 Helmut Walser Smith, *The Butcher's Tale: Murder and Antisemitism in a German Town* (New York: Norton, 2002).

29 Primo Levi, *The Drowned and the Saved*, trans. Raymond Rosenthal (New York: Vintage International, 1989), 62-67.

Germans paid back the death of any German soldier with the murder of civilians at a ratio of 50, 100, or even 200 to 1.[30] Were they fighting against this system of violence or did they become part of it? Or consider the Jewish woman who made the reasonable decision to flee Nazi Germany: is she a survivor or a collaborator? Did she not concede the point to Hitler that Jews and Germans cannot live together in peace? Did she not help make Germany *judenrein*—"purified" of Jews?

Our point in making these uncomfortable comparisons is not to blame the victims for their own victimization. What we want to emphasize is how fascism ensnares its victims in absurd paradoxes. These systems leave ordinary people with what one scholar called "choiceless choices": no matter how one responds to genocide, one only seems to accelerate its deadly cycles of violence.[31]

This book does not concern collective political strategies. Modern German intellectuals and politicians were rather active in theorizing and practicing many of them: mass mobilization, agitprop, and resistance as well as terror, social engineering, and genocidal war. Scholars have been studying these modes of collective action for some time and think they understand them rather well. Some of these are critical to understanding and preventing genocides in the present; others seem to us to be suspiciously violent in their logic.

In this book we are interested in the contributions of ordinary individuals to these systems of violence—in everyday life, when they are not protected or directed by the group, when they must make decisions on their own, and when they are at their most vulnerable. Responsibility as we see it begins in *selfhood* itself, in our ways of being and making "us." Selfhood is an ordinary part of our daily lives, so it is in the dynamics of everyday life that we look for responsibility.

We should also add that, to us, the ardent Nazis who undermined democracy and built fascism in Germany are the necessary but insufficient condition of this study. Our interest lies instead with the many who lived in this terrorist society and seemed to be co-opted in its crimes. The German version of fascism from the 1930s and 1940s set new precedents for humankind's ability to be inhuman. It provided such extreme situations that even banal actions of everyday citizens seemed to demonstrate an acceptance of violence. Yet Nazis, their collaborators, their sympathizers, and even their passive "bystanders" did not represent a circumscribed population that acquiesced to violence in any simple way. The process of becoming an Aryan involved *changing the self.*

---

30   Doris L. Bergen, *War and Genocide: A Concise History of the Holocaust* (New York: Rowman & Littlefield, 2003), 143.

31   Langer, *Survival*, 67-129 at 72; s. a. Bauman, *Modernity*.

And yet it is the relationship between selfhood and violence that is still not adequately understood.

Modern ideologies across the political spectrum disguise assumptions of violence in utopian promises of human liberation.[32] If we draw particular attention to the fascist and racist Right in this book, we are not suggesting that we should withhold our criticism from the Left, whose self-righteous categories of enlightenment have led just as readily to violence; or from the Center, whose assumptions about normalcy have served as surprisingly effective means of destroying human beings with impunity. Our criticism is directed more generally at modern ways of being, believing, and behaving; our point is that they excuse all sorts of violence. These actions serve our narcissistic desire to break the constraints of everyday life not just for personal liberation but in order to act with impunity.

The Self

The violence we wish to interrogate begins with us. We are looking for modes of selfhood without mastery. Responsibility, we argue, stems not from a coherent self abstracted from history or bound to the progress of history towards some utopia, but ironically from a fragmentary self riven by ambiguities, contingencies, deceptions, doubts, humilities, parodies, and skepticisms.

Western notions of selfhood tend to be "outside in," beginning with a theory of the self and applying it to lived experiences. Our approach is "inside out," building our theory of selfhood and responsibility by looking at how actual selves are lived, experienced, and remembered. We are particularly interested in the choices made in concrete historical circumstances that expose both the influences on persons and their intentions at an existential level. People have a working definition of the self; decisions made in the moment provide the points at which this definition opens itself up to ambiguities and challenges. This study turns on those responses which give shape to both our selfhood and our responsibility.

We also take *the self* here quite literally: the four of us cannot avoid self-scrutiny as human beings, as world citizens, as authors, and as academics. Many of the modes of cultivating the self that frustrate us the most are in fact the myths on which our respective disciplines were founded. Let us revisit that story as a way to open ourselves to criticism. It begins way back

---

32 The Socialist Unity Party in East Germany was a tragic example. See Paul Steege, *Black Market, Cold War: Everyday Life in Berlin, 1946-1949* (Cambridge: Cambridge University Press, 2007); and Mark Landsman, *Dictatorship and Demand: The Politics of Consumerism in East Germany* (Cambridge: Harvard University Press, 2005).

in Western civilization, but it can be abbreviated best by returning to the end of the eighteenth and beginning of the nineteenth centuries.

This transitional period witnessed the popularization of a new kind of self defined as an *individual*. We have our doubts about the Romantic genius who struggles in a sublime mode for creative self-expression and liberty against overwhelming forces.[33] We are also skeptical of the universal rationality of the Enlightenment individual who passes objective judgments over the world as a member of a rather exclusive republic of letters.[34] In both, the cultivation of a modern self requires a degree of mastery on the part of the historical subject over his object, be it the natural world, other human beings, or himself.

The archetype of the heroic individual is fundamental to the modern world. Whether pursuing his own interests or cultivating his personality through the use of reason or intuition, this self is first and foremost *autonomous*—released from the web of mutual rights and responsibilities that had conditioned Western civilization for centuries. And it is *heroic* in that this individual is carving out a place for the self in the world of volition and with a quest-like sense of orientation towards some grand goal at the end. That both the Enlightenment and Romanticism imagined this heroic individual as male goes without saying, but it does not preclude the intended universality of their claims.

For all his autonomy and courage, the heroic individual is plagued by self-doubt. For centuries Westerners had imagined that their actions could and would be measured ethically on the basis of transcendental laws authorized by God. Imagine the anxiety felt by the promoters of human liberty when they decided that it was more ethical to question those traditions and base their behavior instead on their reason, genius, or happiness. German intellectuals from Hegel to Martin Buber shared this concern over the loss of ethical standards once the pursuit of self-interest and self-cultivation became the dominant habits of the emergent civil society.[35]

Hegel sought to restore an ethical substance to the self by synthesizing these two modern traditions of Enlightenment and Romanticism. At the cornerstone of his solution lay history. His philosophy sublimated the heroic individual into larger, putatively ethical, collective subjects—families, states, and ultimately the spirit of freedom itself. They allegedly became ethical through

---

33 Friedrich Schlegel, *Philosophical Fragments*, trans. Peter Firchow (Minneapolis: The University of Minnesota Press, 1991).

34 Immanuel Kant, *Critique of Pure Reason*, trans. Paul Guyer and Allen Wood (Cambridge: Cambridge University Press, 1999).

35 Martin Buber, *I and Thou*, trans. Walter Kaufmann (New York: Charles Scribner's Sons, 1970); G. W. F. Hegel, *Phenomenology of Spirit*, trans. A. V. Miller (Oxford: Oxford University Press, 1977); Hegel, *Elements of a Philosophy of Right*, ed. Allen W. Wood, trans. H. B. Nisbet (Cambridge: Cambridge University Press, 1991).

historical processes, though these utopias of enlightenment and freedom can never in fact be realized. Such claims to mastery only thinly disguised a terrible violence. Hegel here was harkening back to Rousseau:

> Whoever refuses to obey the General Will shall be compelled to do so by the whole body. This means nothing less than that *he will be forced to be free*.[36]

Those who stood on the side of history were judged wise by the wise. Those who did not became collateral damage.

By the start of the twentieth century, these dialectical games ensured the terrible majesty of patriarchal families, capitalist markets, nation states, classes, and races. Different historical subjects subordinated human beings to different masters depending on their politics. Yet across the boards, heroic individuals planned, led, volunteered for, and suffered under grand projects of social engineering orchestrated by and for these historical subjects to remake everyday life into a utopia. Only after many decades—after many millions were murdered and many more were wounded bodily and spiritually—did we begin to suspect that, in these historical experiments, the laboratory technician was also the guinea pig.

Academic Traditions

Our academic disciplines are implicated in this problem because of the way we have adopted and propagated modern myths of what it means to be an authentic and responsible self. The academic study of religion is a good example; it also makes good historical sense to begin with theology since the other disciplines developed out of it.

Christians for centuries studied religion for its own sake and accepted it as true beliefs about an external reality. In the wake of Hegel, the philosopher Ludwig Feuerbach argued that religious belief was nothing more than the "projection" of human needs. This argument became popular among other critics of religion such as Karl Marx and Sigmund Freud.[37] As we grow increasingly able to meet these needs ourselves—that is, as we master more of reality—religious beliefs allegedly become neither needed nor rational.

To be sure, nineteenth-century German theologians tried to defend the possibility of religious belief. Friedrich Schleiermacher and Rudolph Otto provided an experiential grounding for it in the feeling of absolute dependence or

---

36 Rousseau, *Social Contract*, bk. 1, ch. 7, our emphasis.
37 Ludwig Feuerbach, *The Essence of Christianity*, trans. George Eliot (New York: Harper, 1957); Sigmund Freud, *The Future of an Illusion*, trans. and ed. James Strachey (New York: W. W. Norton, 1989); Karl Marx, "Contribution to the Critique of Hegel's Phenomenology of Right: Introduction," *The Marx-Engels Reader*, 2nd ed., ed. Robert C. Tucker (Princeton: Princeton University Press, 1978), 53-65.

the encounter with the Holy, respectively. Yet once again, religious beliefs were being treated as needing rational grounding rather than providing a model for living—or for responsibility—themselves.[38] Søren Kierkegaard resisted this dismissal of religious belief, but the price he paid for doing so was being labeled "irrational."[39] As God is by definition beyond the control of the heroic self, belief in God becomes an unreasonable option or is at best considered a private idiosyncrasy. The possibility that a political theology might have something critical to say about selfhood is ruled out in advance.

German letters in the nineteenth century institutionalized the heroic individual in the *Bildungsroman*, or the novel of self-cultivation. Initially developed by J. W. Goethe in *Wilhelm Meister's Apprenticeship* in 1795-96 as the journey of a young man toward true self-knowledge, the orthodox literary canon perpetuated the representation of a coherent, knowable subjectivity. The focus on the (typically male) protagonist encouraged the individual to subordinate the unruliness of the world, acknowledging and incorporating qualities that empower him as an agent while discounting challenges to his capacity to act heroically.[40] The form of the novel displayed this coherent self, triumphing over the historical world, in an ideological manner that suited the dominant groups of the nineteenth century.[41]

The same could not be said of drama. We will have a lot to say about theater in this study because we see the performance of roles on the stage of art as an excellent way to think about how the self operates on the stage of life. Yet the resuscitated dramatic tradition at the end of the nineteenth century portrayed the opposite motif. In this period, the plays of German Naturalism tended to present the incapacity of the protagonist to control his world and his submission to social forces. Still, neither the *Bildungsroman* nor the drama questioned the frequently violent acts undertaken to preserve the heroic self in response to social pressures.

Historians also lionized violence as the best way for historical subjects to promote the progress of history. Over the course of the nineteenth century, the speakers of various German dialects began to imagine their membership within a singular nation, one that needed a state to correspond to it. The *great*

---

38 Friedrich Schleiermacher, *On Religion: Speeches to Its Cultured Despisers,* trans. John Oman (New York: Harper, 1958); Rudolf Otto, *The Idea of the Holy*, trans. John W. Harvey, 2nd ed. (London: Oxford University Press, 1950).

39 Søren Kierkegaard, *Concluding Unscientific Postscript to Philosophical Fragments*, vol. 1, trans. and ed. Howard V. Hong and Edna H. Hong, *Kierkegaard Writings*, vol. XII (Princeton: Princeton University Press, 1992).

40 Johann Wolfgang von Goethe, *Wilhelm Meister's Apprenticeship*, trans. Thomas Carlyle (New York: Heritage Press, 1959); Heinz Schlaffer, *The Bourgeois as Hero*, trans. James Lynn (Lanham: Rowman & Littlefield, 1990).

41 Georg Lukacs, *The Theory of the Novel: A Historico-Philosophical Essay on the Forms of the Great Epic Literature*, trans. Anne Bostock (Cambridge: The MIT Press, 1977).

man of history arose in this context, his self-interest coinciding, as if by magic, with the needs of the human spirit for progress toward freedom. German historians played a particularly noxious role in canonizing this secular creed. It was Ranke and Heinrich von Treitschke who convinced Germans that history is the story of states and nations, and that it was sweet and fitting to die for one's country.[42] Fascism emerged out of this intellectual heritage during and after the First World War; the radical Right responded to the humiliation of defeat with ever more violent forms of mobilization and sacrifice.

The same period engendered a Left Hegelianism with similar calls for sacrifice. Marx replaced Hegel's collective historical subjects with a bourgeoisie and a proletariat that became the new bearers of history.[43] Socialists convinced the bulk of German laborers as well as sympathetic students and intellectuals that only a violent seizure of power, leading to a dictatorship of the proletariat, could force historical progress toward human freedom. Communism emerged out of this intellectual heritage; the First World War split the labor movement into social democrats who sought reform through parliamentary compromise and a radical Left who insisted on revolutionary violence.

These intellectuals ensured that nineteenth-century myths about historical subjects were firmly embedded in Western political culture in the twentieth: on the Left, in the dialectics of critical theory; in the Center, in the invisible hands of civil society; and on the Right, in illiberal categories of nations and races. Although never actually achievable, the totalizing dystopias of modernity legitimized a disproportionate amount of violence in striving to realize their goals: during the policy stage, when movements or regimes actually tried to remake self and society to fit these abstract ideals; in the testing stage, when the straightjackets of revolutionary abstractions for self and society were given their first human subject trials;[44] and already during the conceptual stage, when self and society were first imagined according to fantastic plans. It is here that academics did the most damage. We validated historical development with the authority of science. The moment we framed our human subjects according to these definitions, we encouraged sacrificial violence.

---

42 Berger, *Search for Normality*; J. W. Burrow, *The Crisis of Reason: European Thought, 1848-1914* (New Haven: Yale University Press, 2000), 124-136; George Mosse, *The Nationalization of the Masses: Political Symbolism and Mass Movements in Germany from the Napoleonic Wars through the Third Reich* (New York: Fertig, 1975); the expression at the end comes from Wilfred Owen's 1917 poem, "Dolce et Decorum Est" in *Poems* (Whitefish, Montana: Kessinger, ca. 2004), 14; and ultimately from Horace, *Odes and Epodes*, ed. by Paul Shorey, in the University of Michigan Digital General Collection (January 2006), bk. III, ode ii, ln. 13.

43 Marx and Friedrich Engels, *The Communist Manifesto*, ed. John E. Toews (London: St. Martin, 1999).

44 Helmut Lethen, "The Subject in the Danger Zone," *Telos* 144 (2008): 75-81.

Given the major role played by German intellectuals in manufacturing many of these myths about heroic individualism, it is not surprising that German history itself was implicated in the process. Historians speak of both positive and negative *Sonderwege*: the assumptions, popular at different times and among different populations, that the German *Volk* took a special path and played a unique role in history, either as heroes or as villains.

Only in recent decades have German historians begun to systematically rethink our disciplinary assumptions about historical subjects. Some scholars today no longer believe that the stories of individual Germans can be so easily subsumed into the developmental histories of nations, states, and societies; Germans are far too unruly to be comfortably inserted into the old master narratives. Their memories chide us into recognizing the opposite: that ordinary Germans shaped, and also shattered, those histories and historical subjects in everyday life.[45]

It is worth reminding ourselves that the history of hubris, self-deception, and impunity in modern Germany begins not in 1945, or even 1933, but well before 1914. The Germans repeatedly tried to overcome the trauma of betrayal, dishonor, and death with more self-deceptions, more sacrifice, more destruction, more murder—until, as Paul Celan put it, death itself became "a master from Germany."[46] Here we are thinking of the many German politicians from across the political spectrum who took calculated yet unrealistic risks in their pursuit of domestic and world power; who advocated policies that cynically calculated an unacceptable degree of violence; and who welcomed the chance to contain, undermine, or overthrow democracy.

Germans too often claimed the sovereign right to ignore the human consequences of their actions. During the imperial conquests of territories between 1871 and 1918, both outside Europe and within it, they deceived themselves into believing that they could murder and oppress with sovereign impunity. The Treaty of Versailles punished them for these crimes, but condemnation did not lead to rehabilitation. They almost universally considered themselves unfairly chastised and betrayed by those they had trusted. In the interwar years, the German Sisyphus continued to insist on his right to act as if the laws of gods and man did not apply to him.[47]

---

45 Compare David Blackbourn and Geoff Eley, *The Peculiarities of German History: Bourgeois Society and Politics in 19th century Germany* (Oxford: Oxford University Press, 1984); Jarausch and Geyer, *Shattered Past*; Jürgen Kocka, "Asymmetrical Historical Comparison: The Case of the German Sonderweg," *History and Theory* 38/1 (1999): 40-50; and Maier, *Unmasterable Past*.

46 Paul Celan, *Todesfuge*. Komm. Theo Buck, 2. Auflage (Aachen: Rimbaud, 2002), our translation.

47 Michael Burleigh, *The Third Reich: A New History* (New York: Hill and Wang, 2000); Fritz Fischer, *Germany's Aims in the First World War*, trans. James Joll (London: Chatto & Windus, 1967); Peter Fritzsche, *Life and Death in the Third Reich* (Cambridge: Harvard

These are neither the only German histories that have Sisyphean qualities, nor are we trying to put this account forward as a putative, new master
narrative for German history. Narratives of mastery are the problem. They are
the myths ordinary Germans told themselves to cultivate sovereign impunity.
The origin of German crimes is to be found not just in the inhuman policies of German regimes, or even in the civil societies that failed to rein these
regimes in.[48] The real, though often hidden, source for danger lay in how
ordinary Germans anticipated violent public policies in their personal strategies of selfhood.

The incarnation of Sisyphus we are discussing here is a negative model
of irresponsibility. His decisions are motivated by the pursuit of selfhood
through control. He opportunistically claims credit when good things come
of his actions while he assigns the bad consequences of his own actions to
others or to forces beyond human control. We reject this type of Sisyphus
because he compounds his callously destructive behavior with more violence
in order to forestall critical self-reflection about responsibility.

This cycle of violence and irresponsibility is thus a cause of National
Socialism as well as its consequence. The German Sisyphus made political
violence part of everyday life the moment he coordinated (gleichgeschaltet) his
everyday behavior to the principles and policies of a terrorist movement.[49]
Misreading Nietzsche's Übermensch, the Aryan cultivated his sovereign impunity through a genocidal war for Lebensraum. The Nazi regime sought to
overcome the memory of vain sacrifice and betrayal by controlling Death; and
in Nazi-dominated Europe, the dead walked among the living. Yet it was the
German Sisyphus himself who created that "master from Germany" by allowing his own lies to master him.

To be sure, these lies survived the collapse of the Nazi regime. The German Sisyphus was able to imagine himself the victim after 1945, in part

---

University Press, 2008); Imanuel Geiss, *July 1914: The Outbreak of the First World War:
Selected Documents* (New York: Scribner, 1968). Holger H. Herwig, *The First World War:
Germany and Austria-Hungary, 1914-1918* (London: Arnold, 1997); Isabel V. Hull, *Absolute
Destruction: Military Culture and the Practices of War in Imperial Germany* (Ithaca: Cornell
University Press, 2005); Lars-Broder Keil and Sven Felix Kellerhoff, *Deutsche Legenden: Vom
"Dolchstoß" und anderen Mythen der Geschichte* (Berlin: Ch. Links, 2002); Vejas Gabriel Li-
ulevicius, *War Land on the Eastern Front: Culture, National Identity and German Occupation
in World War I* (Cambridge: Cambridge University Press, 2004); Klaus Theweleit, *Male Fantasies* (Minneapolis: University of Minnesota Press, 1987); Michael Wildt, *Volksgemeinschaft
als Selbstermächtigung: Gewalt gegen Juden in der deutschen Provinz 1919 bis 1939* (Hamburg:
Hamburger Ed., 2007).

48 Hull, *Absolute Destruction*.
49 Bergerson, *Ordinary Germans in Extraordinary Times: the Nazi Revolution in Hildesheim*
(Bloomington: Indiana University Press, 2004); Fritzsche, *Life and Death*: and Robert
Gellateley, *The Gestapo and German Society: Enforcing Racial Policy, 1933-1945* (Oxford:
Clarendon Press, 1990).

because the United States and the Soviet Union, fighting a new Cold War, paroled him. He had bound himself so closely to these various systems of destruction that it became impossible to extricate his experiences from that history of violence after the fact. Yet our point is that the lies, myth making, and storytelling all began in *anticipation* of violence: as a self-deception that allowed the German Sisyphus to believe his own press and encouraged him to act with impunity.

Our Challenge

For critics at the end of the twentieth century, the Nazi regime and its geno-cidal war began to serve as an archetype for a different problem: what had gone wrong with modernity in general rather than a specific German strength or weakness. Given the role played by the myths of heroic individualism in total-izing movements like that of the Nazis, the postmodern challenge for scholars remains in squaring this circle: theorizing a kind of historical subject who is capable of agency without falling prey to the violence of utopias.

Said in another way, we "postmoderns" have demythologized the total-izing societies and heroic individuals of modernity. Yet that does not leave us much better than we were before. In a new millennium, we face ever more powerful and violent systems without the agency we used to command as royal subjects, religious souls, political citizens, or even the heroic individuals of modernity. We have not rediscovered ourselves as ordinary people respon-sible in the making, and unmaking, of our own violent history.

So long as we continue to adhere to the heroic individual as a founda-tion for selfhood, we leave ourselves ill prepared to act responsibly in the face of either modern or postmodern systems of violence. What we need is an unruly way to read modern German history against itself to prepare the way for responsible selfhood.

The German Sisyphus

One source of confusion here is that we take human beings at their word when they claim to have a coherent self under their command. Historians, for instance, tend to label people as victims, bystanders, or perpetrators;[50] or try to determine, once and for all, if a given German was a real Nazi or just a

---

50 Daniel Jonah Goldhagen, *Hitler's Willing Executioners: Ordinary Germans and the Holocaust* (New York: Alfred A. Knopf, 1996); Martin Broszat and Elke Fröhlich, eds., *Bayern in der NS-Zeit*, 6 vols. (Munich: Oldenbourg, 1977-1983); Raul Hilberg, *Perpetrators, Victims, Bystanders: The Jewish Catastrophe, 1933-1945* (New York: Aaron Asher Books, 1992).

collaborator. They treat the self as if it could be expressed as a simple identity like *a = b*. We presume a coherent self for at least two reasons. There is a sense of nostalgia for a non-fragmentary self, as if we had once been whole and that antediluvian self has now lost its coherence. There is also a contradiction between the whole self we think we want and the plural self that is the only kind we can have.[51] Either way, the myths of a coherent, cohesive individual dangerously oversimplify the way we think about selfhood in everyday life.

Human beings are compilations of multiple identities. We are necessarily composed of fragments by virtue of the fact that we act in a variety of different ways in a variety of different situations, and these manifold deeds engender identities as divergent as philosopher and thief. We see these fragments deriving from the *non-conformist* acts through which we cultivate those subjectivities, the *lies* that are an inherent part of living every day, and the *irony* used to negotiate those modern circumstances. In this book we devote a chapter to each of these closely related ways to cultivate a self.

Dipesh Chakrabarty called the inherent contradictions and varieties in modern subjectivities "the plural ways of being human," but he was thinking of the various ways that different kinds of people express the modern condition.[52] We see this plurality in the very nature of modern selfhood. Moreover, the self seems inscrutable to us in the particular and an easy excuse for dangerously homogenizing universalizations in the general. We talk instead about *selfhood* because it emphasizes process. Selfhood is best understood as an action rather than a condition. Ensuring pliability, the dynamism of selfhood enables us to survive the pressures and radical transformations of modernity—even though that means that selfhood can become a tool for impunity.

We also tend to forget that we are political animals, by which we mean that our selfhood depends on others. As moderns we are encouraged to define ourselves by separation and distinction. The Enlightenment gives us a transcendental concept of the self that is universally the same for everyone; the difference from which political subjectivity springs is occluded. Romanticism reacts against Enlightenment transcendental formalism in the name of uniqueness, something accessible to the individual as much through feeling as reason. Both want us to define ourselves in isolation from others. No wonder our ability to respond to others is so difficult to realize.

Ideological categories like classes, genders, or races are not better substitutes. If they recognize our inherent "species being"—Marx's way of saying

---

51 Dominic LaCapra draws the distinction between absence and loss or lack in the construction of the historical self; see "Revisiting the Historians' Debate: Mourning and Genocide," *History and Memory after Auschwitz* (Ithaca: Cornell University Press, 1998), 43-72.

52 Dipesh Chakrabarty, *Provincializing Europe: Postcolonial Thought and Historical Difference* (Princeton: Princeton University Press, 2000), 241.

that we are dependent on others for our selfhood[53]—they nonetheless subordinate the self to the collective. They do violence to that self while ironically undermining their own prospects for political victory. We need to look elsewhere to discover the means for cultivating a responsible self: to the actual interactions between people.

The Source of Meaning

Camus draws our attention to human relations and human actions in the way he tells the story of Sisyphus. He begins by reviewing the various versions of the myth, highlighting for the reader that these are in fact stories. "Opinions differ as to the reasons why he became the futile laborer of the underworld." Sisyphus is described as both "the wisest and most prudent of mortals" and as a "highwayman." Sisyphus is uppity. He defied the gods to bring water to Corinth, was annoyed by what he saw as the failure of his wife's love, so hated Death that he put it in chains, and refused to return to the underworld when called.[54]

Notice what Camus is doing here. He includes these many labels to get us to stop trying to determine once and for all who Sisyphus "is"; he wants to think about selfhood as a process rather than a state. He is not trying to explain why Sisyphus has been condemned to his rock. Camus is content to cite all these accounts equally rather than emphasizing the one he thinks is the best. In other words, Camus does not work in the manner we have come to expect from historians. He wants us to look at where Sisyphus is *now*—dead and in the underworld suffering the punishment of meaningless and eternal labor.

This shift from past to present is not an attempt to escape responsibility for the past or to deny cause-and-effect relationships in historical existence; after all, the metaphorical rock of the past is always there. Camus wants us to recognize our present condition as the place where we exercise responsibility. Sisyphus's condition will never change, which means it will always be meaningless in objective terms. And Sisyphus is aware of this absurdity—this awareness is what makes his condition tragic.

Reliance on a framework of meaning to give his resistance purpose is not an option for Sisyphus.[55] One source of meaning for Sisyphus, which he brings to the contemplation of his rock, has always been his will, his re-

---

53   Marx, "Economic and Philosophical Manuscripts of 1844," *Marx-Engels Reader*, 66-125 at 75.
54   Camus, "Myth," 88-89.
55   Richard Taylor, "The Meaning of Life," *Good and Evil* (Buffalo: Prometheus Books, 1984), 268.

volt, his *scorn* of the gods: "There is no fate that cannot be surmounted by scorn."[56] And yet, he is not yet responsible when he acts solely with resentment at his plight, since his framework of meaning is still being derived from the gods. The great transformation takes place when Sisyphus finally realizes that *he* is the only source of meaning and morality in his condition. Sisyphus begins the work of responsibility once he realizes that he and only he has the ability to respond to his circumstances. Camus makes it abundantly clear that there is no meaning in his situation for Sisyphus to *find*. Responsibility is rather a matter of what Sisyphus *does*.

Condemned to the underworld for a second time, Sisyphus abandons all metaphysical grounding to which he can appeal in making his decisions. Neither history nor the historical process can provide him with meaning for his labors. All he is left with is his decision. This situation does not mean that Sisyphus can allow himself to fall prey to relativism or subjectivism. That kind of radical nihilism is as politically dangerous as it is self-negating. It is what happened to Carl Schmitt, the brilliant legal scholar who put his political existentialism in the service of the Third Reich. Making decisions for their own sake, or *decisionism*, has led to dreadful irresponsibility in the past.[57]

Our point is that decisions can flow from our responsibility as well—that is, literally from our *response-ability*. It is the human place from which Sisyphus labors: from his *ability to respond* to his condition, to respond to the demands this condition places on him, particularly as these demands come from other people. Only human beings can give human labors meaning.

Slave Narratives

If the German Sisyphus is to learn wisdom, it must be through remembering German history neither as master narratives, nor even as the stories of German

---

56 Camus, "Myth," 90.
57 Carl Schmitt, *Political Theology: Four Chapters on the Concept of Sovereignty*, trans. George Schwab (Chicago: University of Chicago Press, 2005); Schmitt, *Political Theology II: The Myth of the Closure of Any Political Theology*, trans. Michael Hoelzel and Graham Wind (Cambridge: Polity Press, 2008); Jürgen Habermas, "The Horrors of Autonomy: Carl Schmitt in English," *The New Conservatism: Cultural Criticism and the Historians Debate*, trans. Shierry Weber Nicholsen (Cambridge: The MIT Press, 1989), 133, 137; Habermas, "Carl Schmitt and the Political Intellectual History of the Federal Republic," *A Berlin Republic: Writings on Germany*, trans. Steve Randall (Lincoln: University of Nebraska Press, 1997), 107-117; Richard Wolin, "Carl Schmitt, Political Existentialism, and the Total State," *The Terms of Cultural Criticism: The Frankfurt School, Existentialism, Poststructuralism* (New York: Columbia University Press, 1992), 83-104; Wolin, "Carl Schmitt: The Conservative Revolution and the Aesthetics of Horror," *Labyrinths: Explorations in the Critical History of Ideas* (Amherst: University of Massachusetts Press, 1995), 103-122; Steve Ostovich, "Carl Schmitt, Political Theology, and Eschatology," *KronoScope: Journal for the Study of Time* 7 (2007): 49-66.

mastery, but through attending to the many stories of his role in the making of those narratives of mastery. Here we are trying to insist on a role for *slave narratives* in opening the possibility for cultivating a more responsible self.

We are not thinking of Hegel's dialectic of master and slave[58] but the way our understanding of events changes when we view them from different perspectives—most notably, different positions on the spectrum of power and violence. Drawn from the history of African slavery in the United States, the concept of *slave narratives* can be read literally as the testimony of the oppressed. They provide a radically different perspective on historical events than the account we are accustomed to read from the masters. Insofar as *official histories* are often ideological, designed to support the ruling elite in the existing state of affairs, we are using slave narratives to refer to any alternate account that disrupts hegemonic narratives.[59] In the case of the Third Reich, these *dangerous memories*[60] do not always come from the victims; they can even come from perpetrators if their personal experiences contradict and challenge the ideological premises of the official discourse. "In the universe suddenly restored to its silence," Camus writes towards the end of his essay, "the myriad wondering little voices of the earth rise up."

Slave narratives are useful in writing more accurate histories. The history of everyday life, or *Alltagsgeschichte*, listens attentively to the silenced voices of ordinary people whose unruly deeds gave shape to German tragedies.[61] Slave narratives are also crucial if we are to understand the nature of responsibility in everyday life. Like Camus, we wish to focus on the details of what our protagonists are actually doing in everyday life. Both slave narratives and the

---

58 Hegel, *Phenomenology of Spirit*, 111-119.

59 Henry Louis Gates Jr., *The Signifying Monkey: A Theory of Afro-American Literary Criticism* (Oxford: Oxford University Press, 1988).

60 Walter Benjamin, "On the Concept of History," *Walter Benjamin: Selected Writings, vol. 4, 1938-1940*, trans. Edmund Jephcott and others, ed. Howard Eiland and Michael W. Jennings (Cambridge: Belknap Press of Harvard University Press, 2003), 389-400; Johann Baptist Metz, "The Future Seen from the Memory of Suffering: On the Dialectic of Progress," *Faith in History and Society*, trans. J. Matthew Ashley (New York: Herder and Herder, 2007), 97-113; Steve Ostovich, "Epilogue: Dangerous Memories," *The Work of Memory: New Directions in the Study of German Society and Culture*, ed. Alon Confino and Fritzsche (Urbana: University of Illinois Press, 2002), 239-256.

61 In *Search for Normality* (80-82), Berger calls for "a historiography which constantly dissolves and questions our notions of collective identity." In *Human Condition* (42-43), Arendt argues similarly: "The application of the law of large numbers and long periods to politics or history signifies nothing less than the willful obliteration of their very subject matter, and it is a hopeless enterprise to search for meaning in politics or significance in history when everything that is not everyday behavior or automatic trends has been ruled out as immaterial." Gabrielle M. Spiegel challenged historians to narrate "the multi-dimensional, semi-coherent, semi-articulate dynamics of practice" in her introduction to *Practicing History: New Directions in Historical Writing after the Linguistic Turn* (London: Routledge, 2005), 1-31 at 23.

story of Sisyphus insist that responsible action is possible because they draw our attention to our ability, even as slaves, to respond. Adapting Camus, this critical historical practice "echoes in the wild and limited universe of man. It teaches that all is not, has not been, exhausted."[62]

We are also interested in what happens to us—in terms of our selfhood—when we quiet the master's voice and hearken to the slave's. The problem facing the dispossessed and the marginalized is that their suffering does not fit comfortably into the official accounts of historical subjects. In listening attentively to their struggle, we draw attention to how they cultivate a self in contradictory and even absurd situations. Rather than taking the self as a stable foundation on which to base our scholarly account, selfhood itself takes center stage in our investigation.[63] Harkening to slave narratives allows us to treat selfhood as a process rather than a condition. Observing the cultivation of selfhood in turn allows us to think critically about the conditions for a responsible kind of selfhood.

The Nazi Past

We can apply this principle to the very challenging case of Nazi crimes against humanity. One of the great contributions of *Alltagsgeschichte* has been to insist that the German Sisyphus can begin to think about responsibility only after he has begun to recognize the contradictions in his own mythmaking. This story *about* German history is part and parcel of German history since 1945.

Even in the immediate postwar years, there were significant forays into new habits of remembering. Some examples include: the debates surrounding Celan's poem "Todesfuge"; the memorial services held at the graves of former slaves from the Netherlands in Ladelund by former masters from Germany; and the collaborative effort by a Lutheran Pastor and a Jewish-American do-nor to rebuild the destroyed *Michaeliskirche* in Hildesheim.[64] Still, these early efforts towards reconciliation were highly variable in terms of the degrees to which ordinary Germans were willing to take responsibility for the Nazi past.

Germans intensified the work of publicly dealing with the Nazi past after the works of Gruppe 47, the Auschwitz trials, the reception of the *Holocaust* miniseries, and the rise of *Alltagsgeschichte*. Recent German history is riddled

---

62 Camus, "Myth," 90-91.
63 Spiegel, *Practicing History*, 1-31; a point made by Dennis Sweeney in Bergerson, "Forum: Everyday Life in Nazi Germany," *German History* 27/4 (October): 560-579, esp. question 6.
64 John Felstiner, "Paul Celan's 'Todesfuge'," *Holocaust and Genocide Studies* 1/2 (1986): 249-264; *KZ-Gedenk- und Begegnungsstätte Ladelund*, <http://www.kz-gedenkstaette-ladelund.de/>, downloaded September 2007; Manfred Overesch, *Von Hildesheim in die USA: Christ und Jude im Dialog über den Wiederaufbau des Weltkulturerbes St. Michael, 1946-1949* (Hildesheim: Olms, 2004).

with debates about how the Nazi past should be remembered and represented. As in any political scandal, there is an element within the German public sphere that seems shocked when another controversy erupts, particularly when it relates to the disclosure of personal collaboration. Rather than some kind of exception to a putative political normalcy, however, we believe these many public debates mark a regular, and beneficial, cycle within the German public sphere.

Still, much of the popular and academic debate on German history and individual culpability remains within the categories of selfhood that we wish to dispel. There is a certain irony in the fact that historical, literary, philosophical, and theological criticism are on the surface so very concerned with explaining responsibility in such categories as causation, authorship, ethics, and sin. They tend to ignore the problem of historical responsibility in everyday life where it is most difficult to explain. Ordinary people living in many different inhuman states and regimes have insisted that their personal behavior did not contribute significantly to systems of mass destruction. Sometimes they go so far as to suggest that they did not fully appreciate the ethical dilemmas confronting them.

We reject the notion that this naiveté is ever really possible. The consummate skill with which ordinary people negotiate the stickiest situations in everyday life requires an astute appreciation of precisely these kinds of human consequences. Making claims to "not knowing"—the familiar archetype here being Germans during denazification procedures—are better understood as anticipatory self-deceptions designed to allow them to act with impunity in the future than assertions of fact in retrospect. In most cases ordinary people just insist that they themselves were not responsible for those tragedies.

Responsible Selfhood

In recent decades, however, a new cohort of Germans has embraced an ongoing postmodern engagement with the past. Typically they are driven by a powerful personal compulsion to correct a particular historical misrepresentation in the spirit of critical journalism or political activism. The ensuing debates often digress into a political blame game rather than the kind of humble introspection that we are advocating. The Nazi past is an easy trump card to play as retribution against one's political enemies.

Still, in the process of scrutinizing that past, some courageous voices refuse to allow any analytic closure on it. They keep these wounds "open" through manifold everyday habits: ranging from art, monuments, scholarship, and journalism to child-rearing, memorial services, public demonstrations, informal discourse, and narrative interviews. Fighting what seems like a rearguard battle, they shy away from forcing their fellow Germans to remember the past as they do, as much as they might wish it at times, because that mandatory remembrance would contradict their own wisdom about how to construct a historically responsible self.

How do we imagine these Germans acting in everyday life? They are all too aware of their self-deceptions when it comes to taking responsibility for the Nazi past or confronting the Nazi present—and yet they act anyway, out of a sense of indebtedness to the dead. They seek out alternatives to conformity neither out of resentment for the existing state of affairs nor in a realistic hope that they will be able to realize a better world; they do so because they must do something—and might end up doing something worth doing. If they inhabit a place on the margins of their society, they do so not to free themselves from responsibility but to free themselves for it. Like mythic archetypes, they model behavior instead of coercing it. What they insist upon is keeping the process of critical remembering alive in the German everyday as a culturally viable option for how we might live history responsibly.

In recognizing that some Germans are adopting postures in response to the Nazi past and present that are reminiscent of Sisyphus with his boulder, we are not naively ignoring the neo-fascist and other groups who challenge it. There are still far too many Germans who wish to close the door on the violent German past and even some who wish to revive it. Historical responsibility in this quantitative sense will remain an ongoing, uphill struggle.

Even for those who do find their way to an open engagement with the German past, we find compelling reasons not to slap them, or ourselves, on the back for a job well done. The myth of West German "success" in dealing with the Nazi past has mixed with analogous myths about "successful" reunification to legitimize the allegedly complete, and seemingly final, reentry of the Federal Republic into the comity of nations.[65] The German Sisyphus we have in mind would be the first to insist that we can never become so lax. Indeed, we have heard these criticisms firsthand.

Those dangers recognized, we would be remiss if we proceeded with our investigation of historically responsible forms of self-cultivation without recognizing those in postwar German society who have taken it upon themselves to radically transform their everyday habits. In the place of the dominant practices of historical hubris, we see courageous people insisting on an ongoing engagement with their past in the hopes of someday uncovering less violent alternatives to the dystopias of Germanic modernities. Their strategies of selfhood focus on what they can do pragmatically in the face of injustice rather than what heroic strides towards progress might be accomplished if

---

65   A point made by Dorothea Wierling at "Practices and Power in the Everyday Life of the Twentieth Century: Symposium in Honor of Alf Lüdtke," University of Michigan–Ann Arbor, November 9–10, 2007. S. a. Habermas, *Berlin Republic*.

only things were different. This proactive cohort of revisionist citizens set the tools of myth, self-deception, non-conformity, irony, and modeling to work on the Sisyphean task of taking responsibility for the human consequences of human actions.

Ours is an age of unprecedented inhumanity made possible by the systematic weaving of violence into the very fabric of everyday life. Not wishing to associate our strategies for selfhood with crimes against humanity, we find many ways to silence our dangerous memories of collaboration. Memory work becomes one such dead end when it uses authoritative texts to try to close off the meanings that the past has for the present. By contrast, the work of memory that we are espousing here allows the past to continue to challenge us to ask questions about our responsibility in order that we can better remember our ability to respond. Always a work in progress, *this humanistic melancholy closely approximates our hope for a historically responsible self.*[66]

The Sisyphus we see now—the Sisyphus at work, the Sisyphus half way up the mountain—is no longer deceiving himself that he is constrained unfairly by circumstances dictated to him by others. This Sisyphus also rejects the role he used to play: the heroic protagonist of myth who gives meaning to his existence by controlling the people and world around him. Neither a divine condemnation nor a future image of himself can provide meaning for his human condition. If he refuses to conform to the dictates of god and man, he now does so, ironically, by making the burden of his punishment his own.

In subsequent chapters, we will have more to say about treating responsibility as a burden. Welcoming responsibility as a duty can disguise subtle claims to sovereignty that can justify its own forms of impunity. Moreover, there are good reasons to question any confident prescription for responsible selfhood insofar as one of its defining features is skepticism about those kinds of certainties. Rather, we are reading the myth of Sisyphus ironically, as if Sisyphus is engaged in a responsible form of self-deception by refusing to conform to the dictates of the gods even as he does. We believe, as Camus does, that Sisyphus makes responsible use of his time in the underworld. This belief means that he appropriates each moment, each action of his eternal indenture, for human purposes. The expression of his freedom is the very weight of the boulder, the very severity of the task—of cultivating a self responsible for history.

One might think, from looking at him, that this German Sisyphus is suffering. He is rarely sarcastic and has only recently begun to laugh at his

---

66 Insofar as all responsibility involves an awareness of historical processes, our use of the term "historical responsibility" may seem redundant. We use it in the sense of "History": to emphasize the particular kinds of responsibilities that fall to ordinary people in view of historical events, great and small.

own past.[67] Yet Camus's eloquent description of Sisyphus's labors fits many a German Sisyphus as they struggle to cultivate historically responsible selves:

> One sees merely the whole effort of a body straining to raise the huge stone, to roll it and push it up a slope a hundred times over; one sees the face screwed up, the cheek tight against the stone, the shoulder bracing the clay-covered mass, the foot wedging it, the fresh start with arms outstretched, the wholly human security of two earth-clotted hands.[68]

In this description of Sisyphus on the slope, struggling with the boulder, we find the most compelling metaphor for the kind of engaged effort at stake in this book.

The Happy Burden of History

Then Camus catches us off guard. He suggests provocatively: "One must imagine Sisyphus happy."[69] This is our conviction too. History can be a happy burden. This German Sisyphus,

> powerless and rebellious, knows the whole extent of his wretched condition: it is what he thinks of during his descent. The lucidity that was to constitute his torture at the same time crowns his victory.

We should not read this kind of happiness in the terms of popular culture today. In our consumer-oriented society, happiness is often reduced to the satisfaction of wants. That is not what we mean. Sisyphus is happy in his never-ending labors because he has finally discovered that meaning in his life is determined by him alone. He is unable to control the situations that life presents to him, but he is still able to respond to those situations by his will.

Moreover, he is now fully aware of this ability to respond. We see this ability in some contemporary Germans too: the discovery of their humanity in their engagement with their history. It is the measure of his success, not in convincing others but in finally learning wisdom, that Sisyphus does not view his historical responsibilities as a life sentence but as an existential choice. To cultivate a responsible self: "The struggle itself toward the heights is enough to fill a man's heart." To this, "the absurd man says yes and his effort will henceforth be unceasing."[70]

The four authors of this book understand responsibility as an ethical duty to preserve human beings. It involves taking seriously how we go about our lives, and dwelling in the situation reflectively in order to fully appreciate its

---

67   Gavriel Rosenfeld, *The World Hitler Never Made: Alternate History and the Memory of Nazism* (Cambridge: Cambridge University Press, 2005).
68   Camus, "Myth," 89.
69   Camus, "Myth," 91.
70   Camus, "Myth," 89, 91.

potential.[71] It also derives from an appreciation of the human consequences of human behavior: that is, a frank recognition of the endings to which human stories may come thanks to our choices made as agents. These endings are always separated from us in time, sometimes also distant from us in space. Responsibility insists on us imagining the relationships between ourselves here and now, and people—ourselves, others—sometime or somewhere in the future. At its core, responsibility involves an act of sympathetic imagination linking human beings in political relationships.[72]

Responsibility is inextricable from our history, and we are historical beings. Responsibility cannot be measured in abstractions: it cannot exist outside of actual and current circumstances. It is a response to conditions that, in the activities themselves, recognize the roots and effects of that response. We must apprehend our situatedness, understand how that influences and even shapes behavior and selfhood, in order to act in everyday life. Agency would not be possible without this rich contextual knowledge. It is only within our lives that we can make sense of our circumstances and can work sensibly.

Responsibility in a negative sense means refusing to excuse oneself; but in a positive sense, responsibility is simply about a certain pride in one's work. It assumes the stubborn posture of the artisan who insists that all the things he makes, ugly or beautiful, are products of his craftsmanship. Responsibility requires the kind of wisdom that Camus attributes to Sisyphus by the end of the myth: that he "makes of fate a human matter, which must be settled among men."[73] It means welcoming the moral weight of the boulder as mine, as a labor that can be done only by me.

This wisdom should not be misunderstood as redemptive because the sentence of historical responsibility cannot be paroled. It is why we, and Camus, find so fascinating that pause when Sisyphus has finally pushed his boulder to the top of the mountain.

> At that subtle moment when man glances backward over his life, Sisyphus returning toward his rock, in that slight pivoting he contemplates that series of unrelated actions which becomes his fate, created by him, combined under his memory's eye and soon sealed by his death. Thus, convinced of the wholly human origin of all that is human, a blind man eager to see who knows that the night has no end, he is still on the go.

---

71   Maureen Healy's notion, see Steege, Bergerson, Healy, and Pamela Swett, "The History of Everyday Life: A Second Chapter," *Journal of Modern History* 80 (June 2007): 358-378; s. a. Steege, *Black Market*, 287-297.
72   Cf. Marx, "Economic and Philosophical Manuscripts," *Marx-Engels Reader*, 66-125, for instance at 81-93.
73   That is, human beings.

Camus leaves Sisyphus "at the foot of the mountain,"[74] about to take up again his struggle to understand his own fate. Sure enough, another controversy is already brewing for the German Sisyphus. He must take up the burden of history again, and again. We stay with him as he moves up the mountain, shouldering the boulder.

---

74 Camus, "Sisyphus," 91.

Lies

And in any case, one lies well when one loves, about oneself and to oneself: one seems to oneself transfigured, stronger, richer, more perfect, one *is* more perfect—.

— Friedrich Nietzsche, *The Will to Power*, vol. III, aphorism 808, 1906

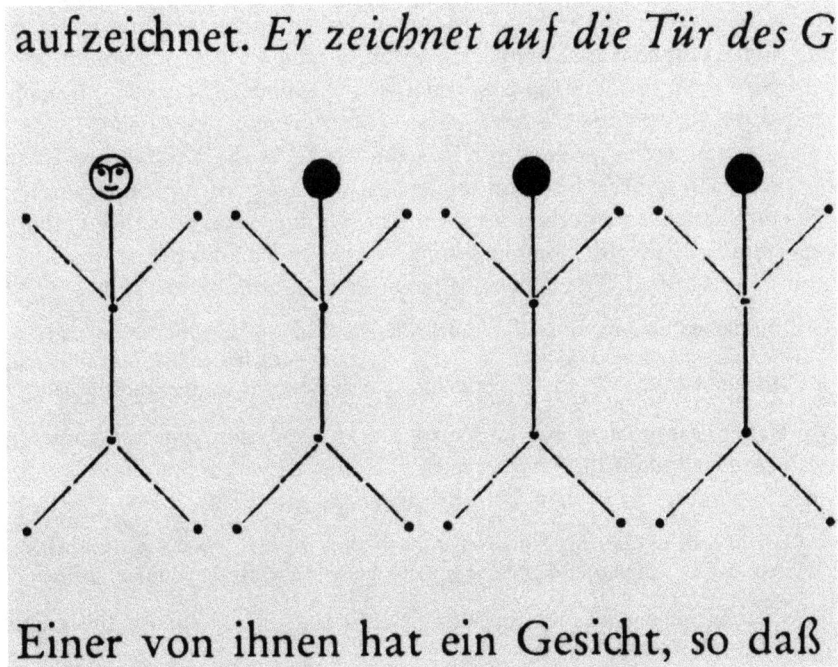

Figure 2. Bertolt Brecht, *A Man's A Man*, Stick Figures, 1925.
Source: Bertolt Brecht, *Mann ist Mann* (Berlin: Suhrkamp Verlag, 1953), 30.

The Kaiser's New Clothes

The reader is no doubt familiar with the story of "The Emperor's New Clothes" by Hans Christian Andersen.[1] A pair of swindlers comes to town posing as master weavers. They promise the Kaiser that they can weave him the most magnificent cloth ever. The clothes made from it have "the special power of being invisible to everyone who was stupid or not fit for his post."

The Kaiser thought this cloth would be useful to him as a tool of state. Clothes made from it could serve as a litmus test to determine the political acumen of his advisors. Yet his ministers, and even the Kaiser himself, each secretly worried that they might not be able to see the cloth either and thus be revealed as unqualified for their posts as well.

Sure enough, they did not see anything when the swindlers claimed to be done with their work since there was nothing there to see. Still, "the courtiers who were to carry the train felt about on the ground pretending to lift it: they walked on solemnly pretending to be carrying it. Nothing would have persuaded them to admit they could not see the clothes." Everyone universally praised the Kaiser's new clothes for fear of being revealed as a fraud.

The same scene repeated itself on the street. As the Kaiser marched in the procession under a beautiful canopy, his subjects praised his new clothes. "Nobody wished to let others know he saw nothing, for then he would have been unfit for his office or too stupid." Never had an Emperor's wardrobe been more admired. The fable ends famously with an innocent child:

> "But he has nothing on at all," said a little child at last. "Good heavens! Listen to the voice of an innocent child," said the father, and one whispered to the other what the child had said. "But he has nothing on at all," cried at last the whole people.

The Kaiser heard their cries. "That made a deep impression upon the Emperor, for it seemed to him that they were right." How did the Kaiser and his ministers respond to the evident fact of their self-deception?

> He thought to himself, "Now I must bear up to the end." And the chamberlains walked with still greater dignity, as if they carried the train which did not exist.

Rather than make a humiliating admission about their duplicity, the Kaiser and his ministers stuck to their lies.

---

1   Hans Christian Andersen, "The Emperor's New Clothes," 1837, trans. By H. P. Paull, 1872, downloaded from *Hans Christian Andersen: Fairy Tales and Stories* <http://hca.gilead.org.il/emperor.html>, October 2008.

Our Lying Selves

Lies are surprisingly important to the self. Both the Kaiser and his court-iers relied on deception to cultivate a particular identity for themselves—of majesty. It was not just the magical quality of the clothes that made them so desirable for the Kaiser and his court; nor was it even their functional benefits for statecraft to ferret out the bad or the stupid. These "clothes" made the Kaiser feel as if he truly embodied on the inside the role he performed on the outside. This allegedly sumptuous raiment projected an image of resplendent sovereignty to his subjects and to himself.

Where did the Kaiser make his mistake? He was probably tempted to blame the swindlers for deceiving him. That is not the moral of this fable, however. It would also be too simple to imagine that their mistake could be reduced to a faulted self-image. Here the presumption would be that it was only the image we have of the self, or give to it, that is a misrepresentation. According to this myth, the self is coherent, secure, and transparent; it is just being displayed falsely for selfish or political purposes.

Andersen's fable is far more critical. It suggests that the self relies in an essential way on deception in order to become the things it claims to be. The Kaiser was *self*-deceived not only because he was lying to himself but also because it was a lie *about* the self. He liked to imagine that his self existed prior to and outside of the social processes by which he invented it—in this case through clothing. He wanted his sovereign majesty to be *natural*, as if he really was the person his clothes made him out to be. Yet that is precisely where he deceived himself the most.

This fable also suggests that lies have political consequences. The Kaiser ignored his role in this elaborate self-deception at the cost of suppressing the obvious; in this sense he only embarrassed himself. Where his lies mattered most was how they spread. His refusal to take responsibility for his self-decep-tions led his ministers to play along; the example of his ministers encouraged his subjects to similar self-deceptions. Self-deceptions are insidious in this way. They invite collusion without responsibility.

Anyone interested in German studies, as we four authors are, spends a considerable amount of time discussing myths and lies, whitewashed pasts and repressed memories. These deceptions seem to betray an insufficient and distorted image of self and society. The remedy for the German neurosis of irresponsibility, accordingly, would seem to be that they must stop deceiving themselves and others—for instance about their Nazi past. In this model of the self, lies are what hinder us from taking responsibility.

We want to suggest the opposite: that we use the myth of a coherent self to disguise our responsibility.[2] Think about it this way: the more we take ourselves as given, the more we do not have to think about our role in our own making; then we can continue to do the things that make us who we are without considering the consequences. The Kaiser made this mistake. He was so taken with the image of himself as an expert statesman and imposingly dressed sovereign that he refused to admit his part in this elaborate lie.

We all know that politicians are prone to lie, but we do not understand why we are prone to believing them. We are particularly interested in the ordinary people who play the role of the *dupe*. A closer inspection of this everyday kind of "duplicity"—by which we mean our willingness to play the dupe—can help us unravel the relationships between selfhood, self-deception, and responsibility.

Our Approach

This chapter combines several forms of criticism in one. Focusing on the playwright Bertolt Brecht, the philosophers Friedrich Nietzsche and Walter Benjamin, and the postwar political theologian Johann Baptist Metz, we recover a heterodox approach to the self within German letters that sees self-deception as necessary for the ongoing construction of selfhood. We apply this abstract model of selfhood to concrete historical examples from the Third Reich, specifically the autobiographic testimonies of two ordinary Germans: Theodora Algermissen and Hans F.

Our goal for this somewhat anachronistic dialogue between ordinary and intellectual Germans is to come to a better understanding of responsible selfhood. The choice to focus on the Third Reich is perhaps obvious. Nazi crimes against humanity intensify issues of self-deception and responsibility, normalcy and genocide. By dealing with the issue of self-deception in the context of the Third Reich, we have taken on, we might say, the very toughest case we could.

From the ancient Greeks we have inherited the notion that the goal of the self is self-knowledge, and that self-knowledge will turn out to be justified, true beliefs. This chapter begins by reviving Nietzsche's attack on this view of the self. Nietzsche insists that lies, false beliefs, and other deceptions are necessary for the constitution of the self. Indeed, lies may become truths through our repeated self-deceptions.

---

2   See Steve Ostovich, "Melancholy History," in *Missing God? Cultural Amnesia and Political Theology*, ed. John K. Downey, Jürgen Manemann, Ostovich (Berlin: LIT Verlag, 2006), 93-101.

The challenge of memory is compounded by the fact that our lies about the self begin during events, not just in retrospect. Following Nietzsche, we view the faculty of memory as a way to shape events as they happen in order to cultivate a coherent, desirable identity for the future. Our point is not that all such self-deceptions are bad—on the contrary. The danger here lies in a lack of critical self-reflection about those deceptions: that is, when we let the lie achieve mastery over us.

In this chapter, we will also draw your attention to the inherently political relationship between the liar and the dupe. In this regard, we will consider Theodora's typically modern and all too ordinary habits of self-cultivation. They illustrate how self-deception encourages liar and dupe to establish a social contract which, we argue, can lay the everyday foundations for fascism. Brecht's play *A Man's a Man* warns of this same danger. Brecht presents us with a self-deceptive protagonist, but he does so to encourage his audience to engage in a kind of self-reflection that could distinguish between who we should want to be and how we should want to act. Hans F., by contrast, struggled to avoid sealing a fascist social contract with Hitler during the Third Reich, but ultimately—like the Kaiser's many ministers, courtiers, and subjects—he let the lie achieve mastery over him. Arguably, these stories are typical of many ordinary Germans.

Deception is an inherent element of our selfhood. The question is: how do we deal with our lies responsibly? Benjamin and Metz can help us here. Both philosophers, grounded in theology, use their own memories to think critically about their self-deceptions. There is no avoiding deception, but we should not deceive ourselves a second time that our lies about ourselves are in a strong sense *true*. Responsibility means recognizing our lies about the self as works of our own creation and making intentional choices about the kinds of lies we tell ourselves—and hence the kinds of people we wish to become.

The Ease of Being Duped

We do not have to apply Andersen's fable to the countless historical examples of *groupthink*[3] in modern German history to see how lies can gain mastery over us. The swindlers who sew the non-existent suit for the Kaiser are clearly *not* the only villains in the story and not even the worst. The Kaiser offends us in his vanity. His courtiers and subjects offend us still more in their cowardly capitulation to the lie. It takes a small child—who does not yet understand and practice the complex lies and self-deceptions that constitute adult life,

---

3   William H. Whyte, "Groupthink," *Fortune* (March 1952), 114-117, 142, 146; adapting George Orwell, *Nineteen Eighty-Four: A Novel* (New York: Harcourt, Brace, 1949).

and especially public, political, adult life—to pierce through this veil of mass deception and self-deception.

What we choose to believe is settled not only on the grounds of what evidence we have for our beliefs. It is also settled on the grounds of what we want to believe and how we direct our attention. It depends on which claims we choose to interrogate and which we merely accept without further investigation. And it is readily influenced by whatever political pressures we happen to feel at the moment. We set the truth aside in preference for other goals. To allow oneself to be deceived is, in many instances, merely a particularly comforting, albeit logically convoluted, form of self-deception.

Nietzsche on Vanity

Among philosophers, Nietzsche stands out as one of the great analysts of deception and self-deception in the modern period. Writing in Germany as it emerged on the international stage as a world power, Nietzsche was scathingly critical of the German middle classes for their uncritical self-deceptions. Living through an unprecedented modernization of German economy and society, he also offers us a strikingly modern approach to our understanding of the self in terms of deception and self-deception.

Nietzsche especially had in mind the social conformity inherent in bourgeois society, but we are interested here in the more general problem of the dupe. According to Nietzsche, our problems come not so much from lying to ourselves about ourselves as much as from deceiving ourselves about the fact that we are liars. As Nietzsche put it: "People lie unspeakably often, but afterwards they do not remember it and on the whole do not believe it."[4] Our problems get worse when we cheerfully believe the lies that other people tell us about ourselves. Yet Nietzsche has surprising things to say about who precisely is lying to whom. Perhaps his most important and controversial insight is that, in many situations, liars and dupes go hand-in-hand.

The Kaiser's deceitful vice is vanity. Nietzsche, not speaking specifically of the story, describes vanity in this way:

> We are like shop windows in which we are continually arranging, concealing or illuminating the supposed qualities others ascribe to us—in order to deceive *ourselves*.[5]

Or, in the aphorism *Vanity*:

> Interest in oneself, the desire to feel pleasure, attains in the vain person to such an intensity that he seduces others to a false, much too high assessment of himself, yet

4   Nietzsche, *Daybreak*, trans. Walter Kaufmann (New York: Viking, 1972), 302.
5   Nietzsche, *Daybreak*, 385.

then submits to the authority of these others: that is to say, he induces error and then believes in this error.[6]

What are the deceptive strategies here? Vain people know that they will not satisfy their need for self-assurance without the opinion of others. They cannot persuade themselves of their own virtues because they do not believe in them. Instead, they manipulate other people into holding them in high esteem—higher indeed than they believe these other people should hold them. Our goal, Nietzsche insists, in changing their opinion of us is to change our estimation of ourselves.

Once vain people—and by this we, and Nietzsche, mean most people—see that the deceived have in fact changed opinions and now hold us in high regard, we allow ourselves to accept their new opinion as good evidence supporting our own desired beliefs. We prefer not to ask ourselves, "Why does this person hold me in high regard?" because that question would interfere with us acquiring the belief we really want to hold. Now we ask, "Does this person esteem me?" And quickly add: "For if so, I must be estimable." Seeing that these liars do in fact esteem us, we dupes forget entirely that we are deceived—forget, indeed, that we practiced the deception. We hold ourselves estimable, so we esteem ourselves. We believe our own press.

There are two orders of self-deceptions here. The *lie of the first order* concerns statements relating to the self directly: that is, the self-deception on the part of vain people that the liar is speaking the truth about us. The *lie of the second order* is a more complicated, and more fascinating, self-deception about self-deception. In this lie, vain people efface their role as dupes in order to render the lie more convincing. As vain people we may be insecure and foolish, but we are not oblivious to the fact that we have become a dupe for a liar. Hence the need for the second-order lie: it erases the memory of our collaboration in deceiving ourselves.

Most people are prone to isolated moments of vanity. We are interested in the more complicated problem of becoming a vain person. It involves making an occasional moral error into a vice. Clearly, one believes one's own press all the more if one hears it often. To make it seem true, however, one must also ignore all the evidence that does not correspond to this conclusion about the self.

That is, a kind of memory work takes place not just in reflection about our vanity after the fact but in the moment of vanity itself. That original labor is to shape what happens, what is known about those events, and the meanings officially ascribed to them in keeping with our aspirations for ourselves for the future. We wish to experience events in keeping with our self-image.

---

6   Nietzsche, *Human, all-too-Human*, trans. Walter Kaufmann (New York, Viking, 1967): Vol. 1, §59.

We not only interpret the world in ways that confirm this self-image but also try to influence events to the same end. Relishing the experience of self-confirmation, we repeat the entire process again and again. Frequency papers over the ill fit between self-perception and reality. In this way, vanity becomes a bad habit.[7]

That vain people remember a lifetime of such events in these self-aggrandizing terms, and then narrate them autobiographically—in interviews, for instance—does not involve an act of selection mediated by *post facto* memory. Like the Kaiser who is still bearing it up to the end, vain people stick to their lies in order to verify their self-image. This dead-end is the revenge of the second-order lie. The self-deception about one's self-deceptions must be upheld at all costs or else the Kaiser would have proven himself unworthy of his post. After years of reiteration, we rely on the same bad habit of vanity to preserve a coherent fantasy of self.

Nietzsche on Hypocrisy

Hypocrisy is another vice of deception that Nietzsche considers. It operates in a similar way and is equally addictive. As Nietzsche writes:

> The hypocrite who always plays one and the same role finally ceases to be a hypocrite; for example priests, who as young men are usually conscious or unconscious hypocrites, finally become natural and then really are priests without any affectation…If someone obstinately and for a long time wants to *appear* something it is in the end hard for him to *be* anything else. The profession of almost every man, even that of the artist, begins with hypocrisy, with an imitation from, with a copying of what is most effective.[8]

Hypocrites begin their deception by acting, by playing a role, by pretending to be something they are not. This form of hypocrisy is familiar to most of us. It is politicians pretending to be virtuous, especially while condemning their own vice in others; it is preachers attacking the sin of gambling while they are fresh off the plane from Las Vegas. Unlike the vain person, however, the hypocrite's deception may not necessarily be, and presumably usually is not, initially motivated by a need for successful self-deception. Hypocrites may expect that the maintenance of their position, given their abilities, will always require this unhappy pretending to be something that they know they are not. They end up living a life as a *poseur*.

---

7   Bergerson, *Ordinary Germans*; Paul Connerton, *How Societies Remember* (Cambridge: Cambridge University Press, 1989). S. a. Judith Butler, *Gender Trouble: Feminism and the Subversion of Identity* (London: Routledge, 1990).

8   Nietzsche, *Human*, vol. 1, §51.

Self-deceptions are akin to *open secrets*: regimes of knowledge and ignorance that facilitate maneuverability in everyday life.[9] In the case of the Kaiser,
the open secret is that he is naked; and yet the Kaiser and his court continue
the parade. Open secrets are also not without danger for those who challenge
them publicly. We do not know what happens to the child who innocently
calls the Kaiser out on his lies.

It is a widely, albeit tacitly accepted understanding that a kind of hypocrisy, a kind of mutual deception about self-deception, is necessary to developing
one's capacities, be they personal or professional. We remember well the first
time that we presented our scholarship in public as budding academics. We
felt very much like *poseurs*. Our senior colleagues knew that and for the most
part were tolerant of our mistakes, allowing us the chance to become what we
claimed to be. Open secrets facilitate maneuverability in everyday life: they afford us the elbow room necessary for self-cultivation without which we would
forever be stuck in the state in which we were born.

To historicize this problem, we could say that it is a condition of modernity.[10] Modernity is contingent upon a changing self and society. From
fictional novels and films to factual history and self-help books, our culture
teaches that true selfhood involves self-cultivation and upward social mobility.
Our society is similarly idealized in terms of development. Conditioned by
temporal disjunctures, or *Ungleichzeitigkeiten*, modernity encourages "great
leaps forward" to promote, accommodate, and even anticipate change.

Modernity offers salves to soothe the wounds that result from persistent
transformation, but the medicine is often worse than the malady. When confronted with fluctuating selves, it is often tempting to place people back into
rigid categories if for no other reason than to make it more comforting for
the self. Modernity enforces regimes of homogenization to counter this sense
of "unevenness" within the present and in contrast to the immediate past.

These dynamics are particularly characteristic of modern German history. Especially before and during the Third Reich, both aspects of modernity
proved to be devastatingly inhuman—trying to make human beings better
and trying to make them all the same. We do a remarkable amount of violence to ourselves and others in the name of modernization; self-deception
makes both the violent transformations of modernity as well as our violent
efforts to control them smoother and more palatable.

---

9   Eve Kosofsky Sedgwick, *Epistemology of the Closet* (Berkeley: University of California Press,
    1990).

10 Ernst Bloch, *Heritage of Our Times*, trans. Neville and Stephen Plaice (Berkeley: University
    of California Press, 1990); Fritzsche, "Nazi Modern," *Modernism/Modernity* 3/1 (1996):
    1-22; Harry Harootunian, *History's Disquiet: Modernity, Cultural Practice, and the Question
    of Everyday Life* (New York: Columbia University Press, 2002); Detlev Peukert, *The Weimar
    Republic: the Crisis of Classical Modernity* (New York: Hill and Wang, 1992).

Nietzsche does not avoid the critical question of whether self-deceptions are good or bad, but he refuses to let his readers off easily by dismissing such deceptions as obviously blameworthy. We would all love to agree: "Lying is always wrong. And that's why I never do it." Both of those statements are false, however. Nietzsche would have us suspect that such normative categories as "lying is always wrong" or "lying is always right" are themselves examples of the vice of hypocrisy. Our brash insistence that we are all truth tellers is in fact just one more convenient self-deception.

Why do we believe liars? We will come back to this question again because the obvious answer is not necessarily the right one. Nietzsche himself offers several, including that our belief in lies is intended to satisfy deeper desires.

> Goodness has mostly been developed by the protracted dissimulation which sought to appear as goodness: wherever great power existed men saw the need for precisely this kind of dissimulation—it inspired a feeling of trust and security.[11]

Here Nietzsche is inverting Plato as he loves to do. The impious fraud becomes a pious truth (*pius veritas*) such that goodness is not identified with truth but depends on deception. To believe that great power—our society, our industry, our government, our culture—is allied with evil would naturally make us feel uncomfortable, as indeed it made some ordinary Germans uncomfortable during the Third Reich. Accordingly we let great power lie to us so that we will not feel this doubt and insecurity. Herein lies one reason why no one, except a child, questioned the Kaiser's nakedness. Hypocrites all, we let the lie pretend to be good, and in duping ourselves, we desperately hope that it is right.

Social Lies

Modern social life is filled with self-deceptions. We dupes and liars need one another to preserve our vanities from public denunciation. It is not enough to simply adopt the habits of our social betters. In a state of incessant change, selfhood is always a work in progress. The modern paradox is that we never quite reach our goal of fulfilled selfhood. It is due not only to the construction of insatiable demands in a mass consumer society but also because the standards for selfhood are constantly shifting. There are no secure foundations for the self in modernity.

For modern Germans, this situation derived not just from the general unevenness of everyday life and the structural dynamics of modernization but also the chronic instability of the modern German political system. Just think

---

11 Nietzsche, *Daybreak*, 248.

for a moment about how many times you had to adjust your sense of self if your grandparents were born in 1830, you in 1880, and your grandchildren in 1930. Your family witnessed the rise and fall of multiple kingdoms, nation-states, empires, soviet republics, parliamentary democracies, authoritarian dictatorships, fascist regimes, and occupation regimes—not to mention a wide range of mutually antagonistic political parties and movements. Each one demanded that you accommodate your sense of self to their principles. It is impossible to cross the finish line if someone is always moving the goalposts or changing the rules of the game. In a context when change is the norm, we must constantly reinvent ourselves just to keep pace.

The result: we come to rely all the more on others to evaluate those changes, to adjust our self accordingly, and then to affirm that reinvention. This collusion amounts to a social contract between self-cultivators. Inscribed in it are not only the terms of what the two partners agree about one another but also what—or more to the point, who—they agree to ignore to cover their tracks. It is this latter self-deception about self-deception that leads most readily to irresponsibility.

To illustrate how self-deception operates in concrete historical situations, we would like to turn now to the example of an ordinary German who struggled to make sense of her responsibility for the Nazi past. Drew, one of our co-authors, conducted narrative interviews from 1992 to 1994 with 38 people who had lived in Hildesheim, a typical provincial town in north-central Germany, during the Weimar and Nazi period.[12] We will look closely at Theodora Algermissen. Drew's first interview partner in Hildesheim, Theodora is interesting to us because of the way she and her family negotiated the challenges of modernity in general, and modern German history in particular, through strategies of self-deception.

Before we get into her testimony, however, we need to explain some things about her historical context. The Weimar Republic was a period of political instability for Germany, but the social structure of Hildesheim was still quite rigid in terms of the cultural constraints placed on individuals to stay in their place. The influx of modern ideas encouraged Hildesheimers to imagine and strive for upward social mobility, but they complained about the social stratification that persisted in spite of the collapse of the *Kaiserreich* in 1918.[13]

---

12 Stadtarchiv Hildesheim Bestand 904-2. Bergerson, "Geselligkeit in Hildesheim zwischen den Kriegen," 126 audio, 13 written interviews on 198 (mostly) 60-minute cassettes conducted mostly in German in Hildesheim, Germany; Tel Aviv and Haifa, Israel; Chicago, Washington, and New York, USA from 1991 to 1994. "G" numbers refer to the cassette side and time signature for the digitized versions available through the Stadtarchiv or Drew.

13 G005b 11:48.

Hildesheimers used the French word *niveau* to designate the kind of status they desired for themselves. They wanted to be seen by their neighbors as "cultivated." Many ordinary Hildesheimers did not have access to these resources or opportunities, however. A university education was the rite of initiation required for membership in the educated bourgeoisie (*Bildungsbürgertum*); property was the key to enter the ranks of the propertied bourgeoisie (*Besitzbürgertum*). The way to square this circle, if you had no formal access to either of these, was to lay claim to *niveau* in terms of how you interacted informally with friends and neighbors. Acting as if you were better afforded you at least the fantasy of status.[14]

Laying claim to *niveau* involved the kind of self-deceptions described here: lies to the self about one's status, followed by lies about one's role in lying. For *niveau* to work effectively, it had to seem completely natural, as if that status was not something that needed achieving but something already embodied. Consider the social consequences of these self-deceptions, however. The more one believes this second lie, the more *other* people seem to embody *niveau* naturally. If we refuse to recognize the degree to which we are *poseurs*, then it makes everyone else seem completely authentic. Taken together, this misapprehension can leave *everyone* feeling like their status is still on shaky ground. We all therefore devote all the more effort to effacing the evidence of our roles in cultivating our exclusivity. In this way our lies perpetuate themselves.

The Algermissen family will be our case in point. To make their *niveau* seem self-evident, they had to work hard to forget the people they climbed over on their way up the social ladder. Herein lies the benefit of looking at a concrete historical example. Theodora's testimony can illustrate how this seemingly ordinary dynamic of modern selfhood involved her in a subtle form of violence.

Theodora's Aspirations

Theodora was born in 1918 to a family with bourgeois aspirations. Her father was a master painter who restored historic churches and half-timbered houses. His profession was certainly respectable. In interwar Hildesheim, historical architecture was prized as the local foundation of a German national culture. Still, his involvement in preserving historical monuments did not assure him the status and power of the culture-bearing bourgeoisie.

The Algermissen family laid claim to *niveau* by surrounding themselves with people of cultivation.[15] Their circle of friends included a structural ar-

---

14   Bergerson, *Ordinary Germans*, chs. 1-2.
15   G001a 11:10. They also invested in property and education for their children as well as ignored their neighbors if they were of lesser status. See Bergerson, *Ordinary Germans*, ch 2.

chitect, a landscape architect, and the owner of a store for musical instruments as well as a bank director and chemist among others whom her parents knew from the prewar *Wandervögel* (the romantic hiking group for bourgeois youth). Theodora let slip that one of her parents's friends had been in charge of reconstructing the Cathedral after the war. Here she reiterated a strategy for cultivating status in Hildesheim that she had learned from her parents as a child.

These friends came together at the home of the Algermissens to play music together. Theodora's mother played the piano or the lute, and friends joined in with violin and flute. They often sang folksongs. Theodora was too small to play along with these adults, but she went to bed listening to their music. Theodora "learned many, many folksongs" from her mother even as a very small child. She sang "along with them, and can [sing] them still today." These musical evenings took place irregularly, when these adults had the time and the inclination. No doubt these evenings were also fun and entertaining. Yet Theodora remembered them so vividly even after many intervening decades arguably because of what these evenings said about her family. They played music with cultivated friends in their home: this fact seemed to confirm the *niveau* they ardently desired for themselves.

Hildesheim's economy boomed after the unification of Germany in 1871. By the turn of the century, Hildesheimers lauded themselves as bearers of German history and culture. Then a series of rapid-fire crises seemed to threaten that status: defeat in the Great War, the Revolution of 1918, the punitive Treaty of Versailles, the democratic constitution of the Republic, and the hyperinflation of 1921-1923. Even after the stabilization of the German economy in 1925, the Algermissen family worried about their finances, feared slipping into the proletariat, and had mixed feelings about the rapid pace of change.

In this typically modern context, it became all the more important for them to find ways to reinforce their claim to *niveau*. From her mother, Theodora learned to stake her identity on her musical cultivation.

> She showed me the note "A" for instance on the piano and showed me also how the notes on the bass clef are written. I then taught myself how to do it a little before I was given piano lessons and then I too could play a few little pieces. I got that from my mother, this stimulus for music.[16]

From her father, Theodora learned to do the same with art. He got together with a group of men once a week after work to discuss the history and culture of Hildesheim.[17] There had been many members of this group, but Theodora remembered two teachers, a hydraulic engineer, and the two directors

---

16   G001a 13:00.
17   G002b 00:00.

of the Roemer and Pelizaeus museums. The people who stuck in her memory were the ones who corresponded to her self-image. Interested in local history and culture, these men met in a country inn to exchange ideas for "how Hildesheim could arrange for this or that to be done."

Like the Kaiser and his courtiers, and the rest of us, these Hildesheimers are vain but self-doubting individuals who formed a social contract to reassure themselves that they are in fact who they claim to be: people of cultivation fit for that "office." We should not be distracted by the fact that some of these people, like the museum directors, already seemed to embody the credentials of membership in the educated bourgeoisie. Arguably, the fact that they appeared so natural in their roles only made the Algermissen family more insecure about their own status—and *vice versa*.

Social Climbing

We "get" the Algermissen family. The four of us are academics who take pride in our cultivation. Some of us play house music and learned folksongs from our parents. We are published authors of fiction and non-fiction. We all love theater, art, and literature; we teach our children to love it as well. We have each achieved tenure and promotion at our respective universities, but that does not mean that we do not still feel the need for confirmation from our readers and our peers. We seek out conversations with others about intellectual topics. We worked over drafts of this manuscript in coffee shops and restaurants quite aware of what might be called the "coolness factor" of our conversation. We were both annoyed and honored by those around us who added their philosophical insights to our discussions.

It is precisely because these practices are so alluring, and yet so ordinary, that they are so powerful. We are accustomed to cultivating an identity for ourselves that corresponds to our self-image. A normal aspect of everyday life, we do not think about these self-deceptions in ethical terms. We tend to ignore their political implications for the same reason that the Algermissen family did—we do not wish to risk being proven unfit.

The Algermissen family experienced these activities as nothing more than enjoyable pastimes. This group was not political, Theodora insisted. Like many ordinary Germans, Theodora distinguished between participating in formal politics, which in the Weimar Republic ranged from rancorous to violent, and participating in the kind of informal struggle for *niveau* that comprised a naturalized part of everyday life. Yet we would be naïve if we did not recognize that this kind of direct personal access to the cultural elite of Hildesheim afforded Theodora's father with both power and profit.

Their performance of exclusivity reinforced social distinctions while it effaced responsibility. The rigid hierarchies of class and confession that persisted in the 1920s were often blamed on pre-war Wilhelmine society. Yet the working classes were wholly absent from this circle of friends. The barriers of religious confession operated similarly though with less rigidly. Theodora's father had been baptized Catholic but her mother was Protestant, and most of their friends were Protestant. Only the structural architect was Catholic.[18] Our point is that the way the Algermissen family strove to climb the social ladder helped perpetuate social stratification.

It made sense that the Algermissen family deceived themselves that their social exclusivity was completely natural. Their *niveau* was predicated on effacing their responsibility for such exclusions. For instance, they did have a Swedish friend who married a Jewish lawyer in Hamburg whom she had met in London. "And their children often came to our house. They were very intelligent. They were great." But they lived in Hamburg.

> So here in Hildesheim, at least in *our* family, Jews played neither a positive or negative role. I was in a class—I sat next to a Jew, but that made no difference at all if she was a Jew or not a Jew. It was just a classmate. Then suddenly one day she was gone, but I heard it said that she is in Palestine. But that really did not play a role in our circle, or in Hildesheim anyway. It was a small, provincial town. There you have it.[19]

Yet Theodora had, in the meantime, become an Aryan. What she left unstated in this anecdote is her dramatic rise in status and power relative to Jews after 1933. Her Jewish classmate certainly noticed her participation in Nazi organizations, perhaps also her vocal support for some of Hitler's policies—a story we will recount in more detail in a later chapter. It was precisely these symbolic shifts in allegiance among their friends and neighbors that encouraged many Jewish Germans to emigrate. Embedded in everyday life, Theodora could imagine that the sudden disappearance of this Jewish girl was not related to her sudden rise in *niveau* as an Aryan.

The example of the Algermissen family illustrates why we should take seriously the relationship that dupes establish with liars. These are not abstract principles but actual ways that we relate to other human beings. This social contract was embedded in the Algermissens' desire for entertainment and a love of culture; but it was fueled by the nagging fear that they could be measured against the standard of *niveau* and found wanting. Unlike the Andersen fable, however, the child does not declare the Kaiser naked. From a young age, Theodora had been fully initiated into the politics of everyday life in order that she could aid her family in raising its *niveau*. They had no intention of losing their membership in this exclusive club even when the rules for membership changed from cultural sophistication to racial superiority.[20]

---

18 G001a 17:00.
19 G0001a 17:20.
20 Even as an adult, Theodora perpetuated her parents' habits of self-cultivation. After her

They did not seem to care whom they stepped on while social climbing. Consider how Theodora framed her father's relationship with a forced laborer during the Second World War.[21]

> My father was issued a prisoner of war, a Frenchman. *Monsieur* Something-or-the-other…My father had fun speaking French with him, and actually it was a rather good relationship with him. He also wrote us [a letter] afterwards.

The Algermissen family may in fact have had a "good relationship" with their French forced laborer—it is hard to tell without comparing this master's narrative to the slave's account. Our argument rests instead on the fact that Theodora used her family's cultural sophistication as French speakers to disguise the underlying power relations in Nazi-dominated Europe. It was easy for a first-order deception about the self, the family's claims to cultural sophistication and social status, to disguise a second-order lie about their role in inhuman systems of violence.

The second-order lie serves as our safeguard. It covers the tracks of the first. It whitewashes the evidence that we cultivate our selves in cahoots with some human beings at their expense of others. It is this second-order lie that bothers Nietzsche the most—and us as well—for it is the lie that allows for sovereign impunity. By erasing the evidence of our agency, it promises that we can lay claim to mastery over others without considering the human consequences.

Fascist Lies

Theodora's example raises the problem of violence in subtle terms. It suggests that we need to take care when a lie about the self becomes a truth. We would like to now consider the particular kind of social contract that can emerge from a society of self-deceivers. Here we are arguing in effect that there were systemic political consequences of this kind of everyday self-deception.

Who precisely deceived whom in the Third Reich? Much hinges on this question. For a long time, historians blamed Hitler and his propaganda machine for indoctrinating ordinary Germans and keeping them obedient.[22] Yet our model for how liars and dupes seal social contracts would suggest that this historical interpretation is incorrect—or at least a secondary matter. Taking Nietzsche seriously, we would say that the radical political leaders of the

---

husband returned from Russia as a prisoner of war, they found new friends and engaged in "culture-oriented" activities and travel that demonstrated her *niveau* (G005b 10:40).

21   G005b 03:40.

22   Ian Kershaw, *The 'Hitler Myth': Image and Reality in the Third Reich* (Oxford: Oxford University Press, 1989).

Right were not the only, or even the primary, agents of duplicity. Propaganda, elections, ideology, peer pressure, and terror all aside, once a majority of the German people sealed this kind of fascist social contract in practice, as so many dupes, they became equally committed to that self-deception.

The Sincere Deceiver

The Third Reich best illustrates the remarkable longevity of such lies, the way they drove liar and dupe to a fascist posture in the first place, and the very real danger that this inherent logic to self-deception can and did lead to global warfare and genocide. Ordinary Germans did not simply repress the memory of collaboration in Nazi crimes against humanity after the fact in response to their guilty conscience. They committed themselves to self-deception after, during, and even before the Third Reich. They wanted to see themselves as both an Aryan *Übermensch* and an ordinary German. They deceived themselves that they had the right to master others and yet could live a life free from ethical or historical responsibilities for their actions.

Their lies gave rise to obstacles that even many nationalist Germans could never have reasonably hoped to overcome, including a worldwide, multi-frontal, genocidal war. They collaborated in a series of lies again in order to avoid facing or taking responsibility for their own duplicity. Yet even after Stalingrad and Allied strategic bombing, many Germans still did not dare to contemplate the prospect of being self-deceptive, or else they would have had to entertain the truly terrifying notion that the modern Leviathan with whom they had sealed a social contract was no longer acting with their good in mind.[23] Great power began by dissimulating to guarantee its own ends; soon enough, the lie of goodness became an Orwellian truism.

Here it is worth returning to Nietzsche not the least because of the way in which his philosophy has been so often held responsible for the Aryan *Übermensch*. Nietzsche warned us from believing too readily the "sincere deceiver." As he wrote: "One of the commonest false conclusions is this: because someone is true and honest towards us, he speaks the truth."[24] So, for example, because a mother had always been true and honest with her child, the child might assume that she always speaks the truth. Here the principle of deception is the same as that of great power. The dupe believes the deceiver because he is comforted by the apparent attitude of the deceiver toward the dupe.

---

23   E. g., Hans Erich Nossack, *The End: Hamburg 1943* (Chicago: University of Chicago Press, 2004); Friedrich Meinecke, *The German Catastrophe: Reflections and Recollections*, trans. Sidney B. Fay (Cambridge: Harvard University Press, 1950).

24   Nietzsche, *Human*, vol. 1, §53

In the age of mass media, of which the Nazis were sophisticated innovators, we could go further. The dupe believes what the liar says about him because the deceiver offers him an image of what he himself desperately wants to become. There need be no other deception than the self-deception of the dupe: the true and honest speaker who does not in fact speak the truth may not deliberately deceive his audience. It could well be that, while speaking in error, the deceiver supposes himself to be speaking truthfully. In this case we would not say that the deceiver was lying; he was merely misleading while misled himself.

The message of the deceiver nonetheless becomes a lie because—and this is our point—of the interpretive act of the dupe. The dupe accepts the message on dubious grounds, grounds like "I want to believe him," or "I will believe him, because he has been true and honest towards *me*." The dupe, akin to the vain person, seals the lie in a social contract with the liar. The dupe agrees to this arrangement because it verifies his secret fantasies and needs of self.

We think that ordinary Germans made this arrangement with their new *Führer* both during the crucial years from 1930 to 1935 when he won the support of one quarter to one third of the German population as well as over the course of the Nazis's ever-escalating seizure of power. Here we are inverting standard interpretations about Hitler's infamous skills as an orator and charisma as a leader.[25] We are trying to make a case instead for taking seriously both sides of what the Nazis called the "leadership principle." The *Führerprinzip* required not only orders from above but also enthusiasm from below. During the Third Reich, we see a poisonous brew of vanity, hypocrisy, and self-deception from ordinary Germans that, ironically, made Hitler into the kind of leader he always imagined himself to be.

The Dupe's Paradox

Here it may be worth distinguishing between an ordinary dupe and a "sincere dupe." We know that some of Hitler's supporters sincerely believed what Nazi propaganda said about them. They felt that Hitler freed them to become what they most desperately desired: Aryan overlords of a European empire. Hitler gave this violent core of the Nazi party permission to cultivate selfhood through murder and destruction.

Many other Germans were less sincere in their "duplicity." They were attracted to National Socialism because of different factors like economic recov-

---

25 Kershaw, '*Hitler Myth*'; Max Weber, "Charismatic Authority" and "The Routinization of Charisma," in *Theory of Social and Economic Organization*, trans. A. M. Henderson and Talcott Parsons (New York: Free Press, 1947), 358-385.

ery, restoring German national sovereignty, and fighting Bolshevism.[26] They too welcomed the freedom to promote their career and enjoy prosperity. They quickly learned to ignore the fact that their successes resulted from removing Jews, socialists, and others from their positions, or that their prosperity depended on the exploitation and murder of entire social groups.

Even if they did not share the antisemitism of the "sincere" Nazis, then, many ordinary Germans sealed this same social contract with Hitler in the moment that they pursued careers and enjoyed prosperity that depended on Nazi violence. From that moment on, breaking with Hitler would have risked disclosing their collusion in their own vain self-deceptions. This contract proved so very hard to break in the long term because it was sealed, publicly, in the blood of Nazi victims.

So why did they sign this deal with the Devil in the first place? One reason is certainly that a skeptical engagement with the self is painful. Though it does not force us to abandon all hope of changing ourselves to fit our aspirations, it does insist that we consider whether it is reasonable to want to become what we wish to become, or believe about ourselves what we wish to believe. In other words, many ordinary Germans started in all likelihood with a small lie. Some chose on the basis of their critical self-reflection to resist; but they were not typical. Many, if not most, paradoxically anticipated the kind of person Hitler was saying they could be and became that kind of person. And then they were hooked.

Nietzsche's dialectic of deception was prescient in its anticipation of this theater of Hitler, or what Walter Benjamin called the aestheticization of politics.[27] In this passage it seems almost as if Nietzsche had been present at one of the Nuremberg Rallies.

> With all great deceivers there is a noteworthy occurrence to which they owe their power. In the actual act of deception, with all its preparations, its enthralling in voice, expression and gesture, in the midst of the scenery designed to give it effect, they are overcome by belief in themselves…Self-deception has to exist if a grand effect is to be produced. For men believe in the truth of that which is plainly strongly believed.[28]

---

26 A large literature: consider Theodore Abel, *Why Hitler Came into Power* (Cambridge: Harvard University Press, 1938); William Sheridan Allen, *The Nazi Seizure of Power: The Experience of a Single German Town 1922-1945* (New York: Franklin Watts, 1965); William Brustein, *The Logic of Evil: The Social Origins of the Nazi Party, 1925-1933* (New Haven: Yale University Press, 1996); Thomas Childers, *The Nazi Voter: The Social Foundations of Fascism in Germany, 1919-1933* (Chapel Hill: The University of North Carolina Press, 1983); and Richard Hamilton, *Who Voted for Hitler?* (Princeton: Princeton University Press, 1982).

27 Benjamin, "The Work of Art in the Age of Mechanical Reproducibility," in *Walter Benjamin: Selected Writings*, vol. 3, 101-133.

28 Nietzsche, *Human*, vol. 1, §52.

And again, in *The evil moment*, Nietzsche writes: "Lively natures lie only for a moment: immediately afterwards they lie to themselves and are convinced and honest."[29] We lie to others who want to be lied to and in so doing we deceive both them and ourselves. None of us could pull it off without co-conspirators.

Clearly it is misleading to think in terms of an individual lie in some sort of pure form. Once even the simplest self-deception is enacted, it reshapes the social context into one more conducive for achieving subsequent self-deceptions; that dynamic in turn begins to implicate others in the same lie. When the Kaiser insisted on lying to himself about his new clothes, he created a circumstance in which his subjects would be more willing to be duped by holding a parade and marching under a canopy. He "placed all bets" on the lie, believed it in every aspect of his daily life, in the hopes that he might just get away with the deception. In the process, he altered the nature of the public sphere: his ministers and his subjects felt the pressure to adopt the small lie. The more people were involved, the easier it became to continue the lie than to reflect critically and publicly on it.

Ordinary Germans bound themselves to the *Führer* in the same kind of social context. Self-deceptions generated real ethical and historical consequences; and not merely for the liar or even the dupe. Lies colonized everyday life on behalf of the liar and the dupe, creating contexts in which their deceptions were easier to perpetuate. They spread like a plague throughout Germany and much of Europe with a totalitarian logic.[30]

Why We Believe Liars

Thus far we have suggested that there is something called a fascist social contract, and that it is grounded in self-deception. It requires deceivers who tell lies, sincerely or not, about the kinds of persons dupes can become if only they agree to collaborate in exclusion, terror, destruction, and murder. It is not adequate to stop our analysis there, however. We can account for the dynamism and staying power of fascist violence only if we appreciate the role of the dupe in perpetuating this fascist social contract in ever new arenas of social interaction. No doubt the reader can think of contemporary examples which fit this model; we focus on examples from the 1920s and 1930s, as democracy in Germany was undermined by fascism, precisely because we believe that these small lies about the self played a crucial role in laying the foundations for more elaborate forms of violence in the 1940s.

We are not entirely satisfied with Nietzsche's explanations when it comes to why we lie to ourselves. Nietzsche identifies fear as a key motivator in his

---

29   Nietzsche, *Daybreak*, 391.
30   Cf. Hannah Arendt, *The Origins of Totalitarianism* (New York: Harcourt, Brace, 1951).

infamous analysis of the success of Christianity. We experience fear, especially the fear of our own cruel natures, and in an attempt to escape that fear we accept the deceptions told to us by a class of lying priests. He argues that we would rather be secure than know the truth. "Even the sense for truth" he writes, "is really the sense for security…One does not want to let oneself be deceived."[31]

The origin of our desire for truth, he argues, is in a kind of evolutionary advantage that the truth provides. It is in an antelope's advantage, trying not to be the lion's next meal, to know whether or not a lion truly lies in wait beyond the next hill. It is also in our advantage, as hunters, to know whether or not an antelope is hiding in the grasses. The value here is security and success: truth has no value in itself. Similar to truth, lies are neither valuable nor vicious except insofar as they contribute to that security or success.

Fear is a major factor in a terror state like the Third Reich. Yet it would be too simple to reduce our motives solely to various forms of survival. As in Thomas Hobbes's *Leviathan*, security can serve readily to disguise other selfish motives. Hitler justified the Enabling Acts, which established his dictatorship, on the need to respond quickly and aggressively to the burning of the Reichstag building, allegedly by communists.[32] Yet it was not simply due to these "reactive" reasons, to temper fear and provide security, that ordinary Germans believed Hitler's lies about the Aryan *Übermensch*. What the example of Theodora suggests is that these lies were also tied to "proactive" motives like the search for *niveau*.

What we are suggesting is that ordinary Germans made the strategic choice to bind themselves to the Third Reich based on hopes of what the Nazis could offer them. The range of motives was wide: from the chance for status, power, wealth, recognition, or upward social mobility to the chance for heroic masculinity, personal empires, and world power. There is much to be gained in war. Beyond plundered goods, control over resources, power over people, and an exaggerated sense of status, we cannot ignore the often coveted opportunity to break free from the constraints of civilization—to kill and destroy with impunity. Indeed, the freedom to terrorize was part of fascist practice from the beginning, long before a concrete war or genocide was planned or waged.[33]

---

31 Nietzsche, *Daybreak*, 26.
32 Burleigh, *Third Reich*.
33 Wildt, *Volksgemeinschaft*; cf. David Schoenbaum, *Hitler's Social Revolution: Class and Status in Nazi Germany, 1933-1939* (New York: W. W. Norton, 1980).

To put this argument in stark terms, we are suggesting that too many ordinary Germans made a fateful decision sometime early in the 1930s to believe the lies that the Nazis told them. Imagining a Nazi future in which they could prosper and succeed, they welcomed the rise in status and power to *Übermensch* that came with the label of Aryan.

This interpretation marks a departure from standard accounts of the Third Reich. Most historians date the "decision in principle" (*Grundsatzentscheidung*) to exterminate the Jews in 1940 or 1941 and focus on policymakers, perpetrators, and their circumstances.[34] Our reading of German history locates this decision a decade earlier when ordinary Germans signed the violent clauses of this deceptive social contract with their *Führer* and focuses on dynamics inherent in the operation of selfhood in everyday life. This first choice to play the dupe to Hitler set ordinary Germans on a path to future collaboration in violence.

Ordinary Germans did not even have to believe all of what Hitler said about them. Even Nazi supporters joked about the Aryan *Übermensch* without any sense of cognitive dissonance. They became ensnared in an insidious dynamic of collaboration because they chose to act as if their status and power as an Aryan was natural. Here we are referring not just to the pseudoscientific bases for eugenics that gave racial identities an artificial veneer of stability. We are trying to draw the reader's attention to the role played by the willed ignorance of one's role in laying claim to superior status. This second-order lie was made all the more powerful because it was sealed in blood. Once the Nazis began to actually brutalize, deport, and murder in the name of the Aryan, it became all the more important to stick to these lies; and yet, this violence began even before the Nazis came to power.

Theodora's Decision in Principle

Theodora illustrates how this tacit agreement operated in everyday life. She did not have anything particularly against her Jewish classmate, we do not think. We believe Theodora when she implied that she never did anything directly to hurt her Jewish neighbors. What she did was ignore their disappearance once she became an Aryan. The Nazi regime came to her aid by pressuring her Jewish neighbors to leave Germany. It was also convenient for her that more ardent Nazis took on the dirty job of antisemitic violence. They reinforced Theodora's inclination to imagine that her rise in status and power was unrelated to anything that she personally had done. Nonetheless, their degradation was the essential condition for her promotion.

---

34 For instance, the excellent work by Christopher Browning, *The Origins of the Final Solution: The Evolution of Nazi Jewish Policy, September 1939-March 1942*, (Lincoln: University of Nebraska Press, 2004); cf. Wildt, *Volkgemeinschaft*, ch. 8.

In its form, her first-order lie—that she was a person deserving status and power—was not that different from any of the lies we tell as modern selves. We can hardly do without these kinds of lies if we have aspirations of upward social mobility. Theodora started getting into trouble when she agreed to become an *Aryan*—a form of self that is predicated on its innate superiority to others. She ran into real hot water, however, when she imagined that her rise in *niveau* was not of her doing. Yet her identity as an *Aryan* was inextricably bound to systems of racial difference, political terror, and ultimately genocidal extermination. Here is why she needed the second-order lie. On the one hand, it reassured her that she deserved the status and power that she had acquired. On the other, the second-order lie allowed her to believe that her rise in status and power took place without any complicity on her part in acquiring it. By the time her father chatted with a French forced laborer during the Second World War, they had so completely accepted the terms of this fascist social contract that they could act like he was a "good master" in all sincerity.

The status and power of the *Übermensch* was never assured, however; it had to be demonstrated and could even be "lost." In order to get married, for instance, a German couple had to prove their Aryan ancestry through genealogical research. If the marriage involved a member of the SS (*Schutzstaffel*), the elite Nazi paramilitary organization, the volume of documentation became extensive. Yet there was always the chance that an ancestor would be discovered who had a small physical or mental handicap—or worse, was Jewish. The very act of laying claim to the status of *Übermensch* was thus fraught with peril. And even racially pure Aryans could land in concentration camps if their behavior marked them as "work-shy," "asocial," or a political threat.[35] Here is where the second-order lie helps out: it reduced the anxiety relating to one's status as *Übermensch* by making that identity seem natural.

This dynamic of selfhood is remarkably familiar in spite of the obvious differences between the Third Reich and our everyday life. We all imagine that we are *ordinary* by which we mean that we are not responsible for the systematic violence of modern history. In our terms, what makes us ordinary is this second-order lie; we use it to erase the evidence of our self-cultivation. The irony is that, in looking at ordinary Germans during the Third Reich, we are tempted to try to find ways to erase the obvious similarities between us and them. One common way to do so is to treat the claims of ordinary Germans to normalcy as if they are quantifiably measurable. Either Germans were normal and therefore not responsible for the crimes of the Third Reich,

---

35 Elissa Mailänder Koslov, *Gewalt im Dienstalltag: Die SS-Aufseherinnen des Konzentrations-und Vernichtungslager Majdanek 1942-1944* (Hamburg: Hamburger Ed., 2009), 117, 240-252, 439-441; Fritzsche, *Life and Death*.

or they were categorically abnormal because of their collusion and therefore not like us. Either way, we get to ignore the ethical pitfalls of modern selfhood—which amounts to nothing other than laying claim to the same sovereign impunity we criticize in them.

This misguided effort to assess the normalcy or abnormality of ordinary Germans depends on our ability to know for sure if they are liars or truthtellers. This model falls apart once we recognize that modern selfhood itself demands lies. We use *normalcy* in a different sense: as a collective self-deception that facilitates sovereign impunity in everyday life.[36] People imagine themselves as ordinary when they act as if they are the pawns of grander kings. Normalcy is thus a particular, and particularly modern, expression of what we are calling the second-order lie. Through it, we imagine that we have no role in or responsibility for our own making. The whole point of this lie is to enable us to continue to believe our own press and inhabit our position of status and power while also keeping our conscience clean. The more that normalcy facilitates immoral behavior, the more we all have to stick to the same lies.

Here Nietzsche himself played the dupe to a pernicious, yet typical lie of the modern era: that the lies always come from deceptive leaders. The fascist social contract is far more prevalent and devious. It is in our will to be "ordinary," incapable of moral decision-making, that we liars dupe vain politicians into believing that they are the heroic protagonists of history. It was this self-deception that generated the fascist social contract between *Volk* and *Führer*.

In our reading, Nietzsche does not represent the progenitor of Hitler—the self-deluded self-appointed *Übermensch*. By understanding Nietzsche correctly, he can serve as Hitler's gadfly and antidote. When lying, Nietzsche seems to be suggesting, do so willfully, critically, even consciously. And certainly never allow yourself the luxury of believing that you are innocent of self-deception. If you do, you run the risk of giving enormous power to those whom you are willing to believe.

Our mistake lies not in lying *per se*. Modern selfhood requires self-deception. We err in duping ourselves and others into believing that our claims about ourselves are in a strong sense *true*.

The Lie of Normalcy

Like the lies of vanity and hypocrisy, the lie of normalcy reiterates within the deluding self the essential political dynamic of the fascist social contract: of letting the lie master us. According to this lie, Hitler was the sincere deceiver

---

36 Normalcy is different from *normativity*, a category of obedience to social expectations, and from *normative*, meaning representative or typical.

and the German people his unwilling dupes. The relationship of deceived and deceivers is much more complex. The lying began within us, in our selfhood. It is our belief in our own irresponsibility that creates a hospitable environment for fascism.

Let us consider another concrete historical example so that we can better understand how the lie of normalcy facilitated fascism. In some ways it was hard to see Theodora's behavior as a lie because we isolated these episodes from the rest of her biography. We will do a more exhaustive analysis of Hans F.'s autobiographical testimony. In the ninety-minute, English-language interview that Drew conducted with him in 1989,[37] he is explicit about his Nazi past and places his own self-deceptions at the center of his testimony. His life story offers us a chance to interrogate his role in the construction of his own normalcy.

Hans's problem as a young man growing up in the Third Reich was not his inability to act but his failure to recognize his own self-deceptions—indeed his denial of his capacity for critical self-reflection. First deliberately, and then habitually, he let the lie of his own powerlessness achieve mastery over him. He remembered that sense of powerlessness quite corporeally. Indeed, he buried that awareness in his body for the same reason: he did not wish to engage in the kind of sustained, critical self-reflection that takes place in consciousness. A close look at his autobiographic narrative will lead us back through the tissues of compounded lies to the characteristically fascist moment when he first adopted these bad habits.

Hans the Perfect Aryan

Born in Fürth in 1926, Hans was "well-built, strong as an ox and very ideally formed,"[38] so he could readily play the part of the perfect Aryan. In the 1930s, Hitler desperately wished to gain the cooperation of young Aryans like Hans as soldiers for his campaign against communism, democracy, and the so-called Jewish world conspiracy that, Hitler insisted, had caused all of Germany's problems. Just as desperately, however, Hitler wanted Hans to think and act like an Aryan of his own accord: to give up his Christian (Methodist) commitment to love his neighbor and to treat Jews with active disrespect or even violence. As Hans understood, "compassion was considered a Christian virtue inherited from the Jews." In its place the Nazis encouraged brutality. They

---

37 Bergerson, Miscellaneous Interview Collection, M001. Interview with Hans F., one narrative interview on a single 90-minute tape cassette conducted in English in his home in Locust Valley, New York, on 28 December 1989. "M" numbers refer to the cassette side and time signature for the digitized versions currently available only through Drew. Hans stuttered; these were corrected in the quotes to follow.

38 M001a 10:00.

believed "that there is such a thing as a super-race, and that the super-race can only prevail if they are merciless."[39] These were the lies of others, and Hans was not so easily deceived by Nazi ideology.

He was far better at adopting the habits of fascist self-deception. The central motif of Hans's recollections was his feeling that he could do nothing to alter his or his neighbors' circumstances. Even as a young adult, however, he did many things. He was called upon to collect scraps for the war effort, safeguard public buildings on weekends, train for war in summer camps, enter basic training after graduating high school early, and join the army, which he did in 1943 at the age of 17. He spent much of the war in advanced training to be a pilot but never left the ground. He was attached to an anti-aircraft battery at the end of the war.[40]

Instead of describing any of these deeds, he talked about how he volunteered for any opportunity that avoided combat—like signing up for new training courses. "By 1943," he recalled, he was personally convinced "that Germany had lost the war and that there was only one sound thing for a young German like me to do and that is to [sic], by all means, to survive the war." When his division was fighting Patton's army, two commanders surrendered on behalf of "millions of Germans who were taken prisoner at that time."[41] Hans landed in the hands of the Americans, as it were, by default.

Hans narrates his life as if he were the object or even the victim of history. In contrast to the notable absence of any stories of collaboration in violence, Hans vividly recalled an incident from basic training when he had been a victim of Nazi brutality. This experience had "almost visceral implications" for him.[42] His company had been sent on a forced march of about twenty-five miles in full military gear. On the outskirts of Nuremberg, they were ordered to take off their clothes, enter a huge pond, tread water or swim for about half an hour, imagine that this pond was the Volga River and the Soviet army was on the other side, and stay afloat somehow or another. Hans had no problem with the training exercise since he was a strong swimmer, but both of his feet were covered in blisters from his ill-fitting boots. When he tried to walk on the gravel back to his clothes, "it was like walking on eggs."

His feet began to swell, but he still had to put his sweaty socks back on and march back twenty-five miles. When he finally got back to camp, an SS officer in his black overcoat and his mistress greeted the troop. The SS officer

---

39 M001a 01:40; M001b 38:25. Hans believed that Nazi brutality was also encouraged "by Nietzsche's philosophy of the Superman:...the blond beast [who shows] no remorse, no feeling of compassion."

40 M001b 11:40; s. a. Michael Kater, *Hitler Youth* (Cambridge: Harvard University Press, 2004).

41 M001b 14:20, 31:50.

42 M001b 33:00.

ordered the soldiers to goosestep past. He did not like how they marched, so he ordered the company of seventeen and eighteen year old boys to take off their shoes: he proceeded to chase them across a freshly harvested field full of stubbles. "I remember still the pain, walking through this [*sic*][43] with feet of mine and all those blisters." When Hans was finally able to go to the dispensary for treatment, he found some non-commissioned officers playing cards. Very much annoyed at being disturbed, one finally agreed to look at Hans's feet. He took a razor blade, cut crisscross across his blisters, squirted a whole bottle of iodine on them, and dismissed him. This was the "kind of brutality that we experienced."

Already during World War One, ordinary Germans liked to imagine that "little people" like "them" were not responsible in either an ethical or a historical sense for the crimes of "great power." At stake in this ontology is a fundamental self-deception about the nature of human responsibility and historical causation which became particularly salient in the modern historical context of Nazi terror and totalitarianism: the belief that ordinary people do not shape and cannot alter the conditions of their collective existence. Their devotion to their own normalcy did not conflict with doing their part in the world-historical revolution that was National Socialism; on the contrary, it sealed the fascist social contract all the more tightly when they disguised their deeds—from the extremes of extermination to the banalities of careerism—behind the veil of compulsory obedience to Hitler. These are bad and dangerous lies, claims about themselves in which ordinary Germans deceptively concurred.

At stake in Hans's story about "walking on eggs" was not just his claim to the status of victim but also his position *vis-à-vis* barbarism in general. To be sure, Hans admitted that he liked the "strenuous life" afforded him by the *Hitler Jugend*, the Nazi organization for adolescent boys, and the military; but he "abhorred" their "brutality." Like when he watched the Nazis burn down the synagogue in Fürth in November 1938 during the so-called Night of Broken Glass, or *Kristallnacht*. "There was something inside of me that recoiled in horror," he explained. "I could not reconcile that with any values that I held dear." And yet he admitted that "there was a conflict there, yes—."[44] Hans did not clarify. We suspect he was referring to his internal conflict about whether to obey the new norms of the Nazi racial community or stick to his Christian convictions. His confession approaches Nietzsche's claim that one lies to oneself for security—as if he were responding to a violent situation and violent people as a bystander in order to avoid becoming a victim himself.

---

43   *Sic*: he probably meant "to go through something" in the sense of "to endure." It seems
     unlikely that he actually walked when chased by an officer.
44   M001b 42:43.

We believe that Hans was on the edge of thinking critically about his role in defending the Nazi regime. The next story he told was how he *almost* became a hero. "Towards the end of the war," he continued, "I would say my attitude toward the Nazis was one almost of blind hatred." Returning to the blisters: when Hans saw the SS officer's "sneering" face, "leaning heavily on his mistress," with something "diabolical" and "hateful" about him, Hans felt the urge to choke him to death.[45] Hans saw himself as the protagonist of his own drama. He wanted to respond to Nazi barbarism with heroic action. But he did not.

Hans was on the verge of disclosing an open secret: that he was not really an ordinary German, constrained by totalitarianism from taking autonomous action or making ethical decisions. He had done many things, but often helping Hitler achieve his policy goals or at least not actively resisting them. The lie that he was just an ordinary German was so very potent and so very functional because it was embodied rather than reflected upon. Ironically, however, he could not ignore those memories of violence after the fact because he still felt them so vividly in his body.

These "rough edges" of his memory are part and parcel of the "unevenness" of modernity in general.[46] To oversimplify the dynamic, Hans began his life as a Christian and was asked to become a Nazi. These incongruities of the self emerged as a result of the adjustments that he made to changing historical circumstances. He remembered *Kristallnacht* in particular because of its violence and the way that that violence challenged his sense of self, but the same could be said of the incident with the blisters.

These divergent selves make the work of memory notoriously difficult. On an individual level memories resist incorporation into smooth-flowing narratives of progress and meaning. Insofar as all memories, like all self-deceptions, implicate selves in human relationships, memory is also a category of responsibility. Hans was perfectly aware that, in remembering *Kristallnacht*, he was obliged to think about what he did and should have done.[47] Whether as the history of a person or a group, memories demand a critical response.

Hans the Bystander

Hans recalled an incident when he was a first taken prisoner by the United States Army that illustrates the problem of self-critical responsibility.[48] He

45 M001b 41:50.
46 Harootunian, *History's Disquiet.*
47 W. James Booth, *Communities of Memory: On Witness, Identity, and Justice* (Ithaca: Cornell University Press, 2006).
48 M001b 42:43.

traveled for three or four hours on a truck standing next to a young Spanish soldier who had had a leg amputated and complained incessantly about the pain. When they finally arrived in Rheims, Hans helped him off the truck and walked behind him slowly as he used his crutches, "trying to give some support to him." At the gate of the camp, a drunk American soldier was using the butt of his rifle to beat prisoners who did not move through fast enough. Visibly enraged at this slow young Spaniard, the G. I. took his crutches away, slapped him in the face, and "virtually" kicked him into the camp. The Spaniard landed in a puddle. "I still remember the sensation that went through me," Hans recalled, but now that it had become discourse in the realm of mind, Hans was obliged to reflect critically on it. "It was almost a repeat of the experience with that SS man," he analyzed, trying to fit these disruptive memories into a coherent autobiography of an autonomous self.

> I went over there, blood has been [sic] drained from my face. I just looked at him, stared at this American with hatred. I knew what he had done, and he was just about to lift his rifle in order to hit me, and at that moment, I mean, one thought went through my mind. "God, don't let him do it, because once he hits you, you know, you lose control, you go for him—and you lose your life." He must have sensed that in me, because his rifle came down again.

His decision to fight against terror, instead of defending it, came after the Third Reich had already been defeated. His compassion was directed to someone with whom he could identify—a fellow POW—not the primary victims of Nazi terror, most notably the Jews. Even in Rheims, Hans stuck to the habit of playing the ordinary German.

Throughout the interview, Hans presented himself in passive terms, as if he were the object rather than the subject of his own biography. An unskilled, Methodist worker, his father heroically defended his son's rights to equal treatment. Hans felt the humiliation of being different. "That ran through me like a knife." His father challenged teachers who accused Hans of being insufficiently fascist; Hans learned that outsiders were vulnerable to abuse. "It made me feel very insignificant and very fragile." He was able to stave off most of the verbal abuse by being a splendid athlete, excelling in boxing, wrestling, skiing. There is much to be gained in collaboration when one fits the Aryan ideal: an exaggerated sense of status for an outsider. Still, Hans assumed the role of non-conformity. He claimed he was always just pretending to be a Nazi; that he felt like a *poseur*.[49] Predictably, the more he played the role, the better it fit. In this respect Hans was typical of many ordinary Germans.

To be sure, Hans got conflicting messages from authority figures. When a Hitler Youth Troop Leader tried to convince him to play hooky from Sunday

---

49   M001a 01:40, 05:18, and 08:15 with quotes at 04:08 and 04:22.

school in order to attend a Hitler Youth rally in Nuremberg, his otherwise gentle father grew overwrought and violent, grabbing the young man by the throat and physically throwing him down the staircase. Hans admired his father "for taking a stand," but Hans preferred to avoid such confrontations entirely, fearing the repercussions. Surprisingly the young Troop Leader never reported the incident to the Secret State Police, or *Gestapo*.[50] Physically active to the point of being wild, a voracious reader of pulp-fiction novels, and a trained pilot, Hans certainly identified with the protagonists of heroic narratives, heroism that he saw reflected in his father's behavior in everyday life. Yet such expectations—and his memories of them—can just as readily inspire feelings of inferiority as inspire great deeds. Hans always seemed to compare his behavior to his father and find himself wanting.[51]

Hans claimed that he experienced the Night of Broken Glass in "vivid" terms, but in fact they were typical of many ordinary Germans for whom these events were extraordinary.[52] The SS threatened him and his other gentile neighbors into silence when the SS "escorted" his Jewish neighbors out of the apartment house in nothing but their pajamas. Still, Hans and his brother ran in the direction of the synagogue to see the commotion. Hans saw flames shooting into the sky out of the synagogue as well as drunken SS troops burning menorahs and *Torah* scrolls on feather beds that had belonged to the Rabbi and Cantor, slit open in the search for hidden Jewish gold. Hans described being horrified by these events, wondering, like some of the adults, why the German firemen did not extinguish the flames but only stood by to make sure that the fire did not spread to the other houses in the neighborhood. Nonetheless, "we went back and continued to school." His fanatical elementary-school teacher told him and his classmates to help spread antisemitic slogans and destroy Jewish shop windows and cemeteries. They were let out of school the same day to these Nazi ends. But his parents forbade him to even leave the house.

Traditionally historians have called such people *bystanders*,[53] but that term is based on a fundamental misunderstanding of the self. The self is cultivated as a series of choices that involve others.[54] Hans would like to have excused himself as a bystander, but even he could not completely convince himself of his crippling sense of powerlessness. Hans, of course, was an adolescent. Historians tend to excuse many of the deeds of youth because, as children,

---

50   M001a 10:23 with quote at 16:10.
51   M001a 13:00, 15:45, 19:58, 22:45, 25:25, 45:35; M001b 30:40.
52   M001a 27:03.
53   E. g., Broszat and Fröhlich, *Bayern*; Hilberg, *Perpetrators*.
54   Koslov, *Gewalt*, 470-475; Wildt, *Volksgemeinschaft*, e. g., 63-68, 96-100, 135-44, 213-217, 352-374.

they were presumably not yet coherent, autonomous, responsible beings.[55] Yet the example of Hans actually helps us appreciate the degree to which young people like him were both constrained by circumstances beyond their control and responsible for signing the fascist social contract nonetheless.[56] The essential lie here concerns this putative absence of agency, when in fact Hans was busy participating in the strenuous life of the Hitler Youth from boxing and wrestling to going to school when his neighbors were being terrorized. The more Hans told these stories, the more he recognized the contradictions in his role as protagonist and victim.

Hans and Heinrich

The memory work of the interview became dangerous for Hans when it interrupted the coherence of his autobiography. It reminded him of the first moment when he signed the fascist social contract and adopted the bad habits of self-deception. Around 1983, Hans read an article about the first return visit of Henry Kissinger, former United States Secretary of State under President Richard Nixon, to his hometown of Fürth. It evoked a rather dangerous memory in Hans of an encounter with "Heinrich" Kissinger who had lived on his street in their youth.[57]

There are many reasons to suspect that this meeting did not take place with Kissinger himself. It is not mentioned in any of the classic biographies of Kissinger.[58] Hans may also have been guilty of inflating the importance of this memory, and therefore of himself, through an association with a future world leader. Yet there is no reason to believe that Hans did not have a similar encounter with another Jewish boy who he then later transposed with Kissinger. The encounter was memorable for the same reasons that *Kristallnacht* had been; Hans was an Aryan and, whoever this other boy was, he was a Jew.

It is important to keep in mind, however, that Hans is the author of this entire anecdote. What appears to be "Heinrich" Kissinger's account of these events are in fact filtered through Hans. According to Hans, after Kissinger attended a soccer game, he gave reporters a rare glimpse into his childhood. Hans retold Kissinger's story in the interview from Kissinger's point of view:

> I [Kissinger] was one of the older Jewish students there, and I was a passionate soccer player. Every so often, the ball would land in enemy territory, across that long wall... And then, it was always the question: who should retrieve that ball.

---

55 Kater, *Hitler Youth*.
56 Wildt, *Volksgemeinschaft*, 211-213, 295.
57 M001b 22:50.
58 Ralph Blumenfeld, *Henry Kissinger: The Private and Public Story* (New York: Signet, 1974), 18-29; Walter Isaacson, *Kissinger: A Biography* (New York: Simon and Schuster, 1992); Marvin Kalb and Bernard Kalb, *Kissinger* (Boston: Little, Brown and Co, 1974).

Since Kissinger had the reputation, even then, of being the most aggressive, the other children always sent him. Most of the time, these excursions into foreign territory were uneventful, but Kissinger remembered one incident in particular.

> One day it was awfully silent on the other [side] and the ball had landed again [over there]…I hesitated to get it back because I thought it was a trap that someone had set for me.

Reading Kissinger's story, Hans recalled his own experience:

> Suddenly the whole thing stood very clearly before me. Because it was an experience which I have never forgotten either. I was the only boy in the courtyard at that time. And I was near the steps of that Methodist church and the ball had landed right there at my feet. And I knew where it came from. I picked up that ball and waited. And then I saw this boy ["Heinrich"]. He looked to the left and he looked to the right and then seeing me, and then stopping in his tracks. And then we looked at each other. There wasn't a word spoken.

Hans seemed to realize how amazing this account sounded. Kissinger had lived at number 35 on Hans's street; Hans at number 33. "I can show you. I have a photograph of the whole thing." He explained that his mother had also witnessed the entire incident from a window above these courtyards. He believed that she too saw the silent tension that had settled on both sides of this wall.

> Except that she didn't know how I felt inside: I felt a tremendous sense of sadness, because it was clear to me that the boy—he didn't trust me. That he suspected that either I would beat him up, or I would give the signal for the other boys to come out of their hiding and pounce on him. Because there was a tremendous distance between us, as he came closer to us, and we made eye contact, he somehow sensed that I meant him no harm. I didn't say a word. I wordlessly handed him the ball. We looked at each other. He took the ball. And at first, it seemed to me, he wanted to break into a run. Then he stopped himself and he went out with great dignity, holding the ball in his hand.

Hans told similar stories elsewhere in the interview. He recounted, for instance, how a Nazi neighbor had denounced him as a hooligan, threatening deportation to a work camp; but he also recalled other incidents when ordinary Germans and Nazi officials overlooked his family's non-conformity to Nazi antisemitism—arguably in order to keep these Aryans in the Nazi fold.[59] That is, Hans understood that his interactions with neighbors could have serious repercussions for himself and his family, though it depended on what each person chose to do in these interpersonal situations.

Above all, Hans realized that he had the relative freedom to make choices even within situations dictated to him by circumstances beyond his control.

---

59 M001a 00:00, 01:40, 37:00.

Hans could treat Heinrich with respect in keeping with the best principles of a civil society, or he could help Hitler to remake that world into a *Volksgemeinschaft* based on fascist and racist principles.[60] To be sure, Hans did not create the wall that stood between them, the antisemitism that weighed down on them, or the Third Reich that hovered over them. He did not choose to look so Aryan. But he did have to choose which role to play, which contradictory social expectations to follow, which world he wished to inhabit, for himself and for Heinrich.

Needless to say, Hans resented having to make such weighty choices. He was aware that his behavior shaped his social context for both himself and others, but he did not like to be reminded that he was not as powerless as he claimed to be. The incident while playing ball thus served as Hans's personal Night of Broken Glass. It was his "first" encounter with the brutal essence and ethical conundrum of the Third Reich: either collaborate in the Nazi system of terror and violence or risk your own neck. In the end, Hans chose precisely that kind of self-deception that generated, and propagated, the fascist social contract. He chose neither to fight nor to play with Heinrich. He neither implemented a racist dystopia as such nor preserved his civil society. He made himself into a bystander—and then treated his self-deception as an essential and natural truth about him.

At this stage, Hans did not engage in critical self-reflection. "It oppressed me," he said later in the interview,[61] referring to the antisemitic segregation of the playground, "and yet I didn't give voice to it, perhaps because I was too young. But somehow I knew it was wrong. I did not feel good about it." Instead of acting on his intuition, Hans learned to passively observe as his neighbors suffered from an abstract fascist terror that loomed in the shadows above him, behind the boy who looked the perfect Aryan.

Hans did not seem to be particularly involved in murder. He did not personally kill or hurt any Jews, though he left ambiguous the scope of his activities in an anti-aircraft unit. Our point is that he collaborated in fascist violence nonetheless by letting himself be tyrannized by his own lies, or as Nietzsche put it: by lying from his heart. He remembered incident after incident when the self-deception of his passivity was tied to Nazi barbarities directed at Jews or even himself. This memory nagged because his ethical failure was personal: he saw how his behavior affected actual neighbors like Heinrich. From that point forth, Hans had to remain a committed believer in his own powerlessness, he had to continue to abide by the dictates of this self-imposed autocratic lie, or else he had to admit to his role in a system of racial violence.

---

60   Wildt, *Volksgemeinschaft*.
61   M001b 36:50.

We would like to suggest that a series of self-deceptions lie at the core of the problem of coming to terms with the Nazi past for ordinary Germans like Hans. What became narratives about self-deception after the fact began as habits of self-deception in lived experience. Hans anticipated the troubling questions that would be posed about his behavior by his mother, by his neighbors, by himself. It was the work of memory to transform those events *even as they transpired* such that they preserved his impunity in everyday life. When he let the lie master him, it became a truth about his self. This kind of motivated irresponsibility allowed him to continue to do many things to live his life, including aid the Nazi regime, and yet act as if he was just ordinary.

These self-deceptions were addictive. Hans employed them to deal with a number of new experiences throughout the Third Reich and afterwards. To be sure, he could still remember the contradictions in his own behavior. Hans experienced his inability to act in corporeal terms: walking on eggs, razor blade cuts, blind hatred, blood drained from his face, looking at Heinrich in silence, wordlessly handing him the ball. Hans became the masks he wore; the lie became its own truth.

Performing Lies

A skeptic might dismiss these interviews as purely rhetorical. Theodora and Hans have a clear motive for wanting to present themselves in a particularly sympathetic light. They had every reason to believe that their young American interlocutor suspected them of Nazi collaboration. Aware of the fact that these interviews were part of scholarly research, they were speaking as much to posterity as to Drew. No doubt, Theodora and Hans were intentionally performing a role for their presumed audience.

This theatrical metaphor is worth taking seriously. There is an obvious connection between the problem of self-deception and performance. Both involve the studied manipulation of reality for effect. If we want to make sense of self-deception, particularly in the context of narrative interviews, we need to consider the performative nature of the self in any interpersonal situation.

Goffman on Selling the Self

The scholar who best theorized the role of performance in human social relations was the sociologist Erving Goffman. In his 1959 book *The Presentation of Self in Everyday Life*,[62] Goffman argued that a speaker is always in essence

---

62 Erving Goffman, *The Presentation of Self in Everyday Life* (New York: Doubleday, 1959), 52.

a salesman, less interested in facts and more concerned with what others will find convincing. The ensuing presentation resembles an artistic work in the sense that speech, gestures, and props, in the midst of scenery designed to lend effect, are planned out in advance to the greatest extent possible.

Goffman makes explicit analogies between performances on the stage of art and of life. In social settings, he claims that interlocutors always approach the presentation of the other with skepticism. In anticipation, the speaker selectively edits the presentation to conceal factors that would raise doubts in the audience. Every individual must be capable of playing multiple roles, even during a single communicative act. Goffman describes a spectrum between *sincerity* and *cynicism* in the speaker's self-presentation; we select positions along this spectrum situationally in order to persuade.[63] Like Nietzsche, Goffman implies that every individual has a plurality of masks from which to choose, actively and subjectively, while performing in any given situation. Not only is the self a fragmentary collection of identities, but like actors, we must constantly choose which identities or combination of identities to present to interlocutors.

Goffman recognizes that deception is an integral part of social interactions since persuasion is the underlying intention of communication, whether it is explicitly argumentative or just uses non-verbal signals to create a good impression on others. Yet Goffman does not clearly map *self*-deception onto his polarities of sincere and cynical. He is not interested in determining whether a sincere or cynical performance might not also constitute a lie to the self. Like Nietzsche we argue that there is no gap between self-presentation and self-cultivation. We have no more authentic self behind our masks. We are our own press.

Brecht on Performing the Self

The performativity of selfhood leads us to several conclusions. We are not who we are in this sense of being a true or singular identity. Rather we are how we act among others.[64] This premise lies at the heart of the play *A Man's A Man* by Germany's most famous modern playwright, Bertolt Brecht.[65]

Brecht's title presents us with a tautology: that a man is a man in this straight-forward and singular sense of identity. As with much of Brecht's work, we should read this title ironically. It warns us that he will challenge our assumptions about selfhood. *A Man's A Man* is Brecht's signature work on this

---

63 Goffman, *Performance*, 17-21.
64 S. a. Butler, *Gender Trouble*.
65 Brecht, *A Man's A Man*, trans. Eric Bentley in *Seven Plays by Bertolt Brecht*, ed. Bentley, 69-147 (New York: Grove Press, 1961).

issue. His fourth major play, it was the first to be written over a long period of time, from 1919 to 1925. This long genesis shows how central the issue of selfhood was to Brecht's thinking as an artist and political activist.

When Brecht moved from his hometown of Augsburg to Munich in 1918 to begin his university studies, he was a lukewarm supporter of the revolutionary communist government that ruled Bavaria for the first half of 1919. He began his theater career in this city and then moved to Berlin in 1922 in pursuit of greater opportunities. Both cities had active Nazi cells throughout the 1920s, and Brecht was an emphatic and persistent opponent of their politics. In 1926 he read *Capital*, Marx's critical analysis of capitalism, and declared himself a communist. Although he was not very good at toeing the party line over the next thirty years, he consistently associated with Leftists. The Nazis openly vilified his writings during the Weimar period; he fled into exile the day after the burning of the Reichstag in 1933.

We do not select Brecht just because of his politics. As works of art, his plays expose the relationship between performance and selfhood in ways that are often hard to see in everyday life. In *A Man's A Man*, we want to focus on Brecht's protagonist, Galy Gay. Brecht wanted his audience to read the life stories of his characters as models for everyday life. What we learn from Galy Gay about self-deception on the stage is therefore directly relevant to our discussion of responsible selfhood more generally.

Brecht creates characters that act out situations of everyday life, even if he shifts the "everyday" to exotic locations and cloaks it in absurdly exaggerated conflicts. This play concerns Galy Gay, an Irish porter living in Kilkoa, India. He leaves home one day to buy a fish for his wife to cook, and he ends up becoming Jeraiah Jip, a soldier in the British army. In other words, a man is not self-evidently who he claims to be. Over the course of the play, the audience learns that a man is a man means that a porter is a soldier, Galy Gay is Jeraiah, and, amazingly, a man is even an elephant. We will explain these remarkable transpositions in a moment; here we simply want to note that they occur for us as viewers while watching the play. The fact that the audience can observe these transformations of self helps Brecht make his main point about selfhood: we are the roles we play.

As audience members, we know that we are seeing actors who can play any role called for. The theater context draws even more attention to the performativity of self, though of course Brecht is keen on emphasizing that it is not just in the theater that selfhood operates in this way. Both Brecht and Goffman are making very similar points: the ever-shifting roles we see on the stage of art mirror the kinds of identity fluctuations we participate in every day. Social interactions are intrinsically *an act*.

Galy Gay the Performer

It can help us to think about *A Man's A Man* as a *station play*. A term used by literary scholars, it refers to the fact that the different scenes are relatively isolated from one another. The protagonists reappear in these stations and thus provide continuity for the play; but the different scenes appear to the audience at best as loosely grouped anecdotes from the fictional biography of the characters. These incidents serve as isolated character studies and are designed to invite in-depth analysis of character without the distractions of plot. This kind of play suits our purposes perfectly as analogies to the anecdotes available to us as scholars working with narrative interviews and the flashes of memory available to us as ordinary people struggling with the past.

Typical of the beginning of a play, Brecht gives us some information about Galy Gay in the first scene that will help us understand him at these later stations. His wife tells him as he leaves their home: "You're like an elephant, the most cumbersome beast in the world of beasts, but, when it comes to running, he runs like a passenger train."[66] Only later do we come to understand why Galy Gay is like both an elephant and a passenger train. Close to the end, to avoid selling a stolen elephant, Galy Gay sheds his name in favor of becoming a soldier. The British army immediately ships him out to the front by train, where Galy Gay distinguishes himself for his ferocity. The symbolic connection between an elephant and a train thus strikes at the very heart of the existential message of the play. Right from the beginning, Brecht warns his audience that, once Galy Gay takes on a role, he plays it to the hilt.

Galy Gay also fits Goffman's model. He is like a salesman who only wants to solicit agreement from others, but he has his own self-interest in mind. He enters into agreements only when there is something in it for him. Soon after leaving home, for instance, he meets the widow Begbick, who runs a traveling cantina for the soldiers of the British army. Instead of going to market to buy the fish, he carries Begbick's vegetable basket for three hours back toward the soldier's camp. Begbick has promised to pay him for carrying the basket. What Brecht shows the audience is that Galy Gay is a man who will do anything for money.

Yet Galy Gay is also not sophisticated enough to work out the fine points of these deals and often gets taken advantage of. Walking back with Begbick, she manipulates their conversation to convince him to do this same service for free. Brecht depicts Galy Gay as a man who believes other people's lies because he is a liar himself. It would be kind to think that Galy Gay learns the habit of lying from his encounters with people like Begbick, but he gives reason to believe otherwise in this first encounter with her. He mentions to Begbick: "I

---

66 Brecht, *A Man's*, 72.

have an imagination, let me tell you. For example, I've often had enough of a fish before I've even seen it."[67] Galy Gay's great imagination allows him to create fictions. Yet his claim is without a doubt *untrue*, for he is hungry and he had been on the way to the market to satisfy that hunger.

Galy Gay is thus a bit of a departure from Goffman's model. In his progression through the stations of the play, he learns to refine his creativity to become a better liar. Still, he complies with the lies of others because he tells lies and expects other people to believe him. In other words, Galy Gay is so committed a liar that he makes himself vulnerable to the manipulations of others. He becomes completely gullible. There is a sense in which Theodora and Hans seem to have fallen into this trap. Brecht uses the fictionality of art to depict this all-too-human fault in an extreme form.

Galy Gay and the Soldiers

Though his commitment to lying makes him vulnerable to the lies of others, Galy Gay uses his own lies in a surprisingly self-aware manner. He gladly changes his identity if there is anything in it for him. Yet he is completely aware that he is a liar who uses deception for personal gain.

In our terms, Galy Gay refuses the second-order lie. He knows that he is lying and does not dissimulate about his role in reinventing himself. On the whole, this contradiction in Galy Gay's character is absurd. It seems unrealistic that he is so very aware of his manipulation of lies for his own personal gain while remaining so very vulnerable to the lies of others. This contradiction, however, is precisely what Brecht wishes to emphasize.

Brecht explores this issue in Galy Gay's relationship with the three soldiers—Polly, Jesse, and Uria. They repeatedly exploit Galy Gay through lies, and he alters his identity accordingly. In an earlier scene, the four soldiers had robbed a temple; the original Jeraiah Jip, one of the four, was partially scalped while trying to escape. Since his deformed scalp would have incriminated them at the next roll call, his three comrades chose to abandon him; but even his absence at roll call will land them in hot water with their sergeant. So they need someone to act as if he was Jeraiah Jip.

Here is where Galy Gay proves useful to them. The three soldiers secretly watch Galy Gay's conversation with Begbick and draw the conclusion that he is a man "who can't say 'no'."[68] His inability to resist makes him an easy target for a scam. The soldiers agree to pay him in cigars and beer for taking on the role of Jip. But more than the pay alone motivates Galy Gay:

---

67 Brecht, *A Man's*, 80.
68 Brecht, *A Man's*, 80.

I did these gentlemen a good turn. Isn't that what really matters in this world? You send up a little balloon—saying 'Jeraiah Jip' is no harder to say than 'Good evening'—and *you're just the man people wish you to be*—it's not difficult at all.[69]

Up to this point, Galy Gay had been lying to get the things he wanted. Now he comes to understand that the best way to improve his situation is to become what other people want him to be. He is no longer lying about facts but about who he is. Still, if he is happy to deceive others about his identity, he does not lose sight of the fact that he is not Jip for real. He deceives others but resists becoming *self*-deceived

At this stage, Galy Gay can still opt out of these deceptions: he can still choose between being Galy Gay or Jeraiah Jip. The story gets really interesting when the soldiers decide to trick him once again in order to compel him to stick to his lies. They hoodwink Galy Gay into selling a fake elephant that he does not own in order to irredeemably tarnish his original name "Galy Gay." This situation is similar to the swindlers and the Kaiser: the soldiers are trying to create a situation where it will be hard for Galy Gay to escape the social contract of liar and dupe.

Figure 3. Bertolt Brecht, *A Man's A Man*, "Elephant Sale," 1925.
Source: Akademie der Künste, Berlin, Bertolt-Brecht-Archiv, BBA-FA 2078/022.

---

69 Brecht, *A Man's*, 88; our emphasis.

Typical of a Brecht play, things never go as planned and the story gets quite complicated, with circumstance working out ironically in ways no one anticipated. When Galy Gay first sees the fake elephant that the three soldiers have hastily pieced together, he circles it skeptically, wondering how he is going to pawn off such a sickly looking creature. Begbick agrees to buy the elephant if Galy Gay will sell it, so Galy Gay overcomes his skepticism. The soldiers then scatter in the hope that the sergeant will catch Galy Gay red-handed in the process of selling a stolen elephant. The sergeant does not come by, however. Instead, the pause gives Galy Gay time to reflect on his actions.

> My mother used to tell me one knows nothing for certain. But you, Galy Gay, you know nothing, either for certain or otherwise. You went out this morning to purchase a fish; you now have an elephant; and who knows what tomorrow may bring? But it's all one so long as you get paid.[70]

We describe all of these details to highlight the way our protagonist has changed himself strategically to accommodate his ever-changing situation. Galy Gay now has many identities: the man who went out for a fish, and the man who is selling an elephant, Jeraiah Jip and Galy Gay. And he is good with that. He uses his flexibility of self to get what he wants. When Begbick and the others return, he creates a detailed story of the fake elephant's noble birth, its youthful and strong condition, and its value as an investment. Galy Gay is growing bold in his deceptions. Indeed, he is now lying *like an actor*. He is both playing the role and aware of his role-playing.

Galy Gay differs from the other examples in this chapter. He insists on staying aware of his own role in his own self-deceptions. Moreover, he insists on making his audience aware that these are performances as well. Never once does he afford himself the luxury of deceiving himself about his own lies. Here is Brecht's point. In performing our many different selves, we should never take our roles so seriously that we forget that we are actors.

Galy Gay the Poseur

Galy Gay spins lies like yarn about the wonderful qualities of this elephant. We are reminded of the swindlers who described their cloth to the Kaiser in similarly aggrandizing prose. Yet Galy Gay admits to himself in the play, and thus to the actual theater audience, that he is just performing. Why does he intentionally undermine this second-order lie? Finding an answer to this question seems pertinent, given the fact that Theodora and Hans stuck so religiously to their deceptions about their own deceptions.

---

70   Brecht, *A Man's*, 115-116.

The reason Theodora and Hans lied to themselves about their lies is that they wanted to believe that they really were the things they claimed to be—and that those identities were theirs naturally. Galy Gay, by contrast, is not interested in understanding himself in terms of how others see him—for instance, as a wealthy man who can afford an elephant, or as a conscientious owner of a healthy animal, or even as a businessman who only sells the finest of products. Galy Gay understands lying solely in existential terms as a means of survival. He is poor. This money will allow him to return to his wife with the ability to buy food, or alternatively to stay in Begbick's cantina to drink and smoke. The point is also not to see Galy Gay as a particularly noble or good man. He is an excellent survivor. In one version of the end of the play, the soldiers have to stage his mock execution and funeral before he will finally become Jeraiah Jip. Galy Gay is too crafty otherwise; the soldiers must close off the possibility of his returning to that role. The point remains: Galy Gay never forgets that he is a *poseur*.

The duplicitous soldiers are the foil for both Galy Gay as a character and a counter-example for Brecht's claims about critical self-awareness. In an exemplary scene early in the play, the four soldiers, including the original Jip, rob a temple and shoot it up with their machine gun. Here is when Jip gets scalped and left behind by his comrades for fear that they would be held responsible for their crime if his wound were seen by their superior officer. Once they used Galy Gay to avoid punishment, the three soldiers come back to the temple to find Jip, whom they prefer to Galy Gay.

Wang, the temple priest, lies to them about holding Jip captive. He then tells them a curious story:

> The man you are looking for is not here. But that you may see that the man who you say is here—and who I do not know to be here—is not your man, permit me to explain it all to you with the aid of a drawing. Allow your unworthy servant to draw four criminals with chalk.

In this complicated way, Wang is telling the soldiers that, if Jip were there, then he would be the proof that the four of them robbed his temple. Notice though how Wang is not referring to them by name, as if to emphasize that identity is a fluid and situational thing.

Brecht then gives this stage direction to Wang: "He draws them on the door of the prayer box." This image reinforces the effect of his speech: to suggest to the audience that identity is nothing more than how we represent ourselves. The published version of the play comes with an illustration; we use it as the frontispiece for this chapter as it seems to capture visually the inherent duplicity in selfhood. Wang explains:

> One of them has a face, so that one sees who he is, but three of them have no faces. They cannot be recognized. Yet the one with the face has no money, therefore he is

no thief. But the ones with the money have no faces, therefore they cannot be recognized. That's how it is as long as they are not together. But when they are together, the three headless men grow faces, and other people's money will be found in their pockets. I would never be able to believe you if you said that a man who might be found here was your man.[71]

A representation of the fluidity of selfhood, this performance of performances reminds us that who we are is only situationally true. Selfhood depends on who we choose to be and with whom. And if we "grow faces" only when we "are together," we also discover our responsibility—this temple priest reminds us—only in social situations.

The actual story Wang tells about the other characters is only provisionally true, however. The soldiers incriminate themselves by being at the temple in possession of the donations that they stole. His parable is also full of deceptions. If Jip has no money on him to prove that he is a thief, it is not for lack of trying; and Wang does not need the soldiers to hang around for faces to grow on them in order to know that they are the thieves. His story is also prefaced in this scene by lies. It ends with a lie about Jip, whom everyone can hear moaning in the very box Wang draws on. As the soldiers reluctantly leave the temple, they exchange more lies with Wang. The point of all of these lies is that everyone knows that everyone is lying to everyone else. The way he tells this story certainly reinforces that conclusion with the theater audience. Wang even publically recognizes that each of the characters need the others in order for their lies to operate. Nonetheless, they all act as if these lies were not lies.

Galy Gay is different from the soldiers and the priest. While they insist on deceiving themselves about their own deceptions, Galy Gay admits that he is lying. Galy Gay is Brecht's protagonist for this reason: he shows us that *awareness of our lying selves is the first step on the path to responsibility.*

Galy Gay the Murderer

Galy Gay is a model not without its problems. Here is a man who has convinced himself that he can pass himself off as the soldier, Jeraiah Jip. Indeed, Galy Gay actually *becomes* Jeraiah Jip in all of the endings to the play. In one version, Galy Gay takes this role so far that he buries his old identity—literally eulogizing himself over his grave. In the other, he takes the lead when his unit destroys the fortress of Sir El Dchowr at the end of the play. The first ending results in a fictive death of his prior self; the second in the deaths of hundreds of other people. In 1936, Brecht even reconsidered this ending again such that

---

71 Brecht, *A Man's*, 91.

Galy Gay the Murderer appeared in a Nazi uniform.[72] In this third version, he made an explicit link between his play and Hitler's coming war for *Lebensraum*.

Brecht's theater thus raises the core questions of this chapter about the relationship between lies and violence. What does Brecht want us to make of the violence at the end of this play? And what is he telling us about the circumstances which seem to compel Galy Gay into believing these lies so sincerely? He surely does not condone Galy Gay's violent acts, but he does not want us to believe that Galy Gay's self-deception *automatically* leads to violence. The whole point of the play is to show that a man is not preset into his role and that we remain responsible for the roles we play.

Self-deception liberates us from the constraints of our society; it is up to us to decide what we do with this liberty. Galy Gay is not compelled to only be a murderous soldier just as Hans was not compelled to only be a Nazi. The Galy Gay who destroys the fortress, or the Galy Gay who eulogizes himself, is a Galy Gay who can assume many roles. By presenting the audience with the many different masks that Galy Gay wears, Brecht offers his protagonist to us as an illustration of our relative freedom of self-cultivation. We have the ability to play roles. Acting gives us the freedom to become the person we wish to be. It is up to us to consider how to do so responsibly.

Galy Gay is not the protagonist of the story because he is a good man; he is a model for us, even when he chooses to kill, because he does so from an existential position *aware of his own choices*. The soldiers and the temple priest are his foils because they deceive themselves without reflecting critically on their own lies. They perform their roles with a sense of sovereign impunity: refusing to recognize their role in their own selfhood and with the hopes of mastery. Galy Gay murders *en masse*, but at least he fully recognizes that he and only he is responsible for making himself into a murderer.

The road to responsibility begins with *a humble and skeptical reflection on the lies we tell ourselves about ourselves*. Yet this awareness by itself is not enough. If we are, as Brecht intended, now confronted with the necessity of lying in order to cultivate our selfhood, we still remain responsible for the way we perform those roles. Nevertheless, we have yet to determine the conditions under which our self-deceptions can become ethical. To conclude this chapter, we turn to theology, and what philosophy can learn from it. We argue that we are more apt to act responsibly if we recognize two things: *the role we play in the construction of our self* and *our dependence on others for who we become*.

---

72 See Brecht, *Grosse kommentierte Berliner und Frankfurter Ausgabe* (Frankfurt: Suhrkamp, 1988-2000), here vol. 24, 51. Henceforth: *GBA*.

The Lie of Coherence

Our conversations with Brecht, Hans, Nietzsche, and Theodora suggest that one of the underlying motives for self-deception is freedom. We lie in order to liberate ourselves from the constraints of our society and human relations. Historical circumstances may make these constraints seem quite awesome; modern German history is full of circumstances that seemed to compel ordinary Germans to particular kinds of actions against their will. Yet the drive for autonomy lies actually at the very core of the modern notion of selfhood. In response we try to define ourselves as prior and external to these conditions as a way to gain some sense of control over them.

The paradox here lies in the fact that we can only develop ourselves in cahoots with other people. We are dependent on others for who we become. Hans recognized his dependency on Heinrich. It was how he behaved *with Heinrich* that determined who Hans became—a Christian or a Nazi. Even his choice to become a bystander rested on abandoning his neighbor to the Nazis. Still, he could not forget that his self-cultivation as a bystander had consequences for others. Theodora, by contrast, tried to forget precisely that: the fact that her new identity as an Aryan master required the creation of a Jewish victim. In other words, there is a strong temptation—for people involved in role-playing, which is to say, all of us—to deny our connection to the audience on whom we depend for applause.

The modern obsession with autonomy all too often leads to violence. It offends our individuality to think that we can only be who we wish to become with the help of others. One easy response is to erase the memory that our selfhood was ever *contingent*. If we can forget our dependence on others for our self-cultivation, we can make ourselves seem not only more authentic but more sovereign. A further response is to pretend that the self is *coherent*. We take our selfhood as given in order to preserve our autonomy in the face of our actual experience. We ignore all of the multiple selves that we have been and can be. We act as if our identity existed prior to our performance of it. We ground our selfhood in an ontological condition outside of our actions so that we do not have to bear responsibility for the human consequences of its process.

The coherence of the modern individual is clearly a lie—and quite often a bad one. If we must recognize that self-deceptions are an essential part of the way selves develop and survive in modernity, we must also admit that the self does not always thrive in the process. All of the examples in this chapter demonstrate that an un-reflective attitude about one's own selfhood is dangerous for others as well as the self. Self-deception lies to us in this way that it will insulate us from danger. In fact, the more we remain uncritical about our role in our own self-deceptions, the more we place everyone at risk. There is also a sense in which these choices are shortsighted; if they seem harmless at all, at best that holds true only in the short term.

Continuing to misapprehend ourselves in the long term only makes matters worse. Particularly in the face of unethical or even criminal behavior in the past, we are tempted to continue to try to erase our responsibility for our own selfhood through forgetting our past actions. By seeking to control or even "master" the past, we once again are trying to liberate ourselves from the other human beings on whom our selfhood was and still is dependent. And just as we imagine ourselves to exist as coherent fixed entities prior to our agency, this false approach to memory imagines the past itself as fixed in the past—that is, as over and done with. We render the past non-threatening by divorcing selfhood from process.

All of this myth-making presupposes that the past places no demands on the present. Our lies show otherwise. We conclude this chapter by turning to Walter Benjamin and Johann Baptist Metz. Benjamin was a Jewish German and close friend of Brecht who also fled the Nazis only to commit suicide on the eve of the Occupation of France. He is a theologically informed philosopher who wrote about the problem of memory. Metz is a political theologian in Germany writing primarily after the war from a Christian tradition about the challenges of dealing with the Nazi past. Both authors help us to rethink how the self operates in time and in relation to responsibility.

Benjamin on History

We need self-deceptions in the violent conditions of modernity. The issue is how to face them responsibly. Our claim is that *the self must always remain fragmentary and open to the possibility of rupture if it is to assume responsibility for its self-deceptions.* Instead of a coherent self, Benjamin offers a model of the self that rejects closure in the name of responsibility. It is most evident in his conception of history as *messianic*.

In his theses "On the Concept of History," he described a "time of the now" (*Jetztzeit*) that is "shot through with splinters of messianic time."[73] For Benjamin, the *Jetztzeit* always contains the possibility of eschatological rupture. "Every second was the small gateway through which the Messiah might enter."[74] Here Benjamin is offering a particular definition of eschatology. He does not mean to imply that we should want to live in the end times—the utopia brought on by the return of the Messiah when the good find their reward and the evil their punishment. Eschatology for him is a process rather than a condition.

---

73 Benjamin, "Concept of History," Thesis XVIII A.
74 Benjamin, "Concept of History," Thesis XVIII B.

Eschatology offers us a way to approach everyday life, open to the possibilities it may offer. Consider the images Benjamin used to describe messianic time: the "arrest" of thought in a "constellation saturated with tensions," the "shock" that crystallizes in a "monad," the "messianic cessation of happening,"[75] the "tiger's leap into the past."[76] These images emphasize an attentiveness to process even as they freeze time in order to examine it closely and critically. They demonstrate his willingness to think through rupture in history.

Figure 4. Paul Klee, *Angelus Novus*, 1920. Source: Courtesy of Israel Museum.
© 2010 Artists Rights Society (ARS), New York/VG Bild-Kunst, Bonn.

75 Benjamin, "Concept of History," Thesis XVII.
76 Benjamin, "Concept of History," Thesis XIV.

These descriptions also communicate his conviction that this kind of thinking is necessary for understanding experience. Thesis IX, the famous *Angelus Novus* of history, proclaimed Benjamin's opposition to understanding history as progressive. Referring to a painting by Paul Klee that he owned, Benjamin described it as "the angel of history. His face is turned towards the past. Where we perceive a chain of events, he sees one single catastrophe which keeps piling wreckage upon wreckage." The problem with historical progress is that it justifies what was, including violence and death, for the sake of what is. But for Benjamin,

> The Messiah comes not only as the redeemer; he comes as the victor over the Antichrist. The only historian capable of fanning the spark of hope in the past is the one who is firmly convinced that even the dead will not be safe from the enemy if he is victorious.[77]

What Benjamin means here is common knowledge: history is written by the winners. The victors will even erase the memory of the dead to justify their conquests. We hardly expect ordinary Germans to do otherwise. It is easier to tell stories of everyday life during the Third Reich from the perspective of the Aryan *Übermensch* than of Nazi victims. These are the master's narratives as well as narratives of mastery. Benjamin refuses to believe these self-deceptions.

Neither is history "empty time" to be filled in with the facts reconstructed by historians.

> Articulating the past historically does not mean recognizing it 'the way it really was.' It means appropriating a memory as it flashes up in a moment of danger.[78]

For Benjamin, "memory work" undermines the narratives of mastery told by the victors to recover what has been silenced. These memories are *dangerous* as they place demands on the present in the name of the dead. "In the voices we hear, isn't there an echo of now silent ones?"[79] The victor's history is a seamless sequence of chronological events safely in the past leading to a justified present. Dangerous memories disrupt both this ideological narrative and the very linearity of secular time with alternate accounts.

Memory work recaptures those who have been erased in the active hope that we can prepare a better future. Yet this hope was "nourished by the image of enslaved ancestors rather than by the ideal of liberated grandchildren."[80] Benjamin's orientation was not towards a utopian future but a responsible present. The way to get there was by living with rupture.

---

77 Benjamin, "Concept of History," Thesis VI.
78 Benjamin, "Concept of History," Thesis VI.
79 Benjamin, "Concept of History," Thesis II. See fn. 60 in Myths for a discussion of dangerous memories.
80 Benjamin, "Concept of History," Thesis XII.

Benjamin on the Self

Living with rupture shows up both in Benjamin's understanding of his own selfhood and the way he narrated it. Benjamin's three attempts to tell the story of his life—*Moscow Diary, Berlin Chronicle,* and *Berlin Childhood around 1900*—can hardly be called an autobiography. Like the station plays of Brecht, he provides the reader with fragments of his life, often frozen somewhere between past and present.

Selfhood for Benjamin remained fragmentary thanks to these ruptures in time, much like Nietzsche's idea of the self, Goffman's idea of self-presentation, and Brecht's advocacy of role-playing. Yet if Benjamin's fragments are formally similar to interview anecdotes, his premise of "living with rupture" stands as a fascinating alternative to the kinds of self-deceptions to which Hans and Theodora habituated themselves. It reminds us more of Galy Gay whose awareness of his own lies means the story of his life will never be simple. It takes us to a place where we might be able to hear the voices of "the silent ones." Above all, living with rupture was not just a philosophical necessity for Benjamin but part of his personal resistance to totalitarianism.

Benjamin located the self as much in body as in mind. In writing the fragments of his life story, Benjamin followed the principle that "language has a body, and the body has a language." Yet Benjamin's corporeal self is resistant to being pinned down. This claim was intentional and political. While Benjamin was writing, the Nazis were politicizing the body. Their eugenic reorganization of Europe, leading to the systematic extermination of entire social groups, was premised on the ability to read identity self-evidently from surface appearances of the body. The Nazis imagined that they had rediscovered a foundational principle—race—that could restore stability to modern selfhood. Here they were making the same mistake that we discussed above: denying that selfhood is a process. As Gerhard Richter recognized, however, "the body prevents its reading from being organized into a closed hermeneutic system. In the moment of reading, it is in a certain sense already a corpse."[81] Hans experienced this problem personally as his body got read by different people in different situations in different ways all of which were beyond his control; and yet he responded to the dynamism of his own body by compressing it into the image he created for it—of the bystander.

Benjamin represents the body as fragmentary like the self. It is in fact useless to systems like fascism "that rely on presence, stability and access to stable meanings." Elaborate charts and complicated race laws did not solve this problem that the Nazis created for themselves. Entire German scientific

---

81   Gerhard Richter, *Walter Benjamin and the Corpus of Autobiography* (Detroit: Wayne State University Press, 2000), 158.

establishments had to be dedicated to clarifying the inevitable ambiguities of race, requiring the hands-on interventions of experts in a growing bureaucratic machinery of murder. "Instead of being employable by a stable network, [the body] renounces its use value as a concept. It is always already shifting into something else."[82] For Benjamin, living without closure in the body made it possible to resist the fascist appropriation of the corporeal self—in this case, quite literally, his "Jewish" body. What in Hans had been dangerous—the intransigent refusal of his memories to conform to what he wanted his biography to be—became in Benjamin the very vehicle of refusing the fascist social contract.

Brecht on Forbearance

Brecht thought about memory in much the same way that Benjamin suggested—through rupture. In the 1930s, the two friends spent significant time together at Brecht's exile home in Denmark. Brecht believed that he was living in one of Benjamin's dangerous moments that will require the work of memory in the future just as it requires ethical choices in the present.

It is worth considering Brecht's response to this conundrum as an alternative to the choices made by Theodora and Hans. Brecht came to understand that future generations, looking back on the behaviors of ordinary Germans during the Third Reich, would expect a straightforward resistance to it. The right thing to do was not always so clear, however. In his poem "To Those Born Later," Brecht wrote:

Oh, we
Who wanted to prepare the ground for friendliness
Could not ourselves be friendly.

...

Think of us
With forbearance.[83]

If the antifascist resistance deviated from its stated ideals, Brecht was willing to recognize it as a necessary action in the larger fight. Yet he also knew that the judgment of future generations may question such justifications.

Brecht never repudiated what he and others did. He knew that antifascist resistance involved violence and in some cases even hurt innocent people. He also felt guilty as an exile that he seemed to be avoiding taking the necessary personal risks and sacrifices that the times demanded of him.

---

82 Richter, *Corpus of Autobiography*, 159.
83 Brecht, "To Those Born Later," in *German 20th Century Poetry*, ed. R. Grimm and I. E. Hunt, trans. John Willet, 84-89, here 89.

For we went,
Changing countries oftener than our shoes,
Through the wars of the classes. Nothing
I do gives me the right to eat my fill.
...
And yet I eat and drink.

As this poem vividly expresses, Brecht was painfully aware of his own self-deceptions in both excusing violence and choosing exile. We may or may not agree with his choices; even he was doubting them. "Those in power/Sat safer without me: that was my hope." As a writer and intellectual in Germany, he strove to help the antifascist cause; that was his "hope." Yet he suspected that the Nazi regime was happy to be rid of him, and he worried that he could not be as effective in exile. Above all, Brecht, like his character Galy Gay, refused to allow himself the luxury of deceiving himself about his own self-deceptions. In our view, one component of what we mean by responsible selfhood is *this humble insistence on looking skeptically at the human consequences of our own lies.*

Brecht shares Benjamin's critical sensibility with regards to anticipatory memory. Both insist on skeptical self-scrutiny about the choices they make in the present in light of what they will say about themselves in the future. Compare them in this regard to Hans and Theodora, whose anticipatory memory tied their self to narratives of mastery. The latter lied to themselves, and then ignored their own self-deceptions, in order to allow themselves to write a victor's history in which their responsibility for violence was forgotten. Brecht did not just anticipate the critical scrutiny of future generations—us—who call him to account for his self-deceptions in the present. He welcomed this scrutiny.

The poem as a whole reaffirms the centrality of role-playing to selfhood. Self-deception remains a critical tool for Brecht: the capacity to embody a role in contradiction to one's beliefs, even during and after the war. Here Brecht parallels his friend Benjamin in challenging the mass mobilization of bodies by keeping open the alternatives for responsible action.[84] They grounded their

---

84   The very notion of self-cultivation seems to require a kind of violent displacement of the meaning of the self into the future akin to how Jacques Derrida accounted for the *originary* violence of any linguistic sign: the precise meanings of a word can never quite be constrained in the moment that it is posited because we know that those meanings will not be the same in the future. See *Of Grammatology*, trans. Gayatri C. Spivak (Baltimore: John Hopkins University Press, 1976). This displacement can take place where one redefines the self in order to act with impunity; or one could take it as the cornerstone for historical responsibility, insofar as this open-endedness to the meaning of the self becomes a means for humble and critical self-reflection. Derrida himself seemed to believe in the latter. See "Violence and Metaphysics," in *Writing and Difference*, trans. Allen Bass (Chicago: University of Chicago Press, 1978), 79-153.

fight against the Nazi bid for world domination by refusing to let their own lies master them.

Metz on Remembrancing

Both Benjamin and Brecht anticipate the postwar challenges of memory, but they do not resolve them. For even if responsibility in the present involves looking critically at our own self-deceptions, it does not offer an immediate answer to the problem of our past mistakes. The past cannot be changed; the dead can not be brought back to life. The work of memory after genocide is thus complicated by an impossible conundrum.

One of the leading intellectuals in postwar Germany to address this problem is the Catholic theologian Johann Baptist Metz. Born in 1928, Metz was just old enough to be drafted into the *Wehrmacht* as a 16-year old at the end of World War II. His biography has some superficial similarities to that of Hans. Metz's company, made up of youths his age, was given cursory military training and quickly deployed against the Americans who had already crossed the Rhine. One evening his company commander sent him to battalion headquarters with a message. When Metz returned the next day, he found his entire unit had been wiped out in an assault by American tanks and planes. His reaction:

> I saw only the lifeless faces of my comrades, those same comrades with whom I had but days before shared my childhood fears and my youthful laughter. I remember nothing but a soundless cry. I strayed for hours alone in the forest. Over and over again, just this silent cry! And up until today I see myself so. Behind this memory all my childhood dreams have disappeared.[85]

This experience was traumatic for Metz, and he only began speaking of it publicly decades later.[86] What we find interesting about his reaction to this experience is how he refuses to cast himself as victim. The experience has forced Metz to start with the problem of suffering in all his thinking; the suffering that concerns him is not his own, however, but the suffering of others. "I begin not with the question, 'What happens to me when I suffer, when I die?' but with the question, 'What happens to you when you suffer, when you die?'"[87] And as a *German* theologian, he has come to realize that suffering means he has to ask the question of what it means to do theology *after Auschwitz*.

---

85   Johann Baptist Metz, "Communicating a Dangerous Memory," *Love's Strategy: The Political Theology of Johann Baptist Metz*, ed. John K. Downey (Harrisburg: Trinity Press International, 1999), 137.

86   Shoshana Felman and Dori Laub, *Testimony: Crises of Witnessing in Literature, Psychoanalysis, and History* (New York: Routledge, 1992); and Cathy Caruth, ed., *Trauma: Explorations in Memory* (Baltimore: Johns Hopkins University Press, 1995).

87   Metz, "Communicating," 137.

This response to suffering shapes Metz's understanding of the self and responsibility. He understands the self, and faith, not as foundational and private but as politically situated and vulnerable. Metz locates the self in history because his experience with the vulnerability of the self to historical conditions has encouraged him paradoxically to call for that vulnerable self to exercise responsibility for those conditions. The experience of others's suffering also leads him to understand history not in the dialectical terms that he encountered in Marxist-Christian dialogue or in later liberation theology. He locates the self in history in terms of eschatological rupture, the kind of rupture he experienced the morning he found his dead comrades.

Eschatology traditionally is based on future hope; but for Metz, under the influence of Benjamin, it also is a matter of the past. Here is how Metz described dangerous memories in "The Future Seen from the Memory of Suffering":

> There are memories in which earlier experiences flare up and unleash new dangerous insights into the present. For brief moments they illuminate, harshly and piercingly, the problematic character of things we made our peace with a long time ago and the banality of what we take to be "realism." They break through the canon of the ruling plausibility structures and take on a virtually subversive character. Memories of this sort are like dangerous and uncalculable visitations from the past.[88]

Metz's memory of his "silent cry" is one such dangerous memory; Hans's memory of Heinrich Kissinger is another.

Like Brecht, Metz claims these memories have a future content that cannot be subsumed into controlling narratives of historical progress. Like Benjamin, history is not the additive totality of empty time, as if events can be simply inserted into a chronology. Historical meaning exists in the relationships between past and present, relationships between people. Note how he explicitly insists on the need to break through canons of self-evident realism. What he is suggesting is that our own memories can help us to serve this purpose of bringing us towards responsible selfhood. Our memories are dangerous because they unmask the certainty implicit in our un-reflected self-deceptions.

It is perhaps appropriate at this point to emphasize that we take the meaning of *memory work* seriously. We are talking about real labor here, as did Metz and Benjamin. It is why we speak of the German Sisyphus as the figure for responsible selfhood. This kind of critical self-reflection is not easy. More to the point, it is never-ending; for as long as we are alive we are still engaged in self-cultivation and therefore must look critically at our selfhood as a process.

---

88 Metz, "The Future Seen," 105.

More than simply making the past present through remembering, the work of memory involves, as Brecht described in his poem, responding to the future content of dangerous memories and the demands they put on the present. Metz, like Benjamin, uses the term *remembrancing*, or *Eingedenken*, to describe memory work. The German term connotes memory as an active process of thinking that has direct impact on the self. The practice of remembrancing turns to memory not simply as a window on the past but as a skeptical process that disrupts our own attempts to master the past. Metz refuses to subsume it under contemporary plausibility structures whether they are our assumptions about the self or official representations of our collectives.

Metz calls this kind of thinking *anamnestic reason*: that is, thinking that is historically and politically situated, that involves hope for the future on the basis of "solidarity backwards" with the dead, especially the victims of oppression whose past lives continue to demand justice.[89] As Nietzsche liked to do, Metz is flipping the signs of orthodox philosophy. Reason traditionally has been understood in terms of abstract universals. Modern reason in particular involves mastery if not domination. Anamnestic reason uses our unruly experiences to undermine the certainties of our reason and selfhood as well.

When we master anything, especially something as volatile as our selfhood, we lay claim to a form of fascist authority that our own experience obstinately denies. Because of its extraordinary crimes, the Third Reich cannot responsibly be thought through in terms of mastery. It is filled with dangerous memories precisely because it started as a series of ordinary lies that became an extraordinary truth. Anamnestic reason counters the motivated irrationality that made the Third Reich possible by insisting that we look self-critically at our own self-deceptions. Anamnestic reason accepts that we cannot undo the past—which makes the work of memory on-going. Nevertheless, it demands of us that we look critically at our self-deceptions about our own self-deceptions so that, at least now, we no longer allow our lies to master us.

Anamnestic reason is an implicit criticism of the kind of reason that operates through mastery—of others and of the self. Metz argues that "only as anamnestically constituted does reason prevent abstract understanding from taking progressive lack of recollection, progressive amnesia, for actual progress. Only anamnestic reason enables enlightenment to enlighten itself again concerning the harm it has caused."[90] There is a terrible violence in universal

---

89 See Ostovich, "Dangerous Memories and Reason in History," *KronoScope* 5/1 (2005): 41-57.

90 Johann Baptist Metz, "Anamnestic Reason: A Theologian's Remarks on the Crisis in the Geisteswissenschaften," *Cultural-Political Interventions in the Unfinished Project of the Enlightenment*, eds. Axel Honneth, Thomas McCarthy, Claus Offe, and Albrecht Wellmer (Cambridge: The MIT Press, 1992), 191.

categories of reason that lead us to forget those things that cannot be mastered by them.

Living historically entails living without the stability of closure. "I am not thinking of a memory which only serves to affirm us or to secure our identities—rather the opposite: it calls into question our tightly sealed-up identities. It is 'dangerous' memory; it makes one rather 'weak,' it creates an open flank."[91] We are suggesting that, at the very least, *responsibility entails this kind of openness in our thinking about history as well as about the self.* By converting self-deception into lucid and ongoing self- and historical criticism, dangerous memories call for the anamnestic reason capable of thinking through rupture responsibly.

Hans in Fragments

A final concrete example can perhaps help us to illustrate what responsible selfhood might look like in practice. The danger here of course is that you will misunderstand our intentions. Like Brecht, we need to remind you that our protagonists are human beings who make good and bad decisions. The point is not to heroize individuals—which only puts us back into particular roles, as if we are at our best when we are sure of our condition—but to open ourselves to the suffering of others, like Metz and Benjamin.

We suspect that Hans spent most of the postwar period in the former state, sure of his condition and forgetting the self-deceptions that helped him to survive the Third Reich in order to master his Nazi past. After the war he moved to South Africa and then to the United States, where he took a job as a teacher at a private Quaker high school. 1983 seemed to mark a turning point for him. Hans began to tell his story in a number of private and public venues. That alone is evidence of a sustained, self-conscious attempt to make sense of his contributions to the Third Reich—and to do so repeatedly, without hope for closure. He revisited his youth in Germany publicly, he explained to Drew six years later,[92] not because he felt particularly proud of what he had done. After all, he said, it is not "that I feel that I am a hero." He felt compelled to return to his adolescence in the Third Reich, he explained, because he had been raised to respect all human beings, to treat them with decency. Of course, that is precisely what he did not do. What had changed in him was that he had become all too aware of the ruptures in his sense of self.

---

91   Metz, *Hope Against Hope: Johann Baptist Metz and Elie Wiesel Speak Out on the Holocaust*, ed. Ekkehard Schuster and Reinhold Borschert-Kimmig, trans. J. Matthew Ashley (New York: Paulist Press, 1999), 33-34.

92   M001b 30:40.

The timing of this shift makes sense and not simply in terms of the publication of Kissinger's story in a newspaper. By 1983, the culture of history and memory in both the United States and Germany had shifted. It became not only acceptable but laudatory to bear witness to the past in public. Assuming the role of witness can also be tied to vanity, hypocrisy, self-pity, and melodrama; these tropes can easily fall into an irresponsible form of deception and self-deception. We see each of these qualities in Hans's testimony. By placing his autobiography under public scrutiny, Hans laid claim to the status of a postmodern kind of hero willing to face down the skeletons in his own closet before a studio audience.

We could also read this public confession of the self as a way to repress his existential anxiety about his own fractured sense of self. Sure enough, Hans sometimes fell back into the fascist habits of normalcy he had learned as a child. "We were caught up in this turmoil and we were torn here and there," he explained, "against our will, and without having much control over our lives." Had the war not ended, he continued, he would have become very hostile towards the Nazi regime and joined the German resistance in some form or another. "I rejected that whole sordid Nazi atmosphere," he insisted.[93] Hans returned here to the embodied passivity of the bystander that got him into trouble in the first place; it provided him with a sense of coherence when faced with the challenge of a fragmentary self.

Yet all of this messiness in his being is hardly a reason to dismiss what he is doing. The truth about Hans lies not in one or the other historical mask that he is trying on but in the fragmentary self that he was desperately trying to understand. Starting in 1983, Hans struggled to make sense of his self through anamnestic reason. He began to let the dangerous memories of his personal experience challenge his contemporary certainties of his self. He opened himself to the demands of the past, perhaps for the first time in his life.

With evident results. His memory work revealed that he had lied to himself about his sovereign impunity as a bystander. His lies not only helped dehumanize others but even dehumanized himself by letting the lie master him. The war did end before he could actively reject the Third Reich or do anything proactive to help Nazi victims. No wonder then that he almost burst out in rage at the American G. I. in defense of the "innocent." At some time he had to save face—in his own eyes at the time and in memory.

And then the "Heinrich" incident disrupted his life in 1983. To say that a magazine article changed Hans only falls back into the same model of passivity; it would be far more accurate to say that Hans used this article to address a problem in himself that had long been nagging at him. This explanation

---

93 M001b 31:50.

fits, we might add, with the reading we gave earlier that the Jewish boy he met could have been any Jewish boy; Hans may have projected the image of Heinrich Kissinger onto this memory.

What happened in 1983 is that Hans began a process of critical reflection that led him to suspect his own biography as self-deception. Moreover, Hans started to tell the story of his life publicly. Perhaps he shared his story with the students, parents, and teachers in his high school—including Jewish ones—to ask for their forbearance; but he did so always as a teacher, aware of his role as a model for a kind of critical self-reflection that prepares the ground for friendliness. He knew full well that he could not pay back his debt to the dead, that his work of memory was like that of Sisyphus, condemned to his boulder. To Drew it seemed as if he assumed this burden happily. Before he died in 2004, Hans read several earlier versions of this chapter. He welcomed any insight that could help him discover the uncomfortable truths about himself.

What he chose to reject was his self-deceptions about his self-deceptions. One of the principles they teach at a Friends Academy is to take personal responsibility. As a Quaker school, they publicly share that struggle in a supportive, non-judgmental atmosphere of the larger community. If Hans was many things in his life, he was the kind of teacher who took his job as a role model seriously. Interrogating his own self-deceptions in this context probably offered him a way to become someone he never thought he could be. His struggle to understand his responsibility for the Nazi past opened him up to new opportunities to respond to the demands of changing situations.

Owning Up to Our Lies

Sisyphus lied throughout his life. While in the upper world, he used his lies to manipulate the gods for his own personal interest. He never thought twice about the people who got hurt in the process. And he never reflected critically on his own self-deceptions. Even when punished, he refused to accept responsibility for his own selfhood.

Then, like Hans, Sisyphus changed. In the underworld, he tells himself a different kind of lie. He acts as if he is obeying the punishment of the gods by pushing his boulder, the punishment for his past behavior, up the hill for all eternity and doing so *dutifully*. In fact, he is scorning them with a parody of obedience. What Sisyphus has learned is the wisdom that he is the master of his own lies, and that the best way to live the eternity of his constrained existence is with a full, conscious, and even embodied, awareness of his self-deceptions.

Lies are part and parcel of being, especially when cultivating a self in modernity. To erase the memory of the tragic human costs of incessant change, modern selves and societies desperately wish to generate stable centers for coherent identities. Historical metanarratives, foundational philosophies, *Bildungsromane*, and Messianic faiths often serve these myths as do political ideologies like racism and fascism. Herein lies the danger of telling and believing in a single, coherent story that describes "us." The ostensibly coherent selves who serve as the protagonists of our stories and politics can never satisfy their debt in full to those sacrificed for our becoming.

The silenced voices of others are certainly one compelling moral reason to question the ordinary lies we tell ourselves about who we are. The other reason lies in ourselves. Our personal reflections on the traumatic past disrupt any attempt to assert narrative control over our own past. We are thus more apt to discover the silenced voices within ourselves when we hearken to the dangerous memories in our own past.

In both a historical and ethical sense, dangerous memories challenge the simplistic notions of responsibility and judgment lurking behind our self-deceptions in and about the past. Instead of the modern myths of a coherent self, we seek histories, stories, and performances designed to recover the memories of promises broken by our own self-deceptions. We welcome the fragmentary subject of those accounts who can own up to lying without losing a critical sense of responsibility to others for the consequences of lies.

Non-Conformity

Love does not consist in its refusal to take sides, but rather in the way it takes sides, that is, without hatred or hostility toward people.
— Johann Baptist Metz, "Messianic or Bourgeois Religion?" 1981

Figure 5. Jochen Löber, *Portrait of Günther Seidner*, Winter 1944.
Edited for Anonymity. Source: Günther Seidner.

A Walk in the Woods

It was an "unbelievably beautiful" Sunday morning in 1935 when Gerhard Mock led a group of some twenty Hildesheim teens on a hike. Telling this fable-like story during an interview in 1993, Gerhard described how he led these boys and girls across the River Innerste and into the Hildesheim Forest.[1] Gerhard was twenty years old, the son of a wealthy assimilated Jewish merchant and a Protestant mother, the product of one of Hildesheim's elite college preparatory high schools, and the leader of the Hildesheim branch of the Federation of German Jewish Youth. In the otherwise deep forest, they found a clearing where the sun shone through the trees. They bore a guitar like typical German youth groups on a hike, but they did not sing the usual songs. Instead they talked about the no-win situations they faced every day in Nazi Germany.

They did not know how they should greet their teachers at school. Hartmut Teufel was the only Jewish boy going to the *Oberrealschule*. Every morning, he explained, the teacher came in and said *Heil Hitler!* and the whole class responded with upraised arms and *Heil Hitler!* "You said that everyone lifted their arm?" Gerhard asked, hoping he had misunderstood Hartmut. "Does that include you?" Hartmut replied that he had discussed with his father how to greet his teachers. "I don't want to stand out." That is, Hartmut said *Heil Hitler!* with all the rest of the students. Conscious of his disciples around him, Gerhard preached.

> I cannot understand that. I cannot imagine that you begin every day with a lie. Not just a lie—but must you also show disrespect to your fellow students at the same time? For you, as a Jew—and you say to me that you are the only one in this school—you stand there every morning and lift up your arm and say *Heil* to the man, to this man, who wants to annihilate us all? I cannot comprehend this.

"What am I supposed to do!?" Hartmut replied. Gerhard responded with idealistic certainty. "Hartmut, I feel so strongly about this that I hope, when you next lift up your arm, that it falls off! For you commit an unbelievable sin with this gesture."

Gerhard was encouraging what Germans refer to as *Eigensinn*. Etymologically this word connotes a sense (*Sinn*) of one's self (*Eigen*) but also suggests that the meanings being given to the self are unique (*eigen*) or one's own. *Eigensinn* is usually used to mean stubborn disobedience or self-assertion. We are using it here to refer to unruly behavior that refuses to conform to social expectations.

Hildesheimers were raised with the expectation to greet their neighbors with *Good morning* or *Good day*. They did so for many reasons, but at the

---

1   G119a 08:40.

most basic level, a respectful salutation laid the foundations for a civil society. Ardent Nazis refused to greet their neighbors according to tradition. With the enthusiasm of a revolutionary movement, they greeted with *Heil Hitler!* instead. In challenging established conventions, they were being rather *eigensinnig*.

They were also politicizing everyday life. Denying that all of their neighbors deserved an equal share of respect, these Nazi supporters used a neighborly greeting as a way to lay claim to power and status as Aryans in the brave new world of the Third Reich. The so-called German Greeting made clear that they lived in a new kind of Germany in which their Jewish neighbors were no longer welcome. By 1935, this alternative salutation became the dominant one.[2]

Gerhard responded with unruliness of his own. He refused to conform to the Nazi *Volksgemeinschaft* in which Jews were treated as outsiders. Gerhard continued to use the traditional and inclusive greeting, *Good morning*, and encouraged the young people who looked up to him to do the same.

This anecdote suggests that ordinary Germans understood the stakes of non-conformity lucidly. They debated their options frequently, openly, even heatedly. For Jewish Germans, however, none of these options seemed very good. Their intuition told them that taking responsibility for their historical situation had something to do with non-conformity, but the devil seemed to be in the details.

Our Unruly Selves

We certainly sympathize with Gerhard's attempt to oppose the Nazis categorically. The Nazi regime was inherently evil in the way that it treated human beings as the transmitters of racial characteristics rather than having value in themselves. We can hardly imagine a more legitimate circumstance in which armed resistance seems justified than against the Third Reich.

Still, we find it far too easy for what begins as a means to an ideal end to become an end in itself. Gerhard's sermon subtly sanctioned a violence of its own. Oppositional movements often take as their guideposts the very principles they seek to oppose. They are often eager to legislate new norms that others are supposed to emulate. They sometimes tolerate, and in some cases even welcome, the destructive moment of non-conformity as a source for historical and personal creativity. They can justify the use of violence today with messianic promises of the ideal world to come. Yet non-conformity cannot be coercive or violent and responsible at the same time.

---

2   For more on greetings, see Bergerson, *Ordinary Germans*, chs. 1 and 5.

Like lies, non-conformity is also a performance, so it is tempting to measure it according to aesthetic principles. Non-conformists often want us to believe that they are acting responsibly simply because of the creativity and courage they show by performing this oppositional role in public. Yet this astute sensitivity to their audience betrays a narcissism which can lead to ethical dead-ends. Being recognized as an unwavering antifascist seemed a little too important to Gerhard, for instance. Danger arises when the performance of *Eigensinn* is valued more than its effects.

The problem is that non-conformity is one of the key tools of modern and postmodern selfhood. Many of us like to imagine that we are non-conformists. Non-conformity was often needed to negotiate the constraints of modern society; not conforming is now lauded in our postmodern society as a good in itself. Non-conformists often present their behavior in this way, as if it was an ethically superior form of selfhood simply thanks to its alternative posture.

The problem with this assumption is that fascists and racists also see themselves as non-conformists. They ostentatiously perform their revolts against the principles of democracy, civility, and equality in order to promote their alternative vision of society. The Nazis were a particularly violent example of this kind of non-conformity, but the reader can probably think of many other examples from past and present. If both pro- and anti-fascists believed that they were acting responsibly by acting unruly, then we can hardly conclude that non-conformity in itself is a responsible form of selfhood.

The challenge of non-conformity is even larger in a context like Nazi Germany. The Nazi regime sought to mobilize all Aryans for its political projects ranging from Party organizations to a genocidal war. In response, ordinary Germans often depict themselves as having "opted out" as much as possible by refusing to conform to certain Nazi expectations. Most scholars no longer believe the myths of obedient Germans passively abiding by Nazi expectations or Jewish victims marching cooperatively to the gas chambers, but we still tend to think of non-conformity in quantitative terms as a kind of "inner emigration" or passive uncooperativeness that falls somewhere in-between the more active postures of collaboration and resistance.

We argue that most ordinary Germans were in fact non-conformists, but over the course of this chapter we will redefine it to mean something quite different. We will treat non-conformity not as the static position that non-conformists claim to be taking on one side or the other of a given expectation or regime, but as the dynamic process by which they are taking sides. Non-conformity is easily twisted to excuse violence with a sense of sovereign impunity. We will argue, by contrast, that unruliness moves towards responsibility when it discovers the endless possibilities for giving birth to something new without resentment or coercion. It does so interpersonally not for applause or notoriety but out of an awareness of our ability to respond to others. Our responsibility combines an openness, akin to innocence, to the possibilities available to us in everyday life with an awareness, grounded in experience, of the need to stand in solidarity with the victims of history.

Our Approach

This chapter begins by reading non-conformity through the lens of German Idealism. We see Immanuel Kant's categorical imperative as the modern foundation for a principled use of non-conformity. When applied to real-life situations however, Kantian imperatives dictate a new conformity. The non-conformity of resentment is no better. Here following Nietzsche, the non-conformist often depends on and thus remains trapped in the categories of conformity in order to express its revolt. Responsible non-conformity requires something different.

We then look at the closely related issue of how non-conformity is performed. The German theatrical tradition understood the purpose of theater to transform everyday life. We use Lothar Schreyer and Walter Hasenclever as our examples of aesthetic expressions of non-conformity. Their Expressionist theater programs mandated that the audience adopt the utopian features of the staged *New Man*—their projected ideal type of future person who breaks free from the constraints of the past. Expressionist theater itself explodes into the German public sphere at the end of the First World War at the same time as fascism. By making these comparisons, we are trying to suggest certain underlying commonalities in forms of non-conformity that lie at the heart of various modernisms, political and aesthetic.

Non-conformity is so closely tied to modern selfhood because it is an expression of the desire for autonomy and freedom. The everyday Germans whom Drew interviewed in Hildesheim typically succumbed to this modern tendency to rebel against norms. The danger we see comes from using non-conformity to liberate ourselves from responsibility. Hannah Arendt and Nietzsche help us clarify how responsible non-conformity might operate. We conclude with stories that break this pattern, and model a kind of open-ended, creative process that we believe supports responsible action in the world.

Acting on Principle

Our modern assumptions about what it means to be a responsible person come from German Idealism. Gerhard wanted us to believe that there was only one foundation for ethics. Like many of his fellow Germans, Gerhard derived his precepts from Immanuel Kant's categorical imperative.

Kant on Ethics

Rejecting codes for behavior sanctioned by gods, churches, or princes, German Idealists of the Enlightenment looked for new philosophical foundations on which to base their actions but with the same ethical certainty. A *categorical imperative* seemed to provide that certainty. It is a mandate as well as an obligation to act in a particular way because you are sure you are right. An individual must first use his own reason to determine if a categorical imperative exists to act in a particular way, but then they must act accordingly.

The way to determine if a categorical imperative exists is to see if the principle passes three closely related tests. First, individuals must reasonably want the maxim to become a universal rule. That is, they must be willing to live in a world in which everyone acts on the same principle. Second, the action must treat other people as ends in themselves and not as means. More simply, the maxim must ensure that you do not merely use people; you must respect their freedom as you would respect your own. Third, the action must demonstrate respect for morals by voluntarily restricting your own actions to the imperative of reason.[3] There always is a right thing to do, Kant teaches. Even when it proves beyond our ability to do, it is still our duty. A man of principle, Gerhard was convinced that he had to do his duty in trying times, and he tried to convince Hartmut and the others to do their duty too.

Thinking this way is a mark of authentic adulthood, according to Kant, and is part of a rational or enlightened modern life. Kant sums up the meaning of enlightenment in a simple phrase or challenge: "*Sapere aude!*" or dare to think.[4] Raise questions about traditions. Do not simply accept what everyone else thinks is true or good, but think critically for yourself. To Kantians, rational independence in public debate is the sign of a mature mind. Do not conform, or at least not before giving thought to the matter; but once you do, you must stick to your guns. We are used to approaching non-conformity as a psychological or social phenomenon, but Kant is suggesting that the issue here is ontological: it has to do with our being *in* the world. Gerhard serves as a model of what Kant intends here: we should become "hard as diamonds" in conforming our wills to the demands of moral reason.[5]

In essence, Kant defined individuality in terms of an enlightened non-conformity to tradition combined with a principled conformity to the answers

---

3   Kant, *Fundamental Principles of the Metaphysics of Morals*, trans. T. K. Abbot (New York: Prometheus Books, 1987).

4   Kant, "An Answer to the Question: What Is Enlightenment," in James Schmidt, ed., *What Is Enlightenment? Eighteenth-Century Answers and Twentieth-Century Questions*, trans. James Schmidt (Berkeley: University of California Press, 1996), 58-64.

5   See Martha Nussbaum, *The Fragility of Goodness: Luck and Ethics in Greek Tragedy and Philosophy*, updated ed. (Cambridge: Cambridge University Press, 2001), 1-8.

of our own reason. Said in another way, Kant provided us with the liberty to become moderns by disobeying tradition. What remained largely uninvestigated by many of his followers—when they translated this principled nonconformity into aesthetic, intellectual, and political movements—was whether the courage to not conform was in fact a virtue in itself.

Nietzsche on Resentment

If modernity idealized non-conformity, it nonetheless perpetuates conformity. This point has been made at length by Michel Foucault in his criticism of the Enlightenment. Foucault encouraged us to see in modern social technologies the mechanisms of intensified homogenization and governability. Conformity is imposed in part by social institutions like schools or armies, but we also impose it on ourselves in the way we discipline our body, self-image, and behavior to conform to social expectations. We make ourselves more easily governable by fitting ourselves into categories of class, gender, race, and sexuality; in the process, we exclude those parts or people that do not "fit." Many Enlightenment thinkers premised their revolutionary programs—for a free citizenry of rational individuals, a civil society of competing ideas and interests, or ethical nation-states bearing culture and civilization—on radically new forms of exclusion and self-discipline.[6] Here Foucault was revolting against the uncompromisingly categorical quality of Enlightenment thinking—ironically, as a non-conformist.

In the German tradition, the philosopher who disclosed the paradoxical relationship between non-conformity and conformity is that great challenger of modern assumptions, Friedrich Nietzsche. There is no more thoroughgoing critic of the Enlightenment in general and Idealism in particular than Nietzsche; he refers to Kant as "the contemptible spider" of Königsberg.[7] To Nietzsche, Kant spins enormous logical webs that ensnare the unwary reader but serve no purpose but the blood-thirst of its maker. Nietzsche himself refused to live the traditional life of a German intellectual; after a brief stint as a professor in Switzerland he led a wandering, largely friendless, and intellectually isolated life. He despised the Germans as a nation of conformists. His entire philosophy is that of iconoclasm: he likened the way he tested "eternal idols"—by which he meant philosophical ideals—to sounding them

---

6   Barbin, *Memoirs*, introd. Foucault; Foucault, *The Care of the Self: The History of Sexuality*, vol. 3 (New York: Vintage, 1986); Foucault, *Discipline and Punish*; Foucault, *Madness and Civilization*.

7   Nietzsche, *The Portable Nietzsche*, ed. and trans. Walter Kaufman (New York: Penguin, 1954), 577-578.

out "with a hammer" rather than with the careful "tuning fork" of more cautious intellectuals.[8]

Nietzsche's diagnosis of conformity for its own sake is simple: conformity expresses the values of safety and security, and is therefore at odds with his well-known preference for risk, for living dangerously, for challenging oneself. Nietzsche frequently argues, especially in his early writings, that the worst sins of bourgeois society should be laid at the feet of our tendency to think and act like a herd rather than as individuals. This criticism of bourgeois society is typical of modern non-conformists, and Nietzsche became the idol of many.

Where Nietzsche catches us off-guard is when he attacks non-conformists for their conformity. In Nietzsche's analysis, non-conformity tends to express, in a negative way, precisely the values that the conformist embraces. Non-conformity is in a way still worse than conformity because it is derivative of the values that the non-conformist reacts against. Non-conformity thus adds to conformity the attitudes of guilt and resentment.

Recall Nietzsche's criticism of Christian morality. For Nietzsche, the moral context of the birth of Christianity is a social-political situation: there are the powerful whom he calls the masters, and the disenfranchised whom he calls the slaves. The powerful have what they need to flourish in life, and the values of this class reflect the satisfaction of ordinary human needs and desires: strength, friendship, health, wealth, pleasure, and so on. The disenfranchised, however, do not have these human necessities and are incapable of acquiring them.[9]

The priest emerges in this situation. He uses the material impotence of the disenfranchised class to accomplish what Nietzsche takes to be one of the most momentous, and yet regrettable, acts in human history: the inversion of the value system of the powerful. The priest introduces, Nietzsche argues, the moralities of "good versus bad" and "good versus evil," the grand types of "master morality" and "slave morality." The list of virtues and desirable goods for master morality includes wealth, friendship, sex, strength, pride, physical health—above all the goods and virtues of "this world." These are the things and activities that the human animal is naturally drawn toward. The converse list of vices and things to be avoided are not surprisingly things like poverty, solitude, denial of the body, and sickness. These moral hierarchies, Nietzsche argues, provide the opportunity for the priest. He convinces the slaves, who far outnumber the masters, that the masters subscribe to what is in fact an ungodly value system. He then insists that what characterizes their condition

---

8   Nietzsche, *Portable*, 466.
9   See Clancy Martin, "Nietzsche," in *The History of Western Philosophy of Religion*, ed. Graham Robert Oppy and Nick Trakakis (New York: Oxford University Press, 2009).

as slaves—poverty, solitude, denial of the body—is truly the more valuable in the eyes of God.

So the priest turns the old value system of the masters on its head. Everything the powerful masters possess and do is not merely bad, but evil, condemned by God: property, pride, sex, even food. And the life of the disenfranchised slaves is not merely good in the sense of good-for-me-and-mine, but good in a more exalted sense of blessed—good in the eyes of God. Hence the new virtues of poverty, weakness, humility, denial of the body, and chastity become traditional Christian virtues.

This kind of non-conformity originates with *ressentiment*, generally translated as "resentment."[10] The individual or class that operates according to resentment defines itself entirely in terms of what it is not. It does not create anything new; it insists that it is *not that* but rather the very opposite of that. Nietzsche criticizes resentment as a foundation for non-conformity because it remains spiritually, socially, and creatively derivative of the value system it defines itself against. Resentment prevents non-conformity from growing and flourishing. Its self-definition and its goals are entirely negative. Like the fox and the sour grapes in Aesop's fable, the resentful find satisfaction solely in terms of denying the value of that which they know they cannot possess.

In the case of conformism, we adopt a value system not because we ourselves have reflected upon and endorse those values, but because we recognize that in order to be accepted and protected by others we must share and participate in the values they endorse. The motive, familiar to all of us from school experiences growing up, is two-fold: the need to be accepted and liked, and the fear of being rejected and cast out. There is of course a lie here: the conformist cannot admit to conforming for these reasons because the conformist has to pretend to have other, more authentic motives for wanting to belong or risk being thrown out of the group for being a liar. Thus we pretend to follow the values of the group for the sake of the values the group endorses. Nietzsche calls this behavior *herd mentality*. He criticizes it as deceptive and self-deceptive regardless of the particular value system it embraces.

When performed in the spirit of resentment, however, non-conformity is no better than conformity. It might even be worse, as it is conformism with an extra layer of unreflective deceit about its own motivations. For most of his life, Sisyphus was this kind of non-conformist. Highly sensitive to the laws of gods and men, he cultivated a sense of himself as outside of those rules, and yet his every action was dictated by his scorn for them.

---

10 Kaufmann's "Editor's Introduction" to Nietzsche, *Genealogy of Morals*, 5-10.

There is a performative contradiction at work here. Non-conformity seems to be a principled resistance to conforming to what is considered normal, traditional, or acceptable; but in practice it often depends on conformity parasitically for its definition and thereby ends up facilitating conformity. This paradox speaks to one of our over-arching arguments regarding the human condition. We have to take care, when we slaves try to liberate ourselves, that we do not simply negate that which we resent. In doing so, we run the risk of merely replicating the very conditions that oppress us.

This danger is not merely conceptual. We are talking about a process of disciplining the self to conform to the very categories against which the non-conformist is revolting. This subtle conformity does a surprising amount of damage to the complex human beings that we are.

Adolescent Rebellion

It is easy to find examples of resentful non-conformity from the Third Reich. Nazi policies and principles were so offensive to some people that they quickly found imaginative ways to protest them in everyday life. Yet these brave acts of unruliness ironically replicated the Nazis's own categories for who were "real" Germans and who were "outsiders." On closer inspection, what we discover even among these resentful non-conformists are ordinary Germans disciplining *themselves* to fit into Nazi categories.

Martha Paul recalled two incidents from the early years of the Third Reich that illustrate the danger. On 30 January 1933, Martha watched from her grandmother's house as her neighbors marched past at night bearing torches. Celebrating Hitler's appointment as Chancellor, the Nazis were demonstrating their rise to power. "Suddenly everyone and his uncle sprouted a swastika… We didn't know there were so many uniforms." Martha was Jewish and 17 years old at the time. She described herself as "excitable." We took this word as code for "a typical adolescent" in that she liked to challenge the authority of adults. So she and her girlfriend hid in the dark behind the large boxes of geraniums that stood on her grandmother's balcony and squirted water on her torch- and swastika-bearing neighbors with a garden hose. "We wanted to show them we were against that."

Here is a classic example of resentful non-conformity. A Jewish German, Martha rejected Nazi principles and expressed her non-conformity symbolically by dousing the torches of her Nazi neighbors. What she perhaps did not realize is that she was replicating a Nazi style of politics in her own behavior by resorting to "violence"—if only symbolic, in the form of water—to silence her neighbor's right to public expression.

Moreover, Martha in effect enacted a role that the Nazis prescribed for her, which defined her as a dangerous outsider, perhaps even potential terrorist. Here it is important to remember that the Nazis used examples of Jewish violence to great effect to excuse escalations in persecution—most notably in 1938 during the so-called *Kristallnacht*. That she expected violent retribution is evident in her testimony. "Nothing happened," she noted, but not without recognizing: "We got lucky."[11] In this sense, Martha's *Eigensinn* backfired. In taking her cues from the Nazis, her non-conformity added to her feeling of isolation in the new Third Reich.

The second incident took place on 20 April, probably also in 1933. The brother of Martha's girlfriend was turning 22 on the same day as Hitler's birthday. So Martha went shopping in Hildesheim for a gift. On Hoher Weg, she purchased a toy Hitler figure "who could raise his arms...up and down." She wrapped it up in a used film box and dropped it in the milk slot in his door, "completely forgetting that they had a Christian maid." She admitted that she felt sure that this particular maid would not have denounced her, but that did not change the fear she felt. "You don't give a Jew a Hitler figure who raises his arm" in a parody of a Nazi salute.

Martha described her *Eigensinn* as "something terrible" when viewed in retrospect, "though at the time I thought it was a funny joke."[12] This joke backfired as well. The lesson she learned was that she should conform to the Nazi principle that Jews and Aryans should not mix—interestingly, in advance of the legislation that removed Christian maids under the age of 45 from Jewish households in 1935.[13] Here she literally took her cues from Nazi racist principles and adjusted her behavior accordingly.

Sarah Meyer, another Jewish German, recalled a similar incident. She depicted herself in her unpublished memoirs[14] as having a "rebellious nature." She even lied to avoid punishment for her unruliness at school. When her "family lost their businesses and properties to the Nazis," her father found work as a travelling salesman in Essen. Around 1935 she moved there with him.

> One day on my way to a public roller-skating arena, where I loved to figure skate, I saw a lot of people lined up on the street. No one was allowed to cross, there was plenty of police to prevent us from doing so. All had to wait until an on-going parade would pass.

> There was my first and only sight of the hated Hitler. He came through, with everyone raising their hands in the salute, I refused, my hand just wouldn't "lift." Since I was in the middle of a huge crowd of people and rather small, I got away with this

---

11 G097a 23:20, 25:30; G098a 28:15.
12 G097a 23:40; G098a 25:40.
13 Cf. Bergerson, *Ordinary Germans*, ch. 5 to, for instance, Burleigh, *Third Reich*, chs. 3-4.
14 Meyer, "Memoire," unpublished manuscript, ch. 3. The actual name and title have been altered to protect her anonymity. Copies are available from Drew. The grammatical and punctuation errors are hers.

by just standing there and looking inconspicuous. This was a terribly frightening experience.

Sarah responded to the Third Reich with resentment. Yet if her non-conformity seemed involuntary in her account, it did not get her far. It left her feeling less like a German and more like a Jew.[15]

Here we see one reason why German idealism fails in everyday life. Back in the Hildesheim forest, Gerhard Mock sought to realize his duty as an end in itself. Taking his leadership role seriously, Gerhard imposed his understanding of Kantian duty on his followers: strict and rigorous maxims that meet the categorical imperative to be ethical at all times. Gerhard seems to have asked himself: "What would happen if the Hitler greeting became a general practice? If its principles became those of German society?" Since no Jew could reasonably wish to be excluded, dehumanized, deported, or annihilated, Gerhard insisted that no Jew could use the Hitler greeting.

In point of fact, Gerhard resented the Nazi insistence that he was a Jew rather than a German. He used a non-conformist greeting as a way to insist upon a civil society in which one's religious background did not prevent full participation as a loyal and patriotic citizen. Ironically his brash insistence on non-conformity only made him and his young wards feel like outsiders in the new Third Reich. Both non-conformity and conformity led to the same outcome: the social alienation of Jews from their German neighbors.

Working for Utopia

To be sure, Jews were not responsible for creating this situation. It was the Nazis who politicized non-conformity as a vehicle for Aryan self-cultivation. They promoted resentment over the Treaty of Versailles and the League of Nations. Resentful non-conformity motivated their antisemitism too, as they actively encouraged Aryans to exact retribution on Jews for their alleged crimes against Germans. The non-conformity of resentment was so successful as a foundation for their political revolution precisely because the Nazis had no qualms about using violence; indeed, they removed all limits to the expression of German resentment. As a result, resentful non-conformity served as a motor for ever escalating cycles of violence.

As the Nazis illustrate however, resistance to conforming to the current world is frequently motivated by a vision of a better world. The emphasis here is on the future: non-conformity becomes a tool in the construction of a new world order. This utopian element can also be seen in Gerhard's behavior. He

---

15   For another example, see G157b 18:44.

was closely approximating the Kantian ideal for ethical judgment in that he promoted a process of enlightenment by "legislating" the only kind of world he could reasonably inhabit. Gerhard responded to an untenable current situation by framing his action in terms of a future, more ethical world.

Utopian hope is part of the process of constructing an alternate future in response to an unsatisfactory present. We are familiar with this sentiment in others as in ourselves. We hope for an idealized vision of what we might become because we are offended by the current human condition: its suffering, debasement, and disappointment. We become non-conformists out of righteous indignation.

There is also an aesthetic quality to this utopian hope. Modern political and modernist art movements sought to construct a New Man in a better world. In this paradigm, life approximated art in that we are encouraged to live "as if" the new reality were already present in the hope of creating it.[16] Stories like the ones we see in the theater or read in history books play an important role in this paradigm as the future is constructed through narrative. Yet they are fictions, even when the stories are allegedly factual, for utopia is by definition not realizable.

In utopian stories, endings become justifications for unruliness in the present, since non-conformity is framed as serving these future ends. The non-conformist tries to convince us that we too should become non-conformists on the promise of these better outcomes. Moreover, these stories themselves—as narratives—seem to afford the author some control over this historical process: whoever writes the end of the story gets to justify the behaviors in the rest of the story.

Non-conformity for utopian ends is often romanticized as a form of self-assertion or self-expression. Martyrdom remains true to its etymology as "witnessing" to the truth and goodness of one's vision. Messianic tendencies flourish and are nurtured when the sign of being in the right is the degree to which one does not conform to the present. So, if we have seen in the last section that there is a big problem with simple negation in non-conformity, an equal danger lies with the simple affirmation of utopian hopes. Both disguise an irresponsible justification for violence in the name of human freedom.

---

16 On the difference between life according to principles or "as if" versus "as if not" and the danger of the former, see: Giorgio Agamben, *The Time That Remains: A Commentary on the Letter to the Romans*, trans. Patricia Dailey (Palo Alto: Stanford University Press, 2005), 35-43; see also Vincent Geoghegan, "Remembering the Future," in *Not Yet: Reconsidering Ernst Bloch*, eds. Jamie David Owen and Tom Moylan (London: Verso, 1997), 15-32; and David Durst, *Weimar Modernism: Philosophy, Politics, and Culture in Germany 1918-1933* (Lanham, MD: Lexington Books, 2004), 110-111.

Schreyer's New Man

Consider first an example from the arts. The Expressionist writer and stage director, Lothar Schreyer, illustrates well the potential consequences of artistic experimentation that feeds off of utopian non-conformity. His plays repeatedly depicted the destruction of all opposition to the protagonist. If this representation of his intentions sounds radical and violent, then it is appropriately so. Violence was intrinsic to his program for cultural renewal.

Schreyer is a less well-known figure, but he was well-connected to major modernist art movements. He was an intimate of Herwarth Walden, the publisher of the Expressionist journal *Der Sturm* and best-known advocate of Expressionist poetics. After his independent theater endeavors failed, Schreyer taught acting and theater design at the Bauhaus at the invitation of Walter Gropius.

To understand Schreyer, we have to begin with the crisis of language. The late nineteenth-century theater used everyday speech as its most reliable way of communicating meaning. The crisis of language began when intellectuals and artists started to realize that words do not have an inherent link to the meanings they intend to convey. In a landmark series of lectures at the University of Geneva from 1906 to 1911, for instance, Swiss linguist Ferdinand de Saussure argued that the words "tree" and "*arbor*" refer to the same natural object in different languages, and yet these sounds are so different from one another that they demonstrate the "arbitrariness of the sign."[17] It is hard to overestimate what a loss this kind of insight meant to artists, including playwrights, when they discovered that sounds themselves are arbitrary symbols. Schreyer responded to this crisis with a radical solution. He invented a new school of theater that avoided using language to convey meaning.

Enticed by the avant-garde developments in Berlin, Schreyer moved to the capital from Hamburg to contribute original dramatic scenes and articles on dramatic theory to *Der Sturm*. In 1916 he founded the *Sturm-Bühne*, a theater company dedicated to realizing his conception of Expressionist performance. His body of work—comprising literary and theoretical texts as well as stage management and directing—advocates replacing words with bodily actions. Schreyer brings Expressionist acting to its most extreme where the body of the actor replaces words as the most important means of communication. His attempts to create a revolutionary theater were not only non-conformist, in that he was rejecting the use of language for communication, but also utopian in his fantasy that he could replace language through performance.

---

17   Ferdinand de Saussure, *Course in General Linguistics*, ed. Charles Bally and Albert Sechehaye in coll. with Albert Riedlinger, trans. Wade Baskin (New York: McGraw-Hill, 1959), 65-70.

In the theater, the crisis of language led playwrights and directors to pre-fer the body of the actor as a more ideal way to communicate. In traditional theater, things like costumes, body language, and demeanor, especially in the stylized setting on stage, give the audience immediate information about the character. "The actor need only appear onstage and the viewer has immediately received information that allows the represented character to be specifically identified."[18] We then expect the spoken lines to provide the story of the play and identify the role of these characters in it. By contrast, the Expressionists explored facial expressions, body positions, and actor movement across the space of the stage as an alternative rather than a complement to words since they believed that words no longer self-evidently communicated their meaning.

Another way that the Expressionists in the *Sturm-Kreis* responded to the crisis of language was to shift to tonal uses of words. Here the difference lay between the semantic meaning of the words and the way they sound. Schreyer was a leading proponent of this orientation.

> Tone is either individual tone or combined tones. Its artistic power depends on pitch, volume, tempo and sound of the tone. The human tone as language provides the melody of the individual, the group or the masses, based on the melody of the work as a whole. Vocal music stands between these as transition.[19]

In several theoretical essays published in *Der Sturm* in 1916-17 under the title of "The Stage Artwork," Schreyer gave low priority to conventionally structured sentences. Instead, he wrote speeches for his actors that consistently incorporated physical modes of performance. He gave instructions for how to use the body to convey the meanings that used to belong to words. The quote above exemplifies the kinds of detailed, yet nevertheless ambiguous, instruc-tions he provided for combinations of sound, color, light, and movement to replace language as the primary system of signification. As you might imagine, Schreyer largely abandons plot and story in favor of expression.

Schreyer promotes these new ways of communicating as the only way to represent a "vision." It becomes the only admissible content of a dramatic performance. Even though the "language" has changed, the intention remains to communicate with an audience in the theater. By avoiding the restric-tions of words and story, however, Schreyer thinks he can communicate com-pletely new ideas. To do so, Schreyer must carefully orchestrate every word, movement, and image on the stage. His theories empower the *Stage Artist*, Schreyer's term for the writer or author, and the stage director to predetermine the actor's every sound and movement on-stage. He even mandates how to illuminate the actors and their correctly colored costumes to invoke a revela-

---

18   Erica Fischer-Lichte, *Semiotics of the Theater*, trans. J. Gaines and D. Jones (Bloomington: Indiana University Press, 1992), 64.
19   Lothar Schreyer, "Das Bühnenkunstwerk," *Der Sturm* 7, August 1916, trans. Baker.

tion of the "vision"—the image of a revolutionary New Man as the bearer of the future.

There are distant echoes of Romantic aesthetics here, and Schreyer was relying on Nietzschean ideas. He evokes these antecedents by couching his theories in a quasi-philosophical rhetoric of terminological definitions. Yet we can learn more about Schreyer from his vocabulary of mystical initiation and spiritual revelation than from their actual content. He goes so far as to claim that, in theory, language cannot communicate anything; language only has value as sound. Here he distinguishes between using the senses for knowing instead of thinking. "Belief is the conscious deception regarding mediated and immediate knowledge...The believer wants to live in the realm of Spirit; the enlightened one, however, experiences it."[20] For Schreyer belief is a self-deception that mistakenly tries to use cognitive faculties; immediacy of experience is the only guarantor of Truth.

On principle, Schreyer chooses to replace communication with the audience in favor of providing models for them. He believes that actions of the actors on-stage can have no meaning for an audience in the traditional sense. Günter Berghaus has pointed to an important corollary of Schreyer's acting method: "He regarded the actor's personality and individuality as an impediment in the process of shaping this *Kunstkörper* [artistic body]. Only a depersonalized, dehumanized actor could be a medium of art."[21] The reduction of the actor to a tool for the symbolic expression of the Stage Artist's vision not only denigrates the person of the actor. It also expresses ideas in ways that remain, in effect, a "foreign language" insofar as the uninitiated do not understand the meanings being conveyed. It is thus possible to claim that Schreyer does not create a new way of communicating at all, since no one outside of his acting troupe can read these signs. He was clearly deceiving himself when he claimed: "The artist proclaims the vision with symbols which inherently express emotions."[22] Yet he firmly believed that language was a barrier to theatrical expression and grounded his revolutionary aesthetic in those utopian ideals.

In practice, Schreyer's utopian theories had authoritarian consequences. To implement his theories, the director had to micromanage the production to an unprecedented degree. Only late in the nineteenth-century had the German stage director assumed the kind of authority we typically associate with that role; and even so, the director and the actors still engaged in considerable

---

20 Schreyer, "Das Bühnenkunstwerk: Die Wirklichkeit des Geistes," *Der Sturm* 8, May 1917, trans. Baker.

21 Günter Berghaus, *Theatre, Performance, and the Historical Avant-Garde* (New York: Palgrave Macmillan, 2005), 77.

22 Schreyer, "Das Bühnenkunstwerk," August 1916, trans. Baker.

give and take regarding the artistic process.[23] By contrast, Schreyer insisted on an inordinate degree of authority over his ensemble. He refused to employ professional actors, preferring amateurs whom he could train in his own methods. He insisted on countless rehearsals before considering a piece ready for performance. Even then he remained suspicious of outside commentary and criticism, and only reluctantly gave public performances. When financial and social pressures compelled him to return to Hamburg in early 1919, he created a similar apparatus to the *Sturm-Bühne* organization he had developed in Berlin. This time he allowed only initiates to work on the group's projects. Again he produced few public performances, preferring instead the self-trained, intra-group audience who were the only viewers who could truly understand the works, since they themselves had also taken part in them.

The reader perhaps now understands why we selected Schreyer for an example of the non-conformity of utopians. He takes his principles to extremes. Modernist artists often imagine themselves in a generational conflict where they represent the new in revolt against the old. Schreyer's projects exponentially radicalize these "us versus them" qualities. We can also see in Schreyer some typical problems with utopian communities: the authoritarian power of the leader over all aspects of communal life; an exclusive and rapturous language that is incomprehensible to outsiders and marks the community members as belonging to the group; and a tendency to objectify humans as means to ends. As a utopian non-conformist, Schreyer is willing to sacrifice meaning in the service of performing the New Man.

This New Man is no longer human; it is in fact no man. He stands on the stage in a pure form, created *ex nihilo*, as if this kind of self could exist outside of human relations. The characters in Schreyer's plays have no meaningful interactions with one another just as the actors are no longer interacting with the director but simply following his orders. Furthermore, the audience can no longer comprehend what those actors are doing. Schreyer imposes this image of man on his actors and insists on cult-like obedience to his authority. In his reconfigured actor, performing the New Man, he has created an ideal type of human being that existed only in the rarified realm of his imagination. Already perfect in the moment of its enactment, by definition this New Man cannot respond to anyone or anybody, and therefore can never be responsible.

Schreyer represents an extreme that throws into detail the ethical consequences lurking within German Expressionism in particular and non-conformity in general. His vehicle was stage performance but his intention was to revolutionize the self in everyday life. Many would think it convenient to

---

23   Simon Williams, *German Actors of the Eighteenth and Nineteenth Centuries: Idealism, Romanticism, and Realism*, Contributions in Drama and Theatre Studies 12 (Westport: Greenwood Press, 1985), 145-171.

model an ideal on stage and see the audience adopt these behaviors in everyday life. Yet therein lies the problem—that the director is trying to dictate progress to his audience. This kind of utopian non-conformity sacrifices humanity to authoritarian control.

Gerhard and Hartmut

It would be a mistake to think that this kind of authoritarian attitude was limited solely to avant-garde directors or other modernist artists. Here we need to take seriously the German aesthetic tradition that sees an ethical connection between the stages of art and life. Comparing Schreyer's example to everyday life can help us to see how easy it is for utopian aspirations to twist non-conformity into irresponsibility.

Let us return to the incident in the Hildesheim forest. Given their untenable position, we can appreciate why Jewish Germans might have grasped at utopian straws in the search for alternatives to the Third Reich. Yet Gerhard's attempt to approximate the Kantian model for ethical judgment put him in the position of trying to create a utopian future by challenging the orthodoxy of the present. This hubris is most evident in his retrospection, as Gerhard attempted to justify his non-conformity by controlling the end of the tale.

About five minutes after the confrontation between Gerhard and Hartmut, a group of Sunday hunters came walking through the forest. They were wearing their lodge jackets and had their weapons slung across their shoulders. According to Gerhard, they were "conventional, unsophisticated" (*biedere*) Hildesheimers who walked like geese, one after another, because the path past the clearing was a narrow one. Gerhard imagined that the hunters liked how this group of young people sat there with their guitar and admired nature. As the first hunter walked by, he greeted the young people, "as everyone greeted a group in those days: he said, *Heil Hitler!*" Here again, Gerhard emphasized the degree to which his Aryan neighbors were conforming to the Third Reich. "As leader of the group, I replied, very emphatically, *Good morning!*" Gerhard's behavior was pure *Eigensinn*.

It is at the end of the story that Gerhard most clearly validates his non-conformity as a perfect duty. "As the second hunter walked by—he had not heard what was said—he said, *Heil Hitler!* I said again, *Good morning!*" This time, the other hunters passed without saying anything. Then the last hunter reappeared after the rest had gone. The children, especially Hartmut, stared at Gerhard. Hartmut said, "Wait and see. Now you will have to own up to what you just preached to us!" The hunter stood about ten meters from the group when he spoke. "I want to say to you that we did not intend to insult you. We feel sorry for you. *Good morning.*" Then the hunter disappeared into the forest. Gerhard believed he could not have picked a better encounter to illustrate his Kantian arguments to his young audience, which he proceeded to do again in a longwinded lecture to Hartmut about the categorical imperative to not conform to the Nazi greeting.

Gerhard concluded his fable with a moral. During a meeting of the local Hillel lodge the next day, Hartmut's father confronted Gerhard, asking him what he had done to his son. "He was all straightened out, and you got him all confused. Now he does not know what to do in school tomorrow!" Gerhard replied: "Mr. Teufel, if he does not know what he should do now, then he will be lost forever." Gerhard emphasized the fact that Hitler wanted to annihilate the Jews—with the added emphasis afforded by hindsight—and he made it seem as if resolute acts of non-conformity could have stopped Hitler from doing so. All that was needed, Gerhard's story implied, was courageous Germans to stand up to the Nazi bullies and the Third Reich would have crumbled.

Gerhard was certainly taking the right side in not conforming to the Nazis, but we are nonetheless suspicious of how Gerhard took sides. Like Schreyer, Gerhard presented himself as if he had looked ahead to the post-fascist world and tried to legislate his way there through the courage of his own reason. The problem with the ideals preached at the Hillel lodge is that he read the incident from the perspective of the endings of the story. At that moment in 1935, however, the majority of Hildesheimers were greeting their neighbors with *Heil Hitler!* whether out of ideological conviction, opportunism, or cowardice. In doing so, they created a situation for the vulnerable Jewish minority in which they had no reason to hope that any kind of greeting, conformist or not, could significantly affect the power of the Third Reich. More to the point, they had good reason to believe, based on personal experience, that their disobedience would end them up in a far worse situation.

Kantian ethics falls apart when there is no reasonable likelihood of ever achieving the utopia one is self-legislating. In the words of philosopher J. B. Schneewind: "If reason showed the perfect good to be a required but unattainable goal, reason would be at odds with itself." Kantian ethics presumes that "the world must allow *the possibility* of success."[24] The challenge for the German Sisyphus begins precisely here: deep in the Hildesheim forest, without foreknowledge of the future, under the threat of terror, trapped in a totalitarian society, and *without* hope for success. How can one cultivate a historically responsible self when you suspect that your best efforts will be doomed to failure?

---

24   J. B. Schneewind, "Autonomy, Obligation, and Virtue: An Overview of Kant's Moral Philosophy," in *The Cambridge Companion to Kant*, ed. Paul Guyer (Cambridge: Cambridge University Press, 1992), 309-341 at 332-333, our emphasis.

What we discover, if we stay with these Hildesheimers a bit longer while they are still on their own in the woods, is a considerable degree of confusion: not about the political stakes of their choices but about which one was best. Hartmut was as much a collaborator in his own alienation as the last hunter was a resister. The hunter who responded to Gerhard's challenge with a humbled, yet still non-conformist, *Good morning*, did not seem particularly committed to National Socialism; the Jewish children obviously were not. Hartmut chose prudently, like many of his non-Jewish neighbors,[25] to "howl with the wolves" for his own safety, even as he was aware of the fact that he was contributing to his own victimization.

It was this uncomfortable absurdity to everyday life under the Nazis that Gerhard wished to repress. Gerhard may very well have made his decision by a process of existential elimination: he could not support the Third Reich, so he had to fight against it, even if despairing of success. This decision would get him closer to the ethical posture of the German Sisyphus who acts responsibly while lucidly aware of its futility, for whom the work of living is preferable to the happiness promised by this or that utopia.

Yet Gerhard did not present his experience this way to Drew in retrospect. In his historical record, designed for posterity, he asserted control over an unruly set of memories by framing them within a moral tale. He also knew better. At other points in the interview, he recognized the threat to life and limb that could result from a non-conformist greeting in Nazi Germany.[26] In *this* story, however, he ignored that information. In the context of his debate with Hartmut, he erased the memory of existential crisis by presenting this decision in categorical terms.[27]

Gerhard's "clearing" in the woods was overlain with Kantian notions of dispassionate objectivity: culturally, physically, and psychologically distanced from the social expectations of their community. Moreover, he used the ending, in the Hillel lodge, where his choice was "proven" correct, to reassert control over the middle of the story where the situation was far less clear. These debates were unsettling since they raised the troubling specter of not knowing for sure what constituted the safest as well as the right thing to do. Gerhard told his story as a fable, prioritizing the meanings discovered at the end, in order to assert interpretive closure on this inherently ambiguous situation.

---

25   S. a. G121b 01:53; G157b 18:44 at 21:37; G057b 07:25.

26   G110b 15:40.

27   Drew also fell into the alluring trap of categorical imperatives. See Bergerson, "Eigensinn, Ethik, und die nationalsozialistische *Reformatio vitae*," in *Sehnsucht nach Nähe: Interpersonale Kommunikation in Deutschland seit dem 19. Jahrhundert*, ed. Moritz Föllmer (Stuttgart: Franz Steiner Verlag, 2004), 127-156.

Gerhard did not just repress the anxiety of everyday life under Hitler after the fact. We believe that, already while in the forest, Gerhard repressed the anxiety of the no-win situation in which he found himself. Gerhard admitted as much as an elderly man. After decades of retrospection, he satirized the certainty as well as the idealism of his youth.

> I was twenty years old back then, and I had found all of the answers. I was very, very wise, and…I gave [the children in my youth group] no grey answers. I gave them [only] black or white answers. After all, I knew everything. [I] had no doubts as to my wisdom—which I distributed generously.[28]

Yet mocking his own arrogance did not lead him to actually second guess if he had made the right decision in this case. He used generic expectations built into the fable as a morally edifying tale to insulate him from what he did not wish to recall, or recognize, about his life under the Nazis: the existential fear of being a Jew in Nazi Germany.

In the Middle of Things

It is worth pausing for a moment here, in the midst of this complicated situation, as we approach the mid-point of our book, to reflect on the benefits of the perspective from within everyday life. The material presented here and throughout this book has gone through many stages of interpretation. It is not that it has taken us many years, multiple publications, decades of reflection, and years of dialogue to work through this material to a point where we feel we are starting to get a handle on it all. It is that we know from experience that we certainly do not have a handle on it and cannot wish to so master it. More will surely have to be said, considered, and done in the future. The insights about historical responsibility are to be discovered in the process rather than as a finished product.

This story is a perfect illustration. In an earlier version of this material,[29] the analysis ended with Gerhard's version. Paul Steege, a colleague of ours, read it in order to offer some criticism. Then, by pure chance, he met Hartmut Teufel personally. Hartmut mentioned in passing that he had been born and raised in Hildesheim, so Paul recounted Gerhard's story. Hartmut declared that it was in fact *his* story. As a result of this encounter, Hartmut sent his version of the same events to Drew via email on 6 March 2002, but with some notable differences in the interpretive framework. A comparison between the two accounts can help us show how endings can be abused to obfuscate responsibility in everyday life.

---

28 G119a 09:27.
29 See Bergerson, "Neighborliness," 664-668.

Hartmut remembers these events taking place "along a narrow path that led through a meadow just before entering the woods." Hartmut also recalled "the incongruous greetings back and forth [that] repeated themselves with each hunter that passed us." It was Hartmut who insightfully described this situation as "a no-win situation." On the one hand, he described the German greeting as having the authority of a "rule" rather than just a social convention.

> On the other hand, saying *Good morning!* might have been considered a provocation or a sign of opposition which could have brought forth a violent reaction on the part of the hunters.

To be sure,

> the first hunter, having passed us, turned back, thereby increasing our anxiety. To our great surprise, however, he addressed Gerhard and said, "I now realize what kind of group you are. I did not mean to insult you."

Yet Hartmut ended his story with a different fable-like moral: that these young Jews had no choice but to conform.

> You can gauge the measure of our fear because the youngest among us, a kid probably no more than ten or eleven years old, had befouled himself.

The end of Hartmut's fable thus emphasized the danger to which Gerhard exposed his young charges for the sake of his idealism.

We are less interested in the factual question of which account was "true." It is how Hartmut and Gerhard tell their moral tales that reveals the most about everyday life under Nazi rule. Each of these men framed their anecdote in a fable-like ending whose primary purpose was to repress the anxiety produced in the middle of their story. The problem was that their Aryan neighbors were placing these Jewish kids in no-win situations in which they either denied their Jewishness or removed themselves from the community of Germans. Indeed, the story illustrates the degree to which ordinary Germans actually discussed the ethical challenges facing them in everyday life and disagreed over which choice was the right one to make. Both men responded to the existential anxiety produced by this untenable situation by claiming to know the only ethical way to act. Both used the endings of their tales to overcome the absurdity they faced in the middle.

What right do we have to sacrifice others for our ideals? We certainly agree with Gerhard that public support for the Third Reich was wrong. Gerhard knew that someone had to draw a line in the sand, even if his Aryan neighbors did not. Yet we also agree with Hartmut that Gerhard exhibited a rather cavalier attitude towards the likely consequences of his non-conformity for his young wards. Non-conformity feeds into a utopian dream of autonomy just as it proffers a way to challenge authority with impunity. When modern revolutionaries romanticize non-conformity, they tend to justify what is for us an intolerable degree of self-righteous violence.

Both men continued to defend their positions by asserting interpretative control over their own memories. In 2002, Hartmut made no bones about the fact that it was *his* story, not Drew's or Gerhard's, and that he still rejected Gerhard's categorical imperative in favor of his pragmatism. Similarly, Gerhard framed the entire anecdote in a less-than-savory description of the Teufel family: that Gerhard's parents were friendly with them even though they represented, for Gerhard, a dark side of Jewish culture. The Teufels had a "Jewish peddler mentality" by which Gerhard meant that they "measured everything:…what can you do for me, how much is it worth, how much can I get out of you, and so on." [30] Gerhard lost track of Hartmut when they both left Hildesheim for the United States, but he described at length a series of brief and sometimes indirect contacts that, by 1988, confirmed his low opinion of Hartmut. Fifty years after the incident in the Hildesheim Forest, Gerhard concluded, "his character had not changed."[31] Retelling these stories in 1993[32] gave Gerhard the chance once again to criticize Hartmut, to verify his antifascist credentials, and to lay claim to the status afforded to self-righteous non-conformists in our post-fascist society. Both men were still trying to use endings to control their dangerous memories of everyday absurdity.

Gerhard called this episode "*ein unglaubliches Sonderereignis*" which we translate as "an extraordinary, unbelievable experience." What made this walk in the woods into such an extraordinary experience for the Jewish young people and the adult hunters alike was the way in which this public debate about a presumably ordinary habit of daily life had suddenly become politically and ethically loaded. Both Jews and Aryans responded to this breakdown in normalcy with anything from shocked silence to serious discussions about the best response. This experience was something unbelievable, however, because ordinary Germans suddenly discovered two disturbingly contradictory facts about everyday life: that they had a larger scope for non-conformity than they anticipated, and yet even non-conformity seemed to aid their tormentors in their policies of oppression.

Utopian non-conformity promises a way out of the Nietzschean paradox. It appeals because it offers a radical break with the past that resentful non-conformity cannot seem to make. Yet as Schreyer's example illustrates, this solution is make-believe, an invention of his own mind to which he is grasping in the hopes of a racial transformation. It makes perfect sense to us that a young Jewish German like Gerhard would turn to such fictions—as

---

30   G119a 10:44.
31   G119a 20:30.
32   G119a 18:03.

if a proper greeting would overthrow the Nazi regime—given the untenable situation in which he found himself. Like many in his situation, he was growing desperate. Unlike the theater, however, Gerhard could not control the outcome of events or even the behavior of the actors. The problem with these fictions is that they encourage their authors to impose them on others without concern for the damage that they did or could do in the process. Please do not misunderstand us: we know that it would be wrong to blame Jewish Germans for a situation imposed on them by their Aryan neighbors. Nonetheless, Gerhard carefully considered and even debated how to respond to the Nazi dictatorship in everyday life; and in his case, he seems to us to have excused too much.

Hasenclever's Son

The problem with non-conformity is that, in practice, it all too readily becomes the vehicle for irresponsibility. We can see how easily it devolves into violence by the way that Gerhard and Hartmut talked about one another: insisting that only they told the story accurately, that the other was a liar, or even worse. It is a short step from this willingness to use violent rhetoric to actually promoting the use of physical violence. What often bridges the gap between implicit and explicit forms of violence is a messianic faith that one has not only the right but the obligation to force others to be free. Unfortunately, many non-conformists see themselves as prophets as well.

Consider another example from German Expressionism: Walter Hasenclever's *The Son* from 1913. Hasenclever, like Schreyer, was committed to using theater to promote the liberation of individuals from oppressive social structures. Unlike Schreyer's hermetically sealed, authoritarian model of theater, however, Hasenclever participated in the traditional open process of submitting his play to theaters which chose their productions on their basis for potential popular appeal. Dependent on audience appeal, Hasenclever's script relates a story according to conventional language. He does not tell actors how to perform their roles or directors how to direct.

Nonetheless, his language and plot are inflammatory. Hasenclever portrayed the Son, his protagonist, as a proactive non-conformist. The Son fights against the overly abstract presentation of knowledge disseminated by the education system, against the disjuncture between lived experience and the social norms of the status quo, and against his Father who stands as the symbolic and physical enforcer of cultural traditions. The play opens with the Son having failed his final school exams—not because he did not know the material but because he felt himself unable to participate in the process itself. His failure leads the Father to lock him up in the house, but the Son is able to sneak out and attend a midnight rally of disenfranchised youth where he delivers an incendiary speech. He spends the rest of the night with a prostitute in a hotel room only to be arrested for having caused a riot.

The final act brings him to a renewed confrontation with the Father, whose unremitting oppression can only be overcome by violence. The Son points a gun at the Father with the intention to kill him, but the Father dies of a heart attack instead. This *deus ex machina*—a sudden and artificial suspension of the plot in order to provide a happy ending for the protagonist—allows the Son to escape responsibility for pulling the trigger, but this non-conformist had every intention of committing murder for the sake of his ideals. Brecht, you will recall, depicts Galy Gay as making an existential choice to become a murderer, though he could very well have become other things. Hasenclever, by contrast, depicts the Son's attempted murder of the Father as a historical necessity.

Scholars get caught up on Hasenclever's difficult relationship with his own father and tend to read this play psychologically. Yet the Son is much more relevant as a paradigm of the New Man than as a self-representation of the playwright. The Son has a messianic function that is typical of Expressionist protagonists. During the midnight rally, the Son performs for the crowd as a Prophet of a better future. Just to make sure that the audience understands what is happening, von Tuchmeyer, his friend, reports the Son's actions to the others gathered backstage and simultaneously to the audience in the theater.

> Now he has jumped off the podium. He's right among the people. He says—: that we've all suffered under our fathers—in basements and in storerooms—from suicide and doubt—...He says: the fathers who torture us should be brought to justice! The crowd is going crazy—...He is ripping the clothes off his body. He is baring his chest. He is showing the stripes that his father whipped into him—his scars! Now he's impossible to see, so many are gathered around him. Now—they grab his hands—they shout encouragements—...He is calling for a fight against the fathers— he is preaching freedom—! "We have to help ourselves, since no one will help us!" They are kissing his hands—what a commotion! They are carrying him on their shoulders—out of the room.[33]

The Son is obviously a Christ figure but not in the sense of a spiritual regeneration. The audience is encouraged to read him as a Messiah whose Second Coming will bring about the Apocalypse. In these End Days, the sons will kill all of the fathers in order to realize an ideal society. Within the play, preaching leads to active rebellion on the part of the crowd for whom he is performing. By having von Tuchmeyer report these events to the audience in the theater, Hasenclever directs the response of the audience, encouraging them to follow suit.

---

33 Walter Hasenclever, *Der Sohn* (Munich: K. Wolff, 1917), 102-104, trans. Baker.

If Schreyer controlled all aspects of his production in order to guide view-ers to a singular interpretation, Hasenclever directs the audience through the narrative of his play. The Messianic elements of *The Son* not only project a utopian end but, thanks to his position of control at the end, the Son, as Messiah, in effect dictates the middle as well. The return to the Father's house in the final act enables the Son to replay the earlier confrontation with the Father with a more "positive" outcome. By destroying the Father, the Son symbolically remakes the social order according to the values of the younger generation—the non-conformists. Hasenclever's move is similar to the way that Gerhard was able to "return" to the Hildesheim forest at the Hillel lodge. Reading the middle in terms of the end, Gerhard attempted to overcome his untenable situation through interpretive closure.

The Son's advocacy of cultural revolution at the rally and the parricide at the end of the play call the audience to violent revolution. In order to break the cycle of repression and martyrdom, Hasenclever was insisting, the non-conformist must move beyond mere beliefs to actions. The new genera-tion requires the whole person, in private and public, on the stage of art and life, to enact the new values by destroying the old. Reconstruction requires destruction in apocalyptic violence.

In the five-year interval between Hasenclever's completion of the play and its breakthrough staging, popular culture in Germany became more receptive to the ideas of the modernist avant-garde. The 1918 staging of *The Son* in Mannheim under the direction of Richard Weichart is credited with popular-izing an authentically Expressionistic mode of performance.[34] For the length of the play the Son remained in a cone of light at center stage, interacting with the other characters mostly at its shadowy fringes. This staging not only had the effect of dramatizing the Son's condition as an isolated and impris-oned individual, but also encouraged an emotive style of declaration and bod-ily acting through the singular focus on the lead character. After almost four years of suffering and sacrifices required by the war, the missionary zeal of Expressionist plays demanding a New Man and the realization of their fervor in the theater achieved a sympathetic response among the audiences.

Hasenclever eventually came to recognize the flaws in advocating violence. In subsequent plays, such as his 1916 adaptation of *Antigone*, he moved from a position of confidence in ecstatic violence to a more realistic and pessimistic posture. This shift came about in response to his personal experience of war: he served on the Eastern Front during the First World War. This reevaluation also reflects his realization that intransigent insistence on violent conflict could not be a sustainable strategy for social reform.

---

34 Berghaus, *Theatre*, 86.

We have more fundamental doubts. Non-conformity often excuses a terrifying degree of violence thanks to the way that it allows for authoritarian control over everyday life and its denizens. To be sure, on the stage of life non-conformity is typically performed as a form of resistance to precisely these authoritarian demands on the self. Yet that righteous indignation does not mean that the non-conformist can avoid responsibility for his own claims to sovereign impunity. We have spent so much time focusing on Gerhard precisely because he captures this paradox of responsibility. We can learn the most about responsibility, and it is the most pressing, where it is most absurd.

The figures we have looked at so far reflected seriously on the ethics of non-conformity, but they chose to emulate a heroic individual, acting with autonomy and preaching their gospel to others. We see in this heroic individual part of the problem with non-conformity. Non-conformists who base their unruliness on principle are willing to sacrifice the safety of others for the sake of their ideals. Often motivated by utopian hope, they show a terrifying willingness to sacrifice others for the inauguration of the New Man. Whether in art or life, these non-conformists believe that they have the right and duty to direct the action and compel others to be free.

Rejecting Politics

The parallels to Nazi leaders are probably obvious to the reader. From early in his political career, Hitler demanded total control over the Nazi movement. Believing himself to be both an artist and a prophet, he often justified contemporary sacrifices on the part of Germans and righteous terror against political and racial enemies with the promise of a future utopia. He grounded his vision of an ideal *Volksgemeinschaft* in a eugenically perfected Aryan race. The Nazis also depicted themselves as a movement of youthful vigor, rejecting the compromises and inaction of an older generation. The Nazi Party gained political capital from both resentful and utopian non-conformity.

The Nazi *Volksgemeinschaft* in turn placed enormous expectations on ordinary Germans. Redefined as Aryan, they were expected to join Nazi organizations, demonstrate public support for the regime, and participate in Hitler's war effort to conquer a European empire for German colonization. To be sure, the Nazi regime was highly sensitive to the reactions of ordinary Germans; and yet the entire system of state-sponsored terror depended on the collaboration of ordinary Germans in the policing, denunciation, and alienation of their neighbors.[35] It is worth reviewing the situation in which ordinary

---

35   Robert Gellateley, *Backing Hitler: Coercion and Consent in Nazi Germany* (Oxford: Oxford University Press, 2001); Gellateley, *Gestapo.*

Germans found themselves during the Third Reich in order to understand how both conformity and non-conformity fit into this Nazi system of terror.

For the most part, ordinary Germans supported and collaborated with much of the Nazi project. Nonetheless they still saw themselves as autonomous individuals who made careful ethical distinctions between what they agreed with in the Nazi program and where they dissented. In this section we will apply what we have learned about non-conformity from these philosophers, playwrights, and Jewish Germans to the challenge of National Socialism as a political movement—to see if it cannot shed some new light on the problem of responsible selfhood. Adopting postures as non-conformists in response to changing situations provided ordinary Germans with a feeling of being dissidents while accommodating a tremendous amount of collaboration in fact.

The Conviction to Have No Convictions

The Nazis were typical of many modern political movements in depicting everyday life as a cosmic battle between good and evil. At the very least, Aryans were expected to demonstrate their support for the regime by publicly advocating its most essential principles. Moreover, the responsible cultivation of Aryan selfhood also meant volunteering to serve in the conquest of a new racial empire as procreators, laborers, soldiers, and murderers with creativity, initiative, and enthusiasm. Resentful and utopian, the Nazis strove to remake multifaceted and messy human beings into ideal types.

They took quite literally the notion of the New Man. The Nazi apparatus of annihilation from social death to physical extermination can be understood as a mechanism designed to transfigure bodies into what the Nazis imagined them each to be: the dirty Jew, the Polish slave, the Aryan *Übermensch*. One could argue that the Nazi movement sought to reform the German polity by transforming the human subject. The final steps took place on site in Eastern Europe through the violence perpetrated on Jewish bodies, but Nazi sports, schools, camps, and organizations already reconfigured the bodies of non-Jewish Germans into Aryan masters in the 1930s.[36]

---

36 Christopher R. Browning, *Nazi Policy, Jewish Workers, German Killers* (Cambridge: Cambridge University Press, 2000); Fritzsche, *Life and Death*; Elizabeth Harvey, *Women and the Nazi East: Agents and Witnesses of Germanization* (New Haven: Yale University Press, 2003); Koslov, *Gewalt*; Moishe Postone, "Antisemitism and National Socialism," in *Germans and Jews since the Holocaust*, ed. Anson Rabinbach and Jack Zipes (New York: Holmes and Meier, 1986), 302-315. Burleigh emphasizes the spirit of impunity with which the Nazis acted against the Jews prior to 1939 in "a genealogy which owed nothing to war at all" (*Third Reich*, 337).

It is hardly surprising that some Germans responded to this unprecedented politicization of their personhood by assuming a posture of distaste for politics *per se*. Although it is impossible to provide the reader with any firm statistics, it has long been clear to scholars that this form of non-conformity was rather popular in Nazi Germany. When told that they had to choose sides, many ordinary Germans disrespectfully chose not to choose. Rejecting politicization as such, they reinvented themselves as "ordinary" Germans—as if politics was best left to the politicians and pundits.

Notice that we just changed orientations: we have been discussing "active" forms of non-conformity thus far; we now want to shift to examples when non-conformists claim to "opt-out" of compliance. This response expressed a kind of ontological unruliness that refused to conform to principle on principle. Alone the expression of *Eigensinn* was liberating; but non-conformity was also pragmatic. It enabled ordinary Germans to maneuver within the complex demands of everyday life in relative freedom.

Yet it is a mistake to think of non-conformity in quantitative terms, as a degree of compliance or non-compliance to official policies. Ordinary Germans often wish us to see their actions in these terms. In response to the totalitarian demands of the Nazi regime, non-conformity seems to answer the troubling question "how much" with the reassuring answer "not as much as they wanted" or simply "not as much as someone else." Luckily for many non-conformists, there was always a bigger Nazi. We want to suggest a way to use this term to mean something very different—even from what we have been discussing up to this point in terms of resentment and utopianism. We want to treat non-conformity as a category of a wholly different order, measured not in quantitative but qualitative terms. Rather than "how much," it answers the question of "how."

Preserving the conviction to have no convictions was neither opposition nor cooperation; non-conformity was a way of stonewalling the authority of absolutes that justify sacrifice for their cause. Rejecting utopias as dangerous for ordinary people, the only principle held here is to have no principles. In some, this posture could become nihilistic; in others simply pragmatic. Either way, the reader should not be fooled by the non-conformist's slight of hand. This posture outside of politics actually allows the non-conformist to assume remarkably political postures as needed. Indeed, since there is no position in fact outside of politics, the non-conformist always positions herself in both resistance and collaboration. In order to circumvent politicization *per se*, the non-conformist moves between different politicized postures.

The non-conformists who claim to have "rejected politics" are fascinating people, especially in the high stakes context of the Third Reich. They discovered a creative solution to a vexing problem. They used a refusal to respond as an expression of one's ability to respond. Yet we cannot take them at their word when they say that they were actually apolitical. Rather than a passive state of disinterest, this kind of non-conformity is an active strategy for creating room for maneuvering within constraining systems of political identities. This apparent freedom is what makes non-conformity so appealing. When confronted with a radical, violent, and threatening reconstruction of personhood for the sake of a brave new world, it expressed an uncompromising autonomy of the self.

Theodora the Unpolitical

A concrete historical example might help illustrate what we mean. Let us return to the case of Theodora Algermissen who, like Martha Paul, experienced the Third Reich as an adolescent girl in Hildesheim, though from the perspective of an Aryan. When Drew conducted interviews with her in 1993,[37] Theodora repeatedly insisted, regarding her family, that, "we were rather unpolitical." As a youngster she confided her problems in the two "aunties" in her neighborhood with whom she spoke about "*Gott und die Welt*" by which she meant all of the many and wide ranging issues that bothered an adolescent girl. But never politics.

Again, the reader might suspect that Theodora was retroactively altering her memories in keeping with the political norms of the 1990s. Her narrative certainly fits this reading of the data. When Drew asked further questions about her experience of political life, she admitted that her father was involved in politics after all. "But the rest of us did not concern ourselves at all with politics. At least not at that age." She later elaborated:[38]

> Politics was just not part of our lives. That is, it was insofar as my father was a member of the Imperial League of German Officers, and of course they were German Nationals, no?

She was referring to the *Deutschnationale Volkspartei*. The DNVP stood for a conservative, monarchist politics and systematically undermined democracy in the final years of the Weimar Republic. According to this reading, Theodora was uncomfortable with the way her parent's convictions did not fit with democratic principles today, so she was altering her memories in retrospect.

We do not think that she was lying, however, or at least not in any simple way. Theodora's narrative moved fluidly from her father's involvement in the conservative-nationalist Officers' League to a more dangerous memory when "I actually came into contact with politics."[39] Theodora guessed the incident

---

37   G001b 09:35.
38   G001b 26:20; G002a 00:00.
39   G002a 25:35. Cf. Bergerson, *Ordinary Germans*, ch. 4.

took place around or after 1930, when she was about twelve years old. She was racing through town on her bicycle on her way to visit a girlfriend in the Nordstadt. Once she got behind the train station, she saw, hanging from windows and on kids' bicycles, the flags of the *Reichsbanner*. The social-democratic paramilitary organization, its flag had three arrows on a red background. "The opposite party was the Swastika." Theodora flew a flag from her bike that was also black, red, and white, but it was the traditional flag of Prussia, "because my father was *deutschnational*." She laughed. "I did that for about a half of a year," Theodora explained. "And then I got beat up by a *Reichsbanner* and then I gave it up."

This incident scared and disturbed Theodora. During the interview, she did not elaborate at first about it. Upon further questioning she explained that these "hooligans" were around 16 or 17 years old and probably socialists or communists. "They tore off the flag, and I rode further, but they wanted to start a fight, so I started to defend myself." They attacked her, she believed,

> Because I had a different opinion than they did [about politics], which I documented with my black-white-and-red flag even though I—it has to be said in all honesty—had no opinion whatsoever. It [the flag] came—

she laughed again

> —from my father. It was a little bit like "they are this, and we are against it." You know, it was really more like a game…But my father was of that political conviction.

No doubt these young socialists saw themselves as outsiders in a town dominated by the nationalistic, and national socialist, bourgeoisie. We do not know if they attacked Theodora's flag out of political conviction *per se*, hoping to realize their socialist utopia in everyday life, or if this violence was more a matter of defending their working-class milieu from a representative of the middle classes. Yet Theodora experienced it as a political act on the part of ideologically committed non-conformists.

Theodora depicts herself as a non-conformist in turn, though of the converse sort: as a wholly apolitical animal, an ordinary German who kept her distance from all kinds of political convictions on conviction precisely because political convictions were not worth the trouble they attracted. It was through this encounter that she came face to face with the violence inherent in modern political utopias. She responded by rejecting political principle on principle.

Theodora was not at all naïve when it came to politics, even as a young girl. When reminded that President von Hindenburg came to Hildesheim in 1928, she remembered standing in an honor guard with her classmates and cheering. She remembered the economic crisis that followed with the "many, many unemployed people" and the tight budgeting she experienced at home.[40] Politics was not a game for the working-class boys who attacked her.[41] From the condition of their clothes, she understood that they were facing hard economic times.[42] She was also well aware of the rising Nazi movement as the most significant alternative to the socialist proletariat. She could identify which of her neighbors supported the Nazis.[43] For her, the incident in the Nordstadt came to symbolize the civil war that was growing in Germany.

The lesson Theodora learned was that political opinions could get you in deep trouble. The Officer's League was anticommunist and antisocialist, she explained, "but not Nazi. My father was always an opponent of the Nazis," she continued. He voiced his opinion too openly and incautiously. "We always feared for him that the *Gestapo* would grab him." To prove her point about her father's convictions, she recounted how, in 1944, he was enlisted even though he was in his mid-fifties. "The rest of his friends were all assigned as officers wherever." He had to build redoubts in Holland. "Imagine that! So that was pure chicanery."[44] Notice what Theodora is doing here: she was applying the lessons she learned from the bicycle incident to analogous situations thereafter. Her father's political convictions got him into trouble in 1944 just as they got her in trouble in 1930. Non-conformity promised to protect her from such danger. The best response to political violence, she was trying to show, was to have no political convictions whatsoever.

The Algermissen Civil War

In the final years of the Weimar Republic however, this issue got personal. "My mother was pro Adolf Hitler in the beginning," Theodora admitted.

> They were divided on this: my father on the one hand rejecting, though he had more background information, that this did not work or that was not correct and the like; while my mother was enthusiastic at first because she saw this crazy unemployment; and the poverty and the depression back then, they all ended. Suddenly there was a recovery, no? She was for [the Nazis].[45]

Much later in the interview,[46] when asked directly about how politics influenced the relationship between her parents, Theodora spoke slowly, choosing her words carefully.

---

40 G001b 12:35.
41 G001b 28:45.
42 G001b 29:40.
43 G003a 14:00.
44 G002b 02:05; G005b 44:25.
45 G002b 02:49; s. a. G005a 3:00.
46 G003a 16:50.

My mother understood my father and said, "Well yes, he is terribly bound to tradition, and he is always so critical anyway." Which is true. And my father said, "That is completely idiotic. But if you are of that opinion

she continued, speaking in his voice directly to "his" wife

you will see eventually. You all

here he meant the many people who believed in Hitler

will fall on your face.

Perhaps concerned that this dialogue seemed improbable, Theodora concluded in her own voice. "That was what he said."

It strikes us as perfectly believable that a young girl could remember quite clearly when her parents got into a disagreement about the future prospects of the Third Reich. After all, her country was on the verge of a civil war over the same issue. Theodora insisted that this difference of opinion never became a cause for a fight between her parents. Yet this claim strikes us as a normative statement of *official memory* rather than simply a report on actual experiences. We often try to fit our memories into societal, familial, or other expectations. These norms may be those in effect at the time of the memory formation or they may reflect the norms prevalent when the memory is being recalled. In this case, Theodora seems to be making her memory fit the social expectations of the Federal Republic of Germany in 1993 when a claim to having been apolitical during the Third Reich fit postwar democratic values.

The more she remembered, however, the more radical the disagreement between her parents seemed in retrospect. Later in the interviews, she described her father's attitude towards the Jewish question.[47]

He was not some kind of antisemite, but he was not necessarily a philosemite. One cannot say that he tried to help their cause. He was just neutral. But when this persecution of the Jews began, he really found that to be unbelievable. That was also a point against Hitler, while my mother did not yet see it that way.

She said, "Look at this one. Jews sit in all the important positions and are dominating." And my father said, "Yes they work hard, and yes this one sits here but all of them do not sit [in such high places.]" So these were the kinds of conversations that took place. I remember them.

Theodora remembered them because they placed her in an untenable position. Her parents were divided on the most pressing political and ethical issues of their time. She had a close call of her own in the Nordstadt, where she learned that participating in these kinds of public debates about the future of Germany only ended in violence. No wonder that she, like many other Germans in the early 1930s, chose to "give up" on politics. She responded to the civil war in

47   G003a 19:30.

German politics, a civil war that threatened to divide her own family, by refusing to conform to the demand to take sides.

One could perhaps argue that Theodora learned to keep her distance from politics from her parents. Earlier in the interviews,[48] she insisted that, among her parents' friends, political events may have been mentioned but, at least while she was in hearing range, they did not discuss politics as such. "It was mentioned now and again, but it did not have any weight. That is how I would express it." Nevertheless, "the closer it got to [19]33, the louder it was broadcast all around. That is for sure." People talked more about current events: "Did you hear this? Have you heard that? How did this or that take place?" Still, she insisted that they avoided taking sides. "To say that they felt drawn into one of these sides party-politically—I cannot say that." She used the term *parteilich,* which can connote both taking sides in ordinary affairs as well as choosing parties in a political debate. Again the tenor of this statement is general. It is another form of official memory: this time reflecting the normative standards for behavior among her family and friends in the past.

When she recalled a specific incident, her memory punctured the official story to confirm the very opposite. Not only did her parents hold political convictions strongly, but those opinions, when voiced, destroyed relationships.[49]

> Perhaps I have to emphasize one thing here. I said that my father was anti-Nazi, but my mother was enthusiastic about it at first. The headmaster of a middle school and his wife belonged to the circle of my parents's friends before [19]33. And he was very much an anglophile and was horribly anti-Nazi.
>
> And my mother let it be known that she was not at all so adverse [to the Third Reich], "for you can see it here that it has gotten so much better." And this led to a break in the friendship. So, that is the most extreme that I experienced here as a child in terms of political consequences.

This kind of break happened only once, but even so, her mother held Nazi political convictions strong enough to cost her a friendship.

In another interview shortly thereafter, Theodora misheard the question Drew posed to her. She instead answered the question that she was wise enough to pose to herself. "What did I think about this?" She responded: "I was so unpolitical." This response seems to us to be the most telling. Fearing that politics might disrupt her family, Theodora projected her own desire to not take political sides onto her parents who had already in fact taken sides and whose choices were beginning to undermine their social relationships. Her insistence that "we/I were all unpolitical" reflects not an actual state of

---

48   G002b 13:20.
49   G003a 14:00.

affairs in her family but her way of negotiating the civil war brewing in her parental home.

Theodora's non-conformity should not be understood as if she had no political opinions. In fact her language reflects the influence of Nazi propaganda. In the turbulent final years of the Weimar Republic, the Nazis depicted their movement as the sole barrier protecting Germany from a Communist revolution. Theodora was clearly more distressed by the people who were resisting the Nazi revolution than the revolution itself. She saw those who resisted Hitler as the ones disturbing her peace. Theodora described antifascist convictions as "terrible" (*furchtbar*) or even "horrible" (*ganz furchtbar*). By contrast, she described her mother's fascist and antisemitic sentiments in positive terms—saying that Hitler had made life in Hildesheim "so much better." She ignored the suffering of her Jewish neighbors as well as trade unionists, socialists, and others for whom life was obviously worse.

Here we can see why placing non-conformity on the same metric as collaboration and resistance misses the entire point. A posture of non-conformity to the demands of political mobilization allowed Theodora to move fluidly between multiple political positions: German nationalist, pro-Nazi, anti-Nazi. Non-conformity gave her not only a way to express herself in resentment against the political pressures of her adolescence; it also provided her with a sense of coherence in rapidly changing and often dangerous circumstances. If her political identities were fragmentary, non-conformity allowed her to recombine these disjointed elements into a modern *bricolage* of selfhood.

Theodora's problem lay not in her inability to take sides in the German civil war of the 1930s. She chose the German nationalist flag for a while. She would choose the Nazis for a while too. Her problem was that the civil war had spread into her family. The way she reiterated her mother's language suggests to us that she wished to side with her in this disagreement over the future of Germany. Yet that choice required being disloyal to her father and potentially risking the kind of break that was taking place among friends and neighbors. So she made political disinterest into her guiding principle.

Her stance is captured in the way that she repeated expressions like "I was so unpolitical." They have the quality of catch phrases—as if she had used them so many times in the past when confronted by those who wished to nail her down unequivocally. Personal experience contributed to this inclination; over the years, the easy choice became a bad habit. Non-conformity provided her with a considerable amount of maneuverability in everyday life. It enabled her to live her life free from responsibility. Dismissing political principles on principle, Theodora made herself into an ordinary German.

Sovereign Impunity

We admit that we can empathize with Theodora's apolitical style of non-conformity. We have experienced the same kind of "political burn out" at times in our own day. In a sense, she is responding to the utopian non-conformity that we too criticized in which political principles excuse authoritarian self-righteousness and violence. We also like the fact that Theodora, like Gerhard, had discovered that she had a wide range of options in terms of how she might respond to the demands of totalitarian politics. Her narrative reminds us that modern subjects still found ways to cultivate their own sense of self (literally their *Eigen-Sinn*) even within the constraints of totalitarian typologies for proper being, believing, or behaving.

Still, her example brings us to the overarching question of this chapter. If non-conformity can be used to both promote and reject utopian politics, if both fascists and antifascists considered themselves to be non-conformists, indeed if non-conformity necessarily involves moving in and out of these politicized postures as the situation demands, offering considerable latitude in actual political collaboration, then non-conformity in itself cannot be the measure of responsibility. This conundrum is worth repeating, since non-conformity has become such a popular posture in our postmodern condition. In the twenty-first century, we like to believe that we are all non-conformists, as if non-conformity in itself can assure us that we are doing the right thing. So far, non-conformity proves to have the very opposite quality of excusing violence.

We will once again rely on Drew's interviews with ordinary Hildesheimers in the 1990s to provide case studies to explore this issue in concrete historical situations. We have selected the typical examples of two ordinary Germans who faced the intense pressure to participate in Nazi organizations. Their examples will show that, by distancing themselves from carefully selected parts of the Nazi project, non-conformity allowed ordinary Germans to lay claim to the status of Aryan *Übermensch* with a sense of sovereign impunity.

Günther the Non-Conformist

Consider the example of how Günther Seidner found his way into the German army.[50] A patriotic refugee to Hildesheim from the Polish Corridor after World War One, Günther wanted to serve his Fatherland, especially if it could lead to the reconquest of his home town of Thorn. Like Theodora's father, though a generation younger, he was a staunch German nationalist who also

---

50   G083a 26:40; G084a 15:20.

claimed that he kept his distance from the extremes of Nazi ideology, especially its antisemitism. He openly admitted that he had volunteered for one year of service, but he blamed Hitler for forcing him to stay longer, which turned out to be multiple years of military and labor service. In the latter, he worked in Marienburg just south of town regulating the Innerste, the river that flows through Hildesheim.

Günther insisted that he preferred to critically discuss Alfred Rosenberg's *Myth of the Twentieth Century*, the most influential Nazi text after Hitler's *Mein Kampf*, rather than do his work. Like Gerhard, he compared himself to his friends to demonstrate his ethical superiority, particularly to one friend who used to read from the Nazi paper on breaks from their labors. Günther claimed that he had been a non-conformist: during the Third Reich, he had only played the role of a Nazi.

We might wish to consider, however, what kinds of political postures he was able to afford himself thanks to his non-conformity. Günther argued that, because of his unruliness, his friend was promoted and he was not. He also insisted that only the leaders of their group were "more or less Nazis," while he and his friends were "not real Nazis." He vehemently insisted that he struggled to keep his ideological distance by not joining party organizations while still proving that he was "a good German" by serving in the German army. He remained a soldier in the mobile artillery throughout the Second World War.

Like many ordinary Germans, Günther claimed to have had no knowledge of or direct involvement in the Holocaust as a soldier. Just because he did not personally kill Jews, however, does not mean that he is innocent of murder. He preserved a series of photos tracing his wartime activities in 1940. One showed his regiment riding into a French town in 1940. Sensitive to the ruins in the background of the photo, he clarified that "the tanks arrived before us and destroyed the town." He made it seem as if his participation in the German army did not also involve killing and destroying, as if one could separate his service as a soldier in a war of imperial conquest from the role of the perpetrator. Surely the French who witnessed this invasion of an imperial German army laying waste to the land and culture of France did not view Günther as a non-conformist. They saw him claiming mastery in Europe with overwhelming violence.

Figure 6. *Regiment*, France, 1940. Source: Günther Seidner.

The reality is that Günther performed both roles at the same time. His non-conformist posture *vis-à-vis* some of the Nazi program allowed him to participate in the Nazi war for *Lebensraum* without having to take responsibility for that violence. There is a causal connection here. Günther imagined that he could conquer and murder without consideration for the human suffering he inflicted because he was a non-conformist. Non-conformity afforded him the luxury of sovereign impunity.

Günther kept a postcard of Martin Niemöller, a Protestant pastor who spoke out against certain policies of the Nazi regime and was incarcerated during the war. Günther carried Niemöller's image in his pocket in order to prove that he had been reluctant to serve in the German army. Günther still had this postcard with him in 1993. This picture served as a prop to increase the persuasiveness of his performance as a non-conformist to others and perhaps even himself.

His non-conformity is further documented in an oil painting made of him in 1944. The artist had belonged to the replacement troops in Günther's unit and painted its officers however they wanted to be painted, usually with their many laurels visible. In his case, Günther had asked the artist to paint him as the artist saw him. The artist bore witness to Günther's non-conformity by depicting him hiding his Nazi insignia. We find this image so compelling an example of non-conformity, we placed it at the start of the chapter.

This recognition on the part of his peers was crucial for Günther. It confirmed a self-image that he desperately wished to imagine was his real self. Yet his non-conformity did not interrupt his continued performance as a soldier of the Third Reich. Quite the contrary, this mutual self-deception bound their individual acts of non-conformity into a fascist social contract from which individuals could hardly extradite themselves on their own. Implicated in each other's excuses, German soldiers fought Hitler's war to the very end.

In part, Günther's behavior was unethical because he supported the Third Reich at all, the essence of which was violent and inhuman. Yet that argument, focusing on ends, presumes precisely what needs clarification: the relationship between non-conformity and systematic historical consequences. We see Günther's non-conformity as strategic. His opportunistic performances of non-conformity allowed him to seek what he desperately wanted for himself: the role of conquering hero in Hitler's bid for mastery in Europe.

Non-conformity collapses into irresponsibility when it is used to excuse violence. We would like to suggest that Günther was rather typical of many ordinary Germans who adopted a posture of non-conformity in order to excuse their collusion in Nazi claims to mastery at home and abroad. Or more accurately, we suspect that they moved rather fluidly between different variations of non-conformity according to the immediate situation and in response to the changing political fortunes of the Third Reich. What we see in this painting is the German Sisyphus before the fall. Able to finesse difficult situations in everyday life, he was proud of his hubris to defy the gods. Like Sisyphus, Günther wanted it both ways: to support the Nazi war and not be responsible for the violence involved. Non-conformity here is a vehicle for sovereign impunity.

Theodora the Führerin

We would like to offer you another example. Returning to Theodora's biography also allows us to address the issue that we did not treat exhaustively before: her personal involvement in Nazi politics and policies. Where Günther insisted that he kept his distance from only the worst excesses of Nazi politics, Theodora claimed to distance herself from politics entirely. During the second taped interview focusing on friendship, Theodora spoke more openly about the challenges of negotiating the demands for participation during the Third Reich. For instance,[51] she remembered how a girl in her class became a strong anti-Nazi after the girl's father was degraded from district attorney to the position of a "simple judge." This girl "did not participate in anything" by which Theodora confusingly meant that she had joined the Nazi Association

---

51 G004b 17:20.

of German Girls (*Bund deutscher Mädel*) "only in order to graduate from high school." In effect, Theodora depicted this girl as a non-conformist, though that claim makes sense only if we understand non-conformity as we are trying to redefine it here: as a strategic movement in and out of politicized definitions of selfhood.

We suspect that Theodora was trying to admit here that she was less of a non-conformist in fact than this girl. Like Günther, she was measuring herself in terms of degrees of nazification in comparison to those who were more or less compliant. She explained that she became a Leader (*Führerin*) in the Nazi youth organization for young girls (*Jungmädels*) and even enjoyed their activities. Nonetheless, she still tried to pose as a non-conformist by dint of the fact that she left in 1935, now in contrast to her best friend, another girl, who continued even after she graduated high school. Here Theodora's narrative is strikingly similar to Günther's and many others for whom the "bigger" Nazi—always readily at hand—proved the straw man to cast their own behavior in a better light.

Clearly Theodora knew the political stakes of belonging to these organizations. She learned a similar lesson during formal dance class. Families with aspirations to the *niveau* of the educated bourgeoisie sent their adolescent children to *Tanzstunde*. The young man who went with her to these balls was an anti-Nazi like her father, but he did so out of socialist convictions. Socialism "did not come over so well at home, so we did not talk about it."[52] Her father's political convictions were as narrow as they were strong if, in 1935, his anti-socialist convictions were still trumping his antifascism. Again, Theodora learned the lesson that politics can lead to conflict and is best left unspoken.

This silent self-deception was all the more true of the Jewish question.[53] By the time Theodora went to *Tanzstunde*—"that was [19]35. There were no more Jews anymore—that is, none that still came out into the open somehow." This time, however, she mentioned her classmate, Hannah Mendelsohn, by name.

> We got along great. She already had acquaintances or relatives in Palestine. She always used to give me the postage stamps that came from there. I collected stamps back then. We got along really well. She could write good essays in German class and I could do mathematics better, so we would always do it tog—

Theodora suddenly changed topics. "And then one day she was not there anymore. And that was around [19]33." Later she received a postcard from Hannah from Palestine with "heartfelt greetings" as if to show there were no hard feelings. Theodora had not heard Hannah say anything about leaving

---

52 G004b 15:20.
53 G004a 25:58.

beforehand; her friend just disappeared. Theodora presented this matter as if she had not been involved in it personally. The antisemitism that would have accounted for her friend's leaving seemed to be one more item on the list of political convictions that Theodora had, allegedly, ignored.

Theodora's high school also had two Jewish teachers.[54] One "very elegant, really terrific"—she taught French, though Theodora was never in her class. "One day she too just disappeared." The other was a music teacher who was teased "not because she was a Jew but because she was a little strange. But I learned an enormous amount from her." Starting around 1932 or 1933,[55] Theodora noticed a growing division in her class. Some of the girls "switched over and suddenly became extreme Nazis. I remember one girl in particular that right off became a *Führerin*—a Leader. She said hateful things [*hetzte sehr*]" about this teacher such as "*Ach*, the old Jewish hag." The reason why the Jews were leaving, Theodora seemed to suggest, was in response to the antisemitic behavior of the more ardent Nazis around her—not because of anything that Theodora had done.

These stories are designed to imply that, if Theodora was not quite philo-semitic, at least she was not antisemitic. The teacher was fired in 1934,[56] but Theodora's father insisted that Theodora still take private lessons from her in the lute. "And then one day I came to her [apartment] and the door was closed, and [she] was gone." In this case, Theodora knew that she fled to Holland. She told these stories to suggest that she was abiding by the same, seemingly reasonable strategy for avoiding problems during the Third Reich: do not talk about the really politicized issues.

Theodora's non-conformity involved a considerable degree of conformity, however. When she shifted the discussion from her parents' politics to her own,[57] she reiterated her mother's justifications for why she supported Hitler.

> Now I would like to plug myself in here. So I was—. Naturally I saw [these positive changes] too: the poverty came to an end, and all of this suffering was past, and Hitler came to power, and suddenly there was great enthusiasm in school.

Everyone was joining the Nazi youth organizations, she explained, the *Bund deutscher Mädel* for the girls over 14 years old and the *Jungmädels* for the 10- to 14-year olds.

> '34 got me caught up in it too. And because I was already older—I was 15 by then— I was immediately asked if I wanted to be a *Führerin*, and I wanted to be a Leader, though I had the Young Girls [in my charge], the little ones.

---

54 G004a 27:00.
55 G004a 29:27.
56 G004a 27:52.
57 G003a 17:45.

Theodora liked the communal nature of these activities.

> Fundamentally, we—I did it because it was fun. The war games we played with them, the hiking we did with them, the sports we played with them, the singing we did with them—I enjoyed it.

For a time, then, Theodora participated actively in a Nazi organization, "and I also advanced, becoming a higher[-ranked] Leader."[58]

Theodora was aware of the fact that this new organization was something different from what either of her parents offered her—a point she made subtly in terms of the songs they sang.[59] In addition to the traditional folksongs that her parents had taught her from the *Wandervögel*, she sang "more modern" songs in Nazi youth groups that were "newly composed": primarily "The Flag High!" and other songs "that moved in that direction" like "Holy Fatherland." Here we see on a subtle level one of the appeals of Nazi youth organizations: they actively sponsored a sense of independence and even non-conformity *vis-à-vis* parents.

Theodora did not mention that "The Flag High!" was more commonly known as "The Horst-Wessel Song" and was one of the Nazi regime's most popular anthems. Instead she recited fragments of the lyrics: "The flag high! The ranks tightly closed!" She also did not recite the rest of the stanza, which had more overtly political content and specifically directed attention to the civil war that the Nazis were waging for the future of Germany:

> Stormtroopers march with calm, firm steps.
> Comrades, shot by the Red Front and reactionaries,
> March in spirit with us in our ranks.[60]

Here her memories, or her self-presentation, corresponded closely to her self-image as someone congenitally disinterested in politics.

Here is also where her self-deceptions fall apart. It hardly mattered why Theodora joined the Nazi organization for girls, or that she supported Hitler only because of his economics and not his antisemitism. Hannah was wise enough to read in Theodora's behavior evidence of the spread of National Socialism. Like Gerhard and Hartmut, she and her family faced the no-win situation in which they either placed themselves in mortal danger by staying in Nazi Germany or helped Hitler make Germany *judenrein* by leaving. They chose the latter, but the absurd paradox at the core of this chapter is that Theodora and Hannah, each in their own way, became collaborators in the Nazi project while firmly believing themselves to be non-conformists.

---

58 G003a 19:00.
59 G005a 10:00.
60 Daniel Siemens, *Horst Wessel: Tod und Verklärung eines Nationalsozialisten* (Munich: Siedler, 2009), 80-81.

In the Fall of 1935,[61] Theodora decided to leave the Nazi organization. "I remember still, I had crawled my way fairly high up in the meantime. Then I decided 'Nope.'" Theodora never offered a reason why she made this decision, but it is fitting given her self-representation as a person without political convictions of any kind. She is able to make a convincing case for her unruliness by shifting the burden of political convictions to her parents, a strategy she repeated throughout the interviews.

> It was really my father who convinced me [to leave]. He said, "Here, look at this, look at this. This cannot end well. And how can Hitler—" In my opinion, he was also referring to the Jewish Question, though my father was not an outspoken philosemite. You cannot say that either. He was indifferent to it. It was a neutral attitude.

That the so-called Jewish Question remained her supposition again corresponds to her *modus operandi*—staying clear of any overt assertions of political convictions.

Non-conformity gave Theodora the freedom to move dynamically between different political positions in everyday life. She recounted that Hildesheim had many Jewish families and that her mother, too, had befriended a Jewish classmate when she had been in school. They also remained friends with the Swedish woman and her Jewish husband until they left for Sweden.[62] Still, Theodora and her mother went to the Olympics in 1936 "and there, one was still very enthusiastic." The break came, for her mother, "when he started to prepare for war" with the Sudetenland and with the Night of Broken Glass. "Everyone was horrified."[63]

Quite literally, we must imagine Theodora moving fluidly from situation to situation—from a lesson with a Jewish music teacher to her leadership position in the Young Girls, marching in Nazi ranks and even singing their songs but distancing herself from their spirit—without a sense of contradiction. Her refusal to conform to any political convictions gave her this flexibility. Without it, we can hardly imagine her thriving in the Third Reich as she did.

Theodora the Teacher

Theodora discovered her ability to respond to the demands of modern political mobilization. By rejecting political principles on principle, Theodora freed herself from the political constraints of everyday life even in totalitarian circumstances. Yet her non-conformity freed her not only from Nazi pressures to participate but also from responsibility for her collaboration in the essential elements of Nazi policies. In this sense, non-conformity also freed her *for*

---

61   G003a 19:06.
62   G003a 20:30.
63   G003a 21:00.

participation. Following the story of her life into the war years will help us to see the human consequences of non-conformity.

Like Günther, Theodora accrued considerable benefits from her non-conformity. She understood full well that her membership in a Nazi youth organization had opened doors for her in her future career.[64] She insisted that she had nothing more to do with Nazi organizations after she left the Young Girls in 1935—

> Except for the fact that I could attend university, and could do anything thereafter that I did do in terms of my career because I had this certificate, or this, well, this official document, in other words, evidence. I was a Leader in the Young Girls. That made my way smooth thereafter. I would not have been allowed otherwise.

We are struck by this justification after the fact. It is as if she is once again burying her father's doubts about fascism under her mother's pragmatic appeal for economic necessities. Her non-conformity certainly allowed her to reap the benefits of the Third Reich for her career.

That career during the war was not as purely pragmatic as she claimed, however.[65] After completing her studies, Theodora took a post as a teacher in the Warthegau: that part of conquered Poland nestled between East Prussia and Silesia that was directly integrated into the German empire after 1939. Theodora left her experiences during the war rather vague in her testimony, and unfortunately, Drew did not press her to reveal more. Thankfully, historian Elizabeth Harvey has reconstructed what a teaching post in the Warthegau entailed for a young woman from the Reich and even used oral history to do so.[66]

Nazi organizations for women sent young women to Germanize the Germans in ethnically mixed regions who seemed, to the Nazis, in danger of losing their German identity and culture. After the Nazi conquest of Poland, these projects expanded in scope and scale in the territories that were directly annexed to the Reich. By 1941, the Association of German Girls alone had sent some 3500 women to serve, mostly to the Warthegau. These women's motives were multifaceted and ambiguous. They ranged from overt enthusiasm for the Nazi colonial project to desires to "return" to the land, to see the world, to escape from parental authority, to get practical experience, to build a career, to discover opportunities, or just to make the best of the situation. We could call these women non-conformists in the sense that their political positions were typically flexible, allowing them to adopt or adapt, emphasize or ignore, the Nazi ideological context on an "as-needed" basis.

---

64 G005b 05:30.
65 G002b 16:50; G003a 05:55; G004b 00:00.
66 Harvey, *Nazi East*.

It was in the Warthegau that Germans first explored how to implement their dreams of *Lebensraum*. Starting in October 1939, they deported, ghettoized, and murdered some 400,000 Jews and 500,000 Poles to make room for one million "ethnic" German colonizers resettled from Eastern Europe. The latter were designed to serve as a human barricade to protect the fragile German self from the perceived threat of Poles and Jews. German women played a key role in both resettlement and reeducation. They screened populations according to race, cleaned farms for German use after their former inhabitants were removed, provided welfare services for German settlers, helped them with their harvests, and invented programs to promote German community life.

Many of the teachers imported to the Warthegau were recent graduates from teacher training schools or probationary teachers like Theodora. They were often compelled to work there and not allowed to transfer out; and yet many also welcomed the challenge and opportunity. They assumed responsibility for inculcating ethnic Germans in the language, culture, and habits of modern Germans. They developed programs, schools, and curricula to promote German identity, proper gender roles, modern hygiene, secularization, sports, and the segregation of the races as well as explicit Nazi ideology.

German teachers were expressly forbidden to socialize with Poles. Polish children were segregated and given little to no schooling in the express purpose of eradicating the Polish language and culture. By December 1941 when Theodora arrived in the Warthegau, the Nazis were conducting their first experiments in Chelmno with the use of gas for the mass extermination of Jews. Rumors circulated among German teachers there about these new techniques of mass murder.

The Nazi East provided young German women like Theodora with a rare opportunity for the cultivation of a modern self. With so much to do in the Warthegau and so few Reich Germans to do it, these empire builders welcomed new recruits with open arms. Harvey shows that the young women from the Reich were surprised and flattered by the positive reception they received in the Nazi East. The coercive project of colonization actually gave these young women the chance to assume a wide scope of responsibilities, prove their competency, become self-reliant, and be rewarded for their initiative.

The Nazis certainly encouraged these teachers to view themselves as conquering heroes whose central mission was to eradicate Polishness and implant Germanness; but even everyday life as an empire builder reinforced this "attitude of mastery" (*Herrenbewußtsein*). After all, it was the job of Reich Germans to teach ethnic Germans about their racial superiority; the glory of the message reflected well on the messengers. Their position as educators also validated their sense of cultural superiority over the ethnic Germans they were resettling or colonizing. On top of the authority and respect due to any teacher, as representatives of the Nazi regime they also commanded a not insignificant degree of political clout. They were treated like royalty even among their "own" people; and their surprise at this meteoric rise in status and power probably helped reinforce the vanity of racial superiority. In their everyday interactions, it proved all too easy to flatter themselves that they deserved the kind of status and power that they were being shown.

What little we know about Theodora's wartime experience suggests that she too assumed her post in the Warthegau with a posture of self-evident mastery. Her future husband had been soldiering in France, she explained, and he had been wounded. He "only came back to Germany for a half of a year in order to recuperate. That is where I met him." When she said, "to Germany," Drew presumed she meant Hannover, where she had been studying, but she corrected him that they had met in the Warthegau. This comment hints at how much of the Nazi colonial project Theodora had accepted as legitimate.

Theodora described their involvement in the Nazi war for *Lebensraum* as the fact of life that it had become. When he was not serving as a soldier, her husband worked as a notary. They met in a guesthouse where they both took their meals. They married in 1942.

> You did not have the opportunity for a long courtship. You had to decide fast because he was back at war, this time in Russia, after just a half a year. That was generally the case.

The newlyweds set up their residence there in the Warthegau—she corrected herself: their *work* residence—until "the war came and everything was gone [*war hin*]." That is, Theodora could remember having moved to the Warthegau as an empire builder with a sense of sovereign impunity for the coercive violence required to build a life for herself and her husband in the Nazi East.

Theodora thrived in the Warthegau. Like many other ordinary Germans, she later described the heydays of the Nazi imperial project in positive terms. From "shortly before the war…up to the collapse of the Third Reich…things were good."[67] She did not explain what made her life as a colonizer so wonderful, for those memories got dangerous precisely in terms of the people who suffered on account of her success. Given her three to four years of service as a teacher in the Warthegau, however, and her husband's similar service as a soldier to the end of the war, we read these statements of self-satisfaction as indirect evidence that, *in the imperial moment*, she had every intention of doing her part to keep the good times rolling for herself and the Third Reich.

---

67 G005a 42:20.

Here we would like to caution the reader against interpreting Theodora as a liar in any straightforward way as if she is telling a falsehood in the post-fascist present about the Nazi past in order to hide her collaboration. She had been deceiving herself long before she performed her role as a teacher in the Warthegau or presented her lying self to Drew. Theodora grounded her bid for racial superiority on the borderlands of the Nazi Empire in older habits of cultivating cultural superiority, developed in her provincial home town within Germany proper. The cornerstone of this deception lay not in the first-order lie about the self but in the second-order lie about her agency, in which she acted as if she had nothing to do with her own rise to status and power. She duped herself into believing that her *niveau* was self-evident, rather than the product of her callous self-promotion. She did so to insulate herself from responsibility for her sovereign impunity.

Theodora understood herself as a non-conformist in much the same way. It is not just that a posture of unruliness allowed her to move in and out of politicized postures as the situation demanded; she also came to identify herself as a non-conformist. This self-image made it easier for her to adjust to her new role as German colonizer. Sincerely believing her non-conformity facilitated the fantasy that she had not done anything to deserve her power and status as an Aryan *Übermensch*.

Everyday Knowledge

The key to understanding Theodora's non-conformity lies in the untroubled way that she narrated her achievement of mastery in the Nazi East—akin to the disturbing normalcy with which Günther let himself be photographed in front of destroyed French towns. In the imperial moment, a posture of non-conformity afforded these ordinary Germans the conceit that their position of mastery in Nazi-dominated Europe was natural rather than something that they did themselves. In their autobiographical testimonies decades later, they disguised their collaboration in violence according to the same logic because non-conformity had worked so well for them in the past.

The tragedy for Günther and Theodora lay in the fact that they were conscious of the absurdity in their posturing. Towards the end of the first taped interview,[68] Theodora said the following about her Jewish friends and neighbors in Hildesheim after 1938:

> No one was there anymore. And they did nothing. What could one have done, you may ask? I wonder now also what one could have done. That is after all one of those accusatory question that one asks oneself: What could one have done, no? Sometimes one is confronted with such situations.

---

68   G003a 25:00.

In light of what we pieced together about Theodora's career during the war, this description of disappearing Jews now seems disingenuous. She had in fact followed the path of some of her Jewish neighbors to the Nazi East. She avoided discussing it in detail, but she clearly understood the violence they faced there because she played a supporting role in reorganizing this territory according to Nazi racial principles.

Theodora put these things together for herself. Before the final interview, she had become so disturbed by the interviews that she could not sleep the previous night. The logic of the topics for each of the three taped interview sessions—neighbors, friends, and politics—raised the question of agency and responsibility again in her mind: *what should I have done?*[69] Drew did not record this conversation, but once the tape recorder was turned on, Theodora explained that the assumptions of his interview questions were wrong:

> That in the Twenties—in the Twenties I would like to emphasize—that we were thinking a lot more about politics than was actually the case. I am of the opinion that it was precisely because we all were so *un*political that it was possible at all that Hitler was able to come to power at all.[70]

What this statement leaves unanswered, of course, is the degree to which she had been actually thinking about politics during the Nazi war for *Lebensraum*, when the very ordinary way in which she built her career and cultivated a self implicated her in unprecedentedly inhuman systems of violence. Still, we read even this contorted statement as an admission on her part about the dangerously irresponsible consequences of a life lived pleasantly free from the burden of political convictions. We would go further and insist that non-conformity all too readily excused violent claims to mastery.

Like Sisyphus, tragedy entered the stories of Günther and Theodora in their awareness of their condition. To preserve their respectability, they had to constantly twist their experiences into confusing knots of anachronism. They reinvented their contemporary identity by proving their obedience to postwar imperatives transposed back into an interwar reality. Decades later, they remained all too aware of their autonomy and yet behaved as if they were incapable of it. What began for Theodora as a strategy to free herself from having to take sides in the violent beginnings of the Nazi revolution became a strategy for reaping the benefits of Aryan status in the violent culmination

---

69 See Bergerson, "Narrating Enlightenment: oral history and civil society after Hitler," *Issues in Integrative Studies* 16 (1998): 31-55 at 49-52; and Bergerson, "Aufklärung durch Erzählung: mündliche Geschichte und bürgerliche Gesellschaft nach Hitler," in *Inspecting Germany: Internationale Deutschland-Ethnographie der Gegenwart*, ed. Bernd Jürgen Warneken and Thomas Hauschild, 222-249 at 242-248 (Berlin: Lit Verlag, 2002).

70 G005a 00:45. She also listed the economic crisis and the persistence of a Wilhelmine mentality of subordination as additional causes: i. e. things that happened to her rather than her own deeds.

of Nazi hubris. Even though she did not pull the same triggers, she claimed with Günther the same right as a non-conformist to sovereign impunity.

How We Take Sides

A dead-end threatens to arrest our exploration of non-conformity. Either out of resentment for our suffering in the past or in the hope of escaping into a better future, modern individuals often turn to non-conformity as a way to liberate themselves from the constraints of the present. We also respond with non-conformity to the typically modern pressures of political mobilization by "opting out." Though we may claim to reject principles on principle, in fact we move in and out of politicized postures according to the needs of the situation, because there is no place outside of political relationships. There is certainly a lot to be said for this struggle for autonomy; the problem is that it too readily implicates us in violence. Our resentment at our circumstance may be legitimate, and our hopes for the future may be laudable, but that does not justify the use of any means to ensure our freedom.

All too often non-conformity becomes an attempt at mastery. Our resentment is directed at those who oppress us; our freedom seems contingent on releasing us from the ties that bind us to them. Utopian language exacerbates this situation by using endings to our stories to silence the skeptical voices in the middle of our stories who remind us of the human consequences of our actions. Sometimes we even use messianic visions of the future as means to assert control over the far more ambiguous situation in the present. In the name of autonomy, non-conformity compounds our claims to sovereignty with the luxury of impunity, precisely because we are reinventing our self in terms of its independence from others.

There is one laudable aspect to Günther and Theodora's behavior. Like Sisyphus, they worked within existing conditions. They dealt with each situation as it came along with a remarkable flexibility of self. This typical trait of many ordinary people reminds us of our ability to respond to the ever changing situations of life, to other human beings. The problem with Günther and Theodora is that they refused to recognize their responsibility. Also like Sisyphus, they cultivated an almost nihilistic attitude towards the human consequences of their non-conformity.

One way out of this dead end is to recognize the fragmentary nature of selfhood and accept it as a process rather than a condition. In the German philosophical tradition, there is no better source for rethinking the human condition as action than Hannah Arendt. Herself a non-conformist, she was often confronted with the challenge of having to take sides in the political storms centering on the Third Reich. Yet we will read her book, *The Human*

Condition, unconventionally in terms of Nietzsche's Messianic figure of Zarathustra. While we recognize that Arendt was deeply troubled by Nietzsche's
work, they share a common concern as existential humanists with drawing
our attention away from the sides we take as non-conformists and towards
the way we take sides.

Arendt on the New

Hannah Arendt spent much of her life as a non-conformist. She was a German Jew who fled Nazi oppression and ended up writing and teaching in the
United States, although after the war she returned to Germany for extensive
visits. These facts set up certain expectations for how she would lead her life,
but she did not conform to these expectations. As a university student, she
was involved in a relationship with one of her professors, the philosopher
Martin Heidegger. He joined the Nazi Party and accepted the post of Rector
at Heidelberg University in order to lead a reform of German higher education
along Nazi lines. This project failed, and Heidegger was marginalized in the
Third Reich, but the taint of Nazism never left his name. Still, the relationship
between Arendt and Heidegger was restored, albeit on changed terms, after
the war; and although she criticized Heidegger's mistakes, she still supported
him personally.[71]

Arendt was a non-conformist not only in her personal life but in her public stances as well. As a left-leaning intellectual, Arendt's comments about the
Civil Rights Movement in the United States were surprising.[72] She was highly
critical of African-American mothers who allowed their children to be put in
harm's way in the effort to integrate Southern schools. She remains notorious
for what she had to say about the lack of Jewish resistance during the Third
Reich. In her account of the trial of Adolf Eichmann, *Eichmann in Jerusalem,*
she attributed the shortcomings of the prosecutor to the fact that he was an
"Eastern Jew." For the most part, however, Arendt was more concerned with

---

71 See Elisabeth Young-Bruehl's biography of Arendt, *Hannah Arendt: For Love of the World*
(New Haven: Yale University Press, 1982); on Arendt and Heidegger: Arendt, "Heidegger
the Fox" and "Concern with Politics in Recent European Philosophical Thought," *Essays in
Understanding 1930-1954: Formation, Exile, and Totalitarianism,* ed. Jerome Kohn (New
York: Schocken, 1994), 361-362 and 428-447; also Mark Lilla, "Martin Heidegger—Han-
nah Arendt—Karl Jaspers," *The Reckless Mind: Intellectuals in Politics* (New York: New
York Review Books, 2006), 1-46; less helpfully Elzbieta Ettinger, *Hannah Arendt/Martin
Heidegger* (New Haven: Yale University Press, 1995); on the relationship of their thought
to politics, see Dana R. Villa, *Arendt and Heidegger: The Fate of the Political* (Princeton:
Princeton University Press, 1996).

72 For example, Arendt, "Reflections on Little Rock," *Responsibility and Judgment,* ed. Jerome
Kohn (New York: Schocken, 2003), 193-213.

conformity than non-conformity. "As Eichmann told it," she wrote in this *Report on the Banality of Evil*, "the most potent factor in the soothing of his own conscience was the simple fact that he could see no one, no one at all, who actually was against the Final Solution."[73]

Arendt's *The Human Condition* is her most philosophically significant work; it is also the place where she responds critically to the ethical threat of conformity. She begins by contrasting the *vita contemplativa*, the contemplative wonder of the philosopher or mystic, with the *vita activa*, her main concern. Her analysis of "the active life" makes a move not unusual for her. She asks us to draw a somewhat artificial distinction between three terms we use in overlapping ways: labor, work, and action.[74] *Labor*, she writes, "is the activity which corresponds to the biological process of the human body." Like farming, labor concerns "life itself." By contrast, *work* is "the activity which corresponds to the unnaturalness of human existence." Work is the way we construct the "world." To stick with our metaphor, if the way we grow food is labor, the process by which we make the plow is work.

Arendt's main concern lies with *action*, which is not directly related to the things we do for our survival. Action is "the only activity that goes on directly between men." She is referring to the kind of activity that requires human communities. It "corresponds to the human condition of plurality, to the fact that men, not Man, live on the earth and inhabit the world."[75] Here she is trying to get us away from thinking about man in the abstract or as a type, like the New Man. Her model for this kind of activity is the ancient, pre-Platonic Greek *polis*. It is the place where members of the community are free to come together and are confirmed for who they are by appearing before others. In action, our selfhood exists through social relationships.

One way to summarize the story of *The Human Condition* is that it records how action has gradually disappeared from the Western world in the time between the Greek polis and modern society. Arendt is concerned with the consequence of this disappearance—the loss of freedom. Labor is what humans do that is necessary for survival, and the products of the *animal laborans* are therefore meant to be consumed. Work, the activity of *homo faber*, produces things that are used but that are meant to endure. In a modern consumer society, however, work has been collapsed into labor. The economy is driven by consumption and producing objects to be consumed or used up

---

73 Arendt, *Eichmann in Jerusalem: A Report on the Banality of Evil* (New York: Penguin Books, 2006; first Penguin ed. 1977), 116. On the controversy surrounding Arendt and this book, read Amos Elon's Introduction to the 2006 Penguin ed., "The Excommunication of Hannah Arendt," vii-xxiii.

74 We do not stick to her distinctions in the rest of the book; we outline them here solely so that we can understand what she can tell us about responsible non-conformity.

75 Arendt, *Human Condition*, 7.

rather than simply used. Both labor and modern work puts us in the realm
of necessity. It may appear we are free in an economy oriented around goods
and services because we have so many choices as to what we can buy to consume. Yet our consumption always has to do with necessity, the necessity of
mere survival, even when the goods and services we purchase and consume
are useless. Neither affords us much opportunity for freedom.

Moreover, consumer society is mass society for Arendt in which "sameness" is both essential to and a product of laboring and consuming. In order
for economies of scale to work in the production process, there must be
confidence in creating a mass of consumers whose purchasing habits can be
predicted and planned for. Every particle or person in the mass is understood
to be essentially the same. "The sameness prevailing in a society resting on
labor and consumption" is "expressed in its conformity."[76] Arendt reminds us
here of the contradictions of modernity in which we are promised freedom
and equality yet experience constraint and homogenization.

Action, by contrast, is free because it is based on the principle Arendt calls
natality. She defines natality as the uniquely human capacity to give birth to
something new, something of "startling unexpectedness." This kind of inven-
tiveness takes place in human situations in which conditions are present that
are not of our making, but natality reminds us that these conditions do not
dictate the scope of our inventions. To put action in Nietzschean terms, it
does not derive its meaning from that which it resents.

In action, we are the origin and creators of values. Here Arendt is pushing
us to recognize that there is no such thing as "human nature"; the human
condition is embedded in the process by which we discover our self. Action
is the crucial mode by which we reveal "who," as distinct from "what," we
are—as originators of the new.

Action also puts us in the condition of plurality. The disclosure of our
"who-ness" requires witnesses if our lives are to take on meaning. Action
draws attention to our self as performed. We recognize ourselves only when
our actions are recognized and remembered by others. We are political beings.

Arendt's frustration with the modern world is that action has been sup-
planted by *behavior*. The social and behavioral sciences, which have come
to play a major role in understanding what it means to be human, adopted
this approach as their model for the self. In these disciplines critical distance
turns human activity into the behavior we can observe from the "neutral"
standpoint of the investigator. Mathematical certainty is provided through
the predictive control of statistics. These ways of thinking about the world
sacrifice creativity on the altar of authoritarian control.

---

76 Arendt, *Human Condition*, 214.

For Arendt, action is the very opposite of behavior. Where behavior is based on laws, such that human beings react to similar stimuli with similar responses, natality reminds us of the human talent for giving birth to the new and unexpected. "The new always happens against the overwhelming odds of statistical laws and their probability, which for all practical, everyday purposes amounts to certainty." Because we are so accustomed to believing social scientists when they predict human behavior, we are often shocked by human action when it catches us unawares and does something unexpected. "The new therefore always appears in the guise of a miracle," and we know what has happened to miracles in the modern, scientific world.[77]

Modern individuals tend to think of selfhood in terms of behavior rather than action. We no longer seek to disclose who we are as unique individuals living with others in plurality. We seek to be and understand ourselves as manifestations of what is normative. We conform. We may resent this conformity, but even our non-conformity is, in mass society, determined by the norm. Arendt's concern:

> The trouble with modern theories of behaviorism is not that they are wrong, but that they could become true, that they actually are the best possible conceptualization of certain obvious trends in modern society. It is quite conceivable that the modern age—which began with such an unprecedented and promising outburst of human activity—may end in the deadliest, most sterile passivity history has ever known.[78]

Conforming to norms means the loss of natality, action, and freedom.

Arendt provides a vivid description of the threat of conformism to freedom and therefore to responsibility, given the traditional view that the former is precondition for the latter. What interests us here is her response to this threat. Notice that she does not turn to non-conformity as a way to escape the threat of conformism. She knows better in light of Nietzsche's critique of non-conformity as parasitic on conformity. Instead she turns to our capacity to give birth to the new and to be the origin of values. Arendt provides an image of natality that takes the principle almost literally. "The miracle that saves the world, the realm of human affairs, from its normal, 'natural' ruin is ultimately the fact of natality, in which the faculty of action is ontologically rooted."[79] Here she is alluding to the fact that, no matter how hard you might try to press human beings into types, categories, organizations, and movements, they will always find inventive ways to not conform.

In natality, Arendt has come close to our understanding of responsible non-conformity. Not only does she recognize a human capability to create anew, but she takes it as a fact without grounding in any metaphysical frame-

---

77 Arendt, *Human Condition*, 178.
78 Arendt, *Human Condition*, 322.
79 Arendt, *Human Condition*, 247.

work. Natality happens. Our inherent creativity is the source of our hope. "It is this faith in and hope for the world that found its most glorious and most succinct expression in the few words with which the Gospels announce their 'glad tidings': 'A child has been born unto us.'"[80]

Nietzsche on the Child

The theological image of the child takes us back to Nietzsche, in spite of Arendt's misgivings. Nietzsche also believes non-conformity can become a force for liberation and the formation of values. It depends on how we perform it.

In his famous discussion of "The Three Metamorphoses" at the opening of Book One of *Thus Spoke Zarathustra*, he outlines three different ways to think about responsibility: the camel, the lion, and the child. Because of what it shows us about responsible non-conformity, it is worth quoting at length.

> I tell you of three metamorphoses of the spirit: how the spirit becomes a camel, the camel a lion, and the lion at last a child...
>
> What is difficult? So asks the spirit that would bear much; then it kneels down like a camel wanting to be well laden.
>
> What is the most difficult, you heroes? So asks the spirit that would bear much, that I may take it upon me and rejoice in my strength...
>
> But in the loneliest wilderness the second metamorphosis occurs: here the spirit becomes a lion who would conquer his freedom and be master in his own desert.
>
> Here he seeks his last master: he wants to fight him and his last god; for final victory he wants to fight the great dragon.
>
> Who is the great dragon that the spirit will no longer call lord and god? "Thou shalt," is the name of the great dragon. But the spirit of the lion says, "I will."...
>
> "All value has long been created, and I am all created value. Truly, there shall be no more 'I will'." Thus speaks the dragon.
>
> My brothers, why is there need of the lion in the spirit? Why is not the beast of burden, which renounces and is reverent, enough?
>
> To create new values—that, even the lion cannot accomplish: but to create freedom for oneself for new creating—that the might of the lion can do...
>
> But say, my brothers, what can the child do that even the lion could not do? Why must the preying lion still become a child?

---

80 Arendt, *Human Condition*, 247; she seems to be thinking of the Christian reinterpretation of *Isaiah* 9:6.

The child is innocence and forgetting, a new beginning, a game, a self-propelled wheel, a first movement, a sacred Yes-saying.

Yes, for the game of creating, my brothers, a sacred Yes-saying is needed: the spirit now wills his own will, and he who had been the world's outcast now conquers his own world.[81]

At one level, this story recounts the evolution of value systems. The camel represents, to Nietzsche, the Judeo-Christian way of being in the world. The camel wants to be weighed down with its burden—"The Law." A moral code coming from God, the camel willingly accepts a set of values coming from outside itself. It desires an externally generated understanding of the meaning of life and of its role in existence. Note, however, that the camel does not desire this burden for its own protection. It is not a member of a herd. Here Nietzsche is not making his classic criticism of bourgeois conformism. The metaphor of a camel is intentional: although camels do travel in groups, we think of them as solitary animals. The camel wants the weight of conformity precisely because it is difficult to carry this burden. It is a proof of the strength and virtue of the camel that the load it carries is not too heavy for it to bear. The camel yearns for what is difficult: and what could be more difficult than conforming with the law of God? For the camel the burdens of conformity could not be too heavy.

Unlike the animals who belong to a herd, the camel is not conforming because of what others think or how others behave; it is not conforming for the sake of fitting in. It is conforming for its own sake—for the sake of duty. For Nietzsche, the Judeo-Christian morality appeals to us not because the values themselves are natural for us, but just because it gives us something heavy to bear against so that we can prove our strength in conforming with it. We see this kind of conformity often. We conform in order to prove something to ourselves. Nietzsche seems to respect this kind of self-willed conformism, embodying as it does a principle of self-determination.

Still, Zarathustra teaches, the spirit changes. Now we see the lion, an image of the flourishing of the individual's freedom. It represents, at the level of changes in Western values, the Renaissance and Enlightenment. The lion insists on personal freedom and the creative, liberated self. With "the death of God" we find ourselves facing down the dragon of "thou shalt." To Nietzsche, the dragon represents not only Judeo-Christian morality but also Kant's categorical imperative.

The lion presents us, Nietzsche argues, with all the opportunities we are confronted with today. Like the lion, we have many ways to express our non-

---

81   Nietzsche, "On the Three Metamorphoses of the Spirit," in *Thus Spoke Zarathustra*, trans. C. Martin (New York: Barnes and Noble, 2005), 25-26.

conformity to the conditions into which we were born. Yet the lion goes one step further. The lion challenges the notion that all value has already been created, that there is no more value for humanity to discover or create. The lion believes in the *possibility* of natality.

The idea represented by the dragon is that we must derive meaning in our lives from what we are being told we ought to do, rather than ourselves deciding what is valuable. Although the lion cannot itself create value, the lion realizes that it must first free itself from the dragon so that it may be in a position to create its own value. It is the lion, then, that kills God.

The lion's non-conformity should not be misunderstood as resentful. It defies the values of conformity, but simply by refusing to comply. To every authoritarian "thou shalt" it simply roars—offering neither a yes or a no. In other words, the lion creates the spiritual space necessary for the emergence of the child. The lion cannot create, it can only challenge. Were it to attempt to create, we suspect, it would fall back into the negative space of resentment. Hence the need for the child.

The child lives in the land of spiritual opportunity that Zarathustra believes the future will bring. It is the country of Nietzsche's ideal type of human being, the *Übermensch*. The human spirit has not become the child yet, Nietzsche believed; we are still overcoming the "thou shalts" of our spiritual past. To create new values, Zarathustra suggests, to move beyond conformity and non-conformity, we need the freedom to forget the past. We need innocence.

One way of reading Zarathustra is to see Nietzsche falling into the trap of modern prophets. Zarathustra seems to be suggesting that only by controlling the past through a radical break with it, into a wholly new and better world, will human beings become free. Here we see the return of the fantasy that responsibility can be found only in complete autonomy—from others and from the past.

Zarathustra is not naïve, however. He anticipated this reading, and indeed, he presented himself with this problem in the first pages of his book. In "The Prologue,"[82] he reflects on the danger of nihilism inherent in "the last man." The absence of foundational principles for giving meaning to our lives seems to make it likely that we will deny the very possibility of finding meaning at all. In fact, what he wants us to do, in the image of the child, is to become the creators of our own meaning.

What Nietzsche's child shares with Arendt's concept of natality strikes at the heart of responsible non-conformity. We need a child's creative spirit acting entirely on its own out of the pure joy of creating. Nietzsche optimistically argues that we are at a turning point in human history. The freedom created by the lion could plunge us into the confusion and self-destruction that is ni-

---

82 Nietzsche, *Thus Spoke*, 12-14.

hilism and the radical loss of all real value. Or, we may find that this freedom allows us to begin the process of value creation all over again, that our culture may be refreshed by or even reborn in entirely new ways of understanding our spiritual place in the universe. The image of the child reminds us that we have the freedom to create those values for ourselves.

What we take from Nietzsche and Arendt is the figure of the child who is the creative source of its own value. We always have the capacity to begin anew. We see this creative potential in the non-conformist postures of our many German informants, whether they were playwrights and philosophers or just ordinary people. Indeed, here is where Nietzsche got it wrong when he idealized the innocence of a child. The innocence of the child too easily excuses sovereign impunity precisely because it is naïve: it ignores the consequences of our past actions, and acts as if it is unaware of the present consequences. It is in our own dangerous memories, filled with colorful examples of our own ability to respond to our fellow human beings in the widest variety of challenging circumstances, that we remember our responsibility.

We too wish to free our hope in the present for the sake of the future, but only with an attentive concern for the human consequences of non-conformity. Our proposition: *responsibility has a remarkable, child-like openness to the possibilities in natality; yet it acts with a mature awareness of every opportunity to stand in solidarity with the victims of history.*

The Unruliness of the Child

To conclude this chapter, we would like to offer you an example of how the unruliness of the child can be responsible. In doing so, we are intentionally playing on the term *eigensinnig*, which in everyday speech evokes the kind of stubborn disobedience of children that most parents find frustrating. It seems fitting to us since most of our sources for this chapter were stories about, or told from, the perspective of youth.

We will compare three final anecdotes from the lives of German children in Hildesheim during the Third Reich. Born between June of 1928 and January of 1930, these three informants were between 8 and 10 years old by the Night of Broken Glass in November 1938. When they recorded their stories in English-language interviews in 1993-94, they were in their 60s and living in Israel, New Zealand, and the United States. Because they had experienced the Third Reich as very young children, their accounts tended to be vague on many details. Even as small children, however, they could still remember the fear and the violence they encountered in everyday life.

These three different people told remarkably similar stories, in spite of the fact that they lived on three different continents and had had no contact with one another since the 1930s. They evidence the crucial role played by ordinary Germans in creating an atmosphere of terror for their Jewish neighbors. Here we can see how readily utopian non-conformity, in the hands of Nazis, undermined the civility and respect on which democracy depended.

The stories end in different ways, however. The first two end in fear and alienation on the part of the Jewish victims of Nazi non-conformity, who denigrated their Jewish neighbors with a sense of sovereign impunity. The last story deviates markedly from this typical pattern by ending in a sense of relief and release, thanks to a young man who made the very different choice to stand in solidarity with the victims. His non-conformity reminds us of the wide range of possible responses available to us when we approach everyday life with the openness of a child.

Thilly and Sarah

Thilly Tappe described being hit, spat on, and stoned while walking home from the Jewish school.[83] Her neighbors knew she was Jewish simply from the fact that she went to the Jewish school.

> In 1939 already, you know...things were bad. People around in the surrounding areas, old women, used to throw dirty water out of the window and hit me. I used to run away, and run, run, run and got lost in the town. To try to get away from them, you know. Walking home, from school, I would always walk the same ways, that I get so scared, you know. That turned around.

When Drew asked if she could recall a specific incident, she responded

> Yes, yes. I was walking home from school, when kids took big rocks and started to hit me with them, "You are a Jew," [they said,] and whatever. I just kept walking and walking and like I told you. Those were bad experiences that almost stopped me from going to school anymore, which eventually I did, of course.

Thilly responded with fear. "Just keep running, and running and running." It would overstate the case to call this resentful non-conformity. Hers was an almost instinctual reaction to flee. Though not accurate in dates and times, Thilly's experience of racism was immediate, personal, and unrelenting.

Sarah Meyer, who was almost the same age, experienced the same fear while going to market with her family in the center of town.[84] Perpendicular to the Altstädter Markt was a street, Judenstrasse, that "always puzzled" her as a young girl. The street seemed "ugly" to her as a child. Her grandparents told her that it had been the ghetto for Hildesheim's Jews in the Middle Ages and explained what a ghetto meant.

---

83   G122a 11:22.
84   G176b 07:00.

That is as far as they went because I had so many fears. I was always afraid, always afraid. It was just a constant fear. It wouldn't leave. It was a nagging thing and my grandfather was quite protective. He tried to alleviate some of this, but he would have not succeeded if he would have painted things even blacker than they were—which was almost impossible.

Earlier in the interview, Sarah described the route she took from her house to Lappenberg where both the synagogue and Jewish elementary school were located.[85] Her description is remarkably similar to Thilly's.

The neighborhood was not too good, evidently. Or not bad, it was just typical. How can I say it: not low class—that's not nice—a different class. And they saw these little Jewish kids coming up and they would call us some terrible names, throw stones at us and anything else that was throw-able, and abuse us in everyway they possibly could.

Like Thilly, Sarah had a hard time identifying a particular incident. The terms of abuse that Sarah recalled were "Jewish pig" and "dirty Jew." Also like Thilly, Sarah described the problem in abstract terms, suggesting that, for both girls, antisemitic terror was more a matter of the atmosphere of fear created by many small acts embedded within a larger system of violence.

These are things you remember…It happened all the time…I would say on a daily basis. There was nobody there to save you, because they were definitively believers and these are the people that you run into now who say that, "I was never a Nazi." They were Nazis, and the children were brought up that way.

Sarah and Thilly were responding to the dystopian non-conformity of the Nazis: the rejection, on the part of some of their neighbors, of the principles of civility and respect for one's fellow human beings. Yet the fact that they even picked on small girls suggests that these ordinary Germans did not worry that they would ever be held accountable. Sarah responded with non-conformity.

I know how I reacted. We were all not really shocked, because it gets to be a norm, but upset of course, and fortunately or unfortunately it was there. I went to my grandfather…And I say I had been called these terrible names and they keeping on throwing things, and—they hit you: these kids would hit us and beat us up. It was nothing short of physical and mental-emotional abuse, all of it. And that's when he talked to me and I was very young and he told me, "You have to learn to say. *I am proud that I am a Jew*.'"

Sarah expressed this italicized phrase in German, probably because it stuck in her mind in that language. She took her grandfather's advice to heart. She insisted on being proud that she was a Jew in spite of Nazi propaganda and the antisemitism of her neighbors. Modeling her behavior on her grandfather, she

---

85   G176b 01:35.

discovered her ability to respond to a situation beyond her control and fraught with terror.[86] Still, hers was largely the non-conformity of resentment.[87]

Ruth and an Anonymous Hitler Youth

Ruth Busche told a remarkably similar story of being chased home by racist thugs. But this time, the story of ordinary terror ends in release—a release that resulted from someone acting in an unexpected way and doing something new. Ruth's story:

> I must have been four or five, and we still lived on Hoher Weg. One night, at least one afternoon, I went riding my little sleigh and it was Christmas, I remember, because the store was opened late and my mother was so busy she didn't even notice I'd gone. My mother, as I said, put her business before anything else. I think I left when it was still light and it rapidly got dark. By the time I got back it was completely dark.
>
> So I was riding my sleigh and these boys came, these Nazi boys, Hitler Youth boys came and they wanted to beat me up. And a boy—and I don't know to this day what sort of boy he was, whether he was a non-Jewish boy or Jewish boy, he must have been non-Jewish—and he stepped between them and me and protected me and said: "you go home." And they threatened him, but they took off.
>
> And I was so upset, and so frightened and so on, that I wet my pants all the way up Hoher Weg. I was trailing this little sleigh crying my eyes out. When my mother heard that I was outside crying, she thought something terrible had happened to me. And she was relieved to find out that I was fine.
>
> [I was crying] because I've [*sic*] wet my pants. And that was the one time she was very nice to me. She said, "Doesn't matter." I was so relieved, because I thought I was going to get into terrible trouble because I've [*sic*] wet myself, but she was just pleased that nothing terrible had happened to me.

This anonymous boy embodied a performative contradiction: a Hitler Youth who defended little Jewish girls from racist violence. His position in Nazi society was notably vague in her memory, a result of years of official memories in which such paradoxical figures did not fit. His motive was also unclear. He was probably not particularly philosemitic. He had joined the Hitler Youth after all. It makes no sense to view his non-conformity as resentment or utopianism. More akin to Theodora, his response to this situation probably had nothing to do with political convictions at all.

---

86 S. a. the similar account in Meyer, "Memoirs," ch. 2.

87 Around 1943, Johanna Ernst was told that she would be sent to serve as a helper in an anti-aircraft battery in southern Germany. Her future husband suggested that they marry instead and have a child to protect her from this war service. In this case, an act of resentful non-conformity nonetheless had an outcome that was a literal form of natality (G132b 09:15).

Where this anonymous boy differed from all of the examples that we
have seen so far is that he found a wholly new and unexpected way to not
conform. Neither rejecting nor confirming Nazi politics *per se*, he took personal responsibility for a victim in the Nazi present. At least this time, he
surprised everyone by seeing to it that no further harm befell his neighbor
or himself.[88]

This ending to the chapter on Non-Conformity should not be misread
as a renewed attempt at interpretive closure on the ethical ambiguities of
everyday life under Hitler. As the next chapter will suggest, there is always
room for more skepticism. Still, the example of this anonymous Hitler Youth
offers us the best model so far for how we might cultivate a historically responsible self.

Historians might conclude from these stories that Nazi-dominated Europe was a seething nest of non-conformists. Some fought for or against the
Third Reich in the hopes of realizing a utopian future. Many others expressed
their unruliness through resentment. Yet the vast majority moved strategically in and out of politicized roles to make everyday life as comfortable for
themselves as possible and to benefit as much as they could from all that the
Third Reich offered them. Even if it seems contradictory to us in retrospect,
this wide range of non-conformity functioned smoothly to excuse and enable
Nazi violence by affording ordinary people the luxury of sovereign impunity.
Precious few used non-conformity to help those in need.

There might be a more interesting way of reading Ruth's story, however.
As a fable, it can enable new, non-conformist readings of the past, tales
that might inspire creative thoughts about the scope of our unruliness and
inspire us to act with the freedom of natality. Here we are not suggesting,
as Gerhard had, that this kind of non-conformity constitutes a perfect duty
for ordinary Germans, Jewish or not, during the Third Reich. We cannot
imagine that the anonymous Aryan boy from Ruth's childhood had hoped
that his act would somehow create a better world. We imagine instead that
he championed this girl simply because this German Sisyphus could not
abide the alternative.

Whether he did so because he was concerned first and foremost about
the kind of person that his neighbors took him to be, or because he was actually concerned for her welfare, is immaterial. Explanations or rationalizations
are not what count here, nor do principles or utopian vision. Confronted in

---

88 Dora Pröbst recalled a similar tale of a border guard who let her pass the border to Holland, and exile, with her half-Jewish son. If he had checked for valuables in her suitcase, as
required by official procedures, she would have ended up in a concentration camp for trying
to smuggle out three gold items. In this case, however, his non-conformity was probably
related to the fact that he was attracted to her (G126b 20:20).

everyday life with a concrete example of a system of violence in which he was being asked to collaborate, this boy discovered his responsibility in his capacity for natality. In everyday situations beyond his control, he is measured, as are we, *by the unexpected act.*

Irony

Direct your attention to the finish.
— Bertolt Brecht, *In the Jungle of Cities*, 1922

Figure 7. *Air-Reconnaissance Installation*, Lippstedt, Germany, 1940.
Source: Reinhard Oetteling.

Yes, *Hitler,* No?

Theodora Algermissen depicted herself as congenitally disinterested in politics. The way she told the story,[1] all the girls began to join Nazi youth organizations after Hitler came to power. "So, lots of enthusiasm for some, for others not so much." Theodora admitted that, in 1934, she was also "seized" by enthusiasm. Yet she insisted that "the politics really did not play such a big role at all. *Yes, Hitler*—" Theodora said emphatically, raising her arm in a parody of a Nazi salute. "Yes, oh yes, *Hitler,* no?" She meant that she performed the obligatory rituals of fascism but not wholeheartedly. "Fundamentally, we—I did it because it was fun."

This account is troubling, and not just for us. As an Aryan, Theodora was expected to participate in the mass mobilization of the German *Volk* for the goals of the Nazi revolution. She felt like a non-conformist; yet she could recall her own enthusiastic participation. During the Third Reich, she moved in and out of these politicized postures. How do you narrate a self that was both one thing and its opposite? How do you explain all this clever use of ambiguity to a skeptical audience who suspects you of deception?

Our Ironic Self

As Theodora's example illustrates, maintaining the contradictions of self-deception and non-conformity requires a substantial dose of *irony*. Irony enables us to avoid either-or choices between belonging to or rejecting normative expectations. It lets us take ambiguous positions simultaneously on the inside and the outside—for instance of Nazi organizations—to get the benefits of both. The ambiguity of irony also comes to our aid when we try to tell the story of our lives to others and account for contradictions in our selfhood. It was particularly useful for Germans when speaking to an audience that does not have first-hand experience of the tremendous political pressures inherent in a fascist society.

Let us look closer at Theodora's example, for it is typical. At the core of her expression, "Yes, oh yes, *Hitler,* no?" was the way she emphasized the word "*Hitler.*" On the one hand, she reiterated the *Führer*'s name the way ardent Nazis used to say it as part of the *Heil Hitler!* greeting—with enthusiasm. On the other hand, we are to understand that she meant precisely the opposite of what she was doing. By *over*emphasizing his name, she was mocking those who were serious in their adoration.

---

1   G003a 17:45.

Theodora was suggesting that, during the Third Reich, she had belonged to the Association of German Girls but did not share the official enthusiasm for Nazi ideology. The point of her "Yes, oh yes, *Hitler,* no?" was to convey by example her *ironic strategy* for negotiating the totalitarian pressures of Nazi society. In the early years of the Third Reich, she did what she was supposed to do but undermined that obedience by imbuing those acts with the very opposite set of meanings. "Yes, oh yes."

Theodora was also describing an *ironic situation* in which the end of the story contradicted our expectations about the protagonist derived from the rest of her life story. She implied that it should contradict our expectations that a non-conformist was conforming to the Nazi demand for political mobilization. Irony allows for a paradoxical kind of self: one that can be a pro- and anti-fascist at the same time without a loss of integrity. It even made this quite serious situation seem funny.

During the Third Reich, however, Theodora's response to this ironic situation approached *parody.*[2] In parody we perform a role—here, that of the ardent Nazi—with an attitude of mockery of that role. Parody criticizes the very forms it presents. It focuses the audience on the content of the performance, but equally as much on the skill of the performer. Theodora presented herself as talented at acting as if she were a Nazi while nonetheless preserving her critical distance from it. Given her chronic allergy to politics of all kinds, her parody of a Nazi seems a fitting response to her ironic situation.

Furthermore, the way she told this story was ironic. As a *narrative strategy* it certainly makes sense that she chose irony to communicate an ironic experience since there is a certain correspondence between the experience and how she is describing it. This "fit" is not necessary or automatic, however. She chose irony because it still served the function that it had in her past: to provide her with room for maneuverability in relation to the Nazi regime.

Irony has the additional benefit of soliciting the audience's collaboration in the work of interpretation. If we laugh with her at the irony that a non-conformist like her was conforming to fascist principles, then we have tacitly accepted that she had been a non-conformist all along. Irony is subtle in this way. Her statement "Yes, oh yes, *Hitler,* no?" invited Drew, and posterity, to confirm her interpretation of events, as if to say: "am I not correct?" She wants us to recognize ourselves in her situation, and she uses that identification to justify her own behavior. The logic here is seductive. Theodora provocatively reminds us that we are no different from her, that we too use irony to negotiate complicated social situations. If we all do it in everyday life, she implies, then she must not be responsible for doing anything so very wrong.

---

2   Cf. Jonathan Culler, *Structuralist Poetics: Structuralism, Linguistics, and the Study of Literature* (Ithaca: Cornell University Press, 1975), 152-160, who views irony as a species of parody.

We are in fact more like Theodora than we would like to imagine. As we will argue in this chapter, selfhood is inherently ironic. Indeed, irony is particularly appropriate to the paradox of memory since, while remembering, we are simultaneously inhabiting our selfhood at different points in time. The beauty, and the problem, with these layers of irony is that they create a kind of shell game with the truth. Using ironic tropes to describe a parodic response to an ironic situation leave us rather confused about the bottom line. Was Theodora a Nazi or not? Herein lies the purpose of irony: it forestalls every effort at clarity.

The Challenge of Irony

Theodora's use of irony presents us with a serious challenge as scholars. How can we determine the truth about ordinary Germans during the Third Reich if their very sense of self was ironic? More generally, how then can we ever hope to clarify the nature of responsible selfhood? Theodora engaged in ironic strategies for this reason. So long as she could keep people wondering whether or not she was a real Nazi, she could preserve her relative freedom to enjoy the benefits of membership without taking responsibility for its violence.

There are ways to interrogate irony with analytic precision, however; it just requires using the tools of irony ironically. For instance, at the bottom of these layers of irony lies a performative contradiction that is untenable. For this house of cards to stand, Theodora has to convince us that, at least during the interviews, she is being completely candid, sincere, and transparent about all of this irony from her past. Our experience, however, warns us against believing her. If she so often uses irony to such great effect, why should we believe that she is suddenly being straight with us now? In effect, she wants us to believe a curious claim: that she is being completely honest now about her past deceptions.

The parody of a Nazi needed to be *sufficiently* credible, however, if it was going to convince. That meant a considerable amount of actual collaboration. The converse seems just as plausible: that Theodora really *did* support Hitler in 1933 and only acted as if she "switched shirts" after 1945. And whether or not Theodora made this switch, certainly many Germans did. Unfortunately, we cannot know for sure from her testimony—for the same reason that her friends in the Association of German Girls could not know for sure in 1933. That is the whole point of irony: it leaves you wondering.[3]

Our point is not to determine once and for all if ordinary Germans were liars or truth-tellers, conformists or non-conformists, Nazi collaborators or resistance fighters. We need to understand what happens to the self, and our

---

3   Two other excellent examples can be found at: G058b 00:23; M001 37:00.

responsibility, in light of the unavoidable fact that we need self-deception, non-conformity, and as it turns out, irony as well, for our selfhood. This situation is present for modern individuals in general, as modernity often compels us to fit ourselves into particular types which never quite fit the complex and unruly beings that we are. It is particularly pressing for people living in a fascist society or trying to account for their behavior afterwards, since their irony involved negotiating roles that were inherently and often explicitly violent.

Acting *as if* one were a Nazi to avoid becoming one is an imaginative solution to a challenging situation. Irony has something akin to natality about it in that it scandalously ignores normative and politicized categories. Irony promises to liberate the ironist from the constraints of everyday life; and yet irony also seems to liberate ironists from ethical constraints as well. In the place of a clear and coherent explanation of character, they offer a paradox—as if to say: "it is impossible that the person I am today could ever have done the very thing that I did in the past." Irony thus seems to undermine the very possibility of a historically responsible self.

Our Approach

This chapter will suggest the opposite: that irony is a crucial component of responsible selfhood. That irony is an essential element in self-understanding was clear already to Socrates. In some respects the intellectual history of orthodox Western philosophy, like the political history of modern Germany, can be viewed as an attempt to remove the self from the ambiguous realm of irony and give it some stability.[4] At great cost, however—of authenticity, of understanding, of responsibility. We argue against posing these questions of selfhood as black-and-white options: in the case of the Third Reich, as if one could ever really be *either* a collaborator *or* a resistance fighter. The route to a politically responsible self in history lies, we believe, in taking seriously the ambiguous nature of the irony that ordinary people use to negotiate the contradictions of everyday life.

Much like the scholar or critic, ironists position themselves on the margins of everyday life to comment on it. By raising questions about our assumptions, they force their interlocutors to interrogate their own stances and grounds for authority. Irony seems to have as a result an inherent potential to liberate human beings from their assumptions. For good reason, then, irony

---

4   Irony and ironists have been charged with moral irresponsibility ever since Socrates. See Aristotle, *Nicomachean Ethics*, trans. David Ross (Oxford: Oxford University Press, 1998); Hegel, *Phenomenology of Spirit*; Kierkegaard, *The Concept of Irony*, trans. Howard V. Hong and Edna H. Hong (Princeton: Princeton University Press, 1989); Gregory Vlastos, *Socrates: Ironist and Moral Philosopher* (Ithaca: Cornell University Press, 1995).

is often lauded as a means to promote critical thinking, and perhaps even ethical behavior, in others.

Our first task in this chapter will be to define irony more precisely and investigate its potential to liberate. We begin with J. G. Hamann, the heterodox German philosopher from the eighteenth century who used Socrates's criticism of the Athenians to criticize the *philosophes* of the Enlightenment. We illustrate his philosophy with a source that is more contemporary to the matters at hand: Bertolt Brecht's poetic use of irony in his "Salomon Song." Taken from the *Three Penny Opera*, Brecht tried to use irony to liberate his interwar German audience from their conventional ways of being, believing, and behaving.

The danger in this strategy comes from the fact that irony seems to have no limits, opening a Pandora's Box of complete relativism. The second step in our analysis returns us to Drew's interviews in Hildesheim, this time to the figure of Reinhard Oetteling, who used irony in a life-long struggle with selfhood and responsibility. Again trying to suggest a certain similarity between art and life, we treat him as a Brechtian character in his own autobiographical testimony. Our purpose is to expose the danger of nihilism when ironic strategies for the self are taken to an extreme.

Another point of this chapter is to emphasize the relationship between self-deception, non-conformity, and irony. They are not really independent strategies; they are cumulative, in that irony incorporates the others, and modern selfhood requires them all. We include a close reading of an anecdote from the life of Jürgen Ludewig, another Hildesheimer, to illustrate how they operate together to liberate the self from any sense of responsibility for one's actions. We draw attention to those consequences by viewing Jürgen's actions from the perspective of the victims.

How then can we redirect irony from sovereign impunity to responsible selfhood? Ironists tend to avoid this question on principle. Fearing its potential for nihilism, typical theories of irony either stop before addressing the ends to which irony is employed or subvert that potential for freedom by reverting back to didactic modes of transformation. Using irony to promote a politically responsible self seems in itself to be rather ironic; and yet it is one path to a more responsible self. Brecht, Walter Benjamin and Simone de Beauvoir help us work through this paradox. Herein lies the pay-off for the German Sisyphus of an interdisciplinary exchange that compares desirable forms of irony against counterexamples from the Nazi era. Direct your attention to the finish.

Defining Irony

In our usual way of speaking and understanding one another, we tend to make statements with the intent that they are taken at face value. The measure of our speech is typically its *isotropism* with our thought or meaning: that we use words to say what we mean. Irony refutes this self-evident kind of relationship between speech and meaning. It depends on the contrast between an apparent meaning and a hidden meaning different from the apparent meaning. Theodora employed this strategy, using the *Hitler* from *Heil Hitler!* to hint at a hidden meaning the opposite of its apparent meaning. As Friedrich Schlegel famously put in *Critical Fragment* 48, "irony is the form of paradox."[5]

Quintilian, a Roman rhetorician, defined irony as the mode of speech "in which something contrary to what is said is to be understood."[6] Where Quintilian may have gone wrong is in the suggestion that the meaning "to be understood" is merely the contrary of the apparent meaning. Quintilian's definition is closer to *sarcasm*, where one says the opposite of what one thinks in a rather straightforward way. Sarcasm is akin to the non-conformity of resentment, where opposition remains trapped in the terms of that which it opposes.

In irony, the real hope of understanding the statement occurs in an oscillation between the apparent and the hidden meanings. Because irony is intentionally ambiguous, one is never quite sure what is meant. Indeed ironists may not mean either what is said or the opposite of what is said. In some cases ironists may not even be clear to themselves what they are trying to say. As Linda Hutcheon argues, irony "undermines stated meaning by removing the semantic security of 'one signifier: one signified.'" Irony "can only 'complexify'; it can never 'disambiguate.'"[7]

Grounded in ambiguity, irony denies the possibility of making precise definitions of discreet phenomenon; and yet the title to this section of our chapter provocatively suggests the opposite. Indeed, most of our section titles should be read in ironic, subversive, deceptive ways. Since Socrates, irony has been a strategy to compel one's audience to participate in the work of interpretation: to seek out the meaning of the statement, to try to understand what the ironists could possibly mean by that contradiction between statement and purported meaning, and to marvel at the creative way the ironists reconfigured expected outcomes.

---

5   Schlegel, *Philosophical Fragments*, 6.
6   Vlastos, *Socrates*, 21.
7   Linda Hutcheon, *Irony's Edge: The Theory and Politics of Irony* (London: Routledge, 1995), 13.

The power of irony lies in the ironist's uncompromising insistence that the audience must work through the tension between apparent, assumed, and other possible meanings. One often wonders, when reading Socratic dialogues, why Socrates's interlocutors do not simply throw up their hands and run home—and of course, most of the early, ironic dialogues end that way. So we beg your indulgence. Still, you should not have any false expectations of analytic closure or utopian outcomes. Irony's charm and its challenge lie in the fact that it never quite completes the work of interpretation or the work of being human.[8]

Hamann on Reason

We are used to thinking of the self as the foundation for knowing. The self allegedly provides us with a point of stability in the process of understanding and negotiating a complex reality. For Plato this stability derives from the knowing self being in contact with unchanging Forms of eternal Truth. A more modern perspective locates this stability in the structure of reason itself. Kant, the German philosopher who defines Enlightenment, acknowledges that the self is always an interpreting subject. Yet Kant stabilizes that self in shared categories of reason that are "transcendental." These categories—such as causation, space, and time—serve Kant's philosophy as the conditions for the possibility of both individual knowing as well as arriving at consensus between people about the world around us.[9] In his model, this transcendent self remains prior to judgment and a stable foundation for living in the world.

We want to make a case for understanding the self as fragmentary instead. We base our critique of Kant on the work of eighteenth-century German philosopher J. G. Hamann. Hamann was actually a good friend of Kant, somewhat of a mentor, and recognized by both as the intellectual superior of the two; ironically, Hamann became the accidental leader of the anti-rationalist and anti-Enlightenment movement. He had a fundamentally mystical view of the universe and humanity's place within it. Like many a mystic, he had serious doubts about the reach of human knowledge, and he emphasized the importance of our spiritual compatibility with the universe around us rather than our physical or scientific mastery of it. His fundamental stance was that we are finite, confused, humorous, hugely arrogant beings who, for all of our exaggerated notions of self-importance, have been set a tremendous task: making meaning out of life.

---

8   Richard Rorty, *Contingency, Irony and Solidarity* (Cambridge: Cambridge University Press, 1989), xv-xvi.

9   Kant, *Prolegomena to Any Future Metaphysics*, introd. Lewis White Beck (Upper Saddle River: Prentice Hall, 1950).

Hamann argued that Kant mistakenly reified what is only a word, like "faculty" or "concept," into a "thing" that is somehow productive of knowledge.[10] To Hamann, concepts, faculties, and even the self as Kant understands them are nothing more than the miscellaneous parts and products of our language. These words are no more the suitable foundation for knowledge than any one brick, arch, or cornice might provide the suitable foundation for a building.[11] You may insist on one of these as the foundation for your cathedral of selfhood—the Enlightenment liked its definition of reason, for instance—but why not another? In essence Hamann is encouraging us to question the reliability of any possible grounding for characterizing the self other than our ordinary experience of it.

To continue the architectural metaphor, Hamann treats concepts, and words more generally, as tools rather than foundations. They do not exist, he argues, except between persons as a means of communication. Any attempt to extract some sort of extra-subjective, prior basis for knowledge out of them will never work. "Every sentence," Hamann wrote,

> even if it proceeds from the same mouth and heart, is subject to an infinite number of subordinate notions, which are given to it by those to whom it is addressed, in precisely the same way as rays of light become this or that color to our eyes depending upon the surface from which they are reflected.[12]

All knowledge is inextricably embedded in communication between human subjectivities.

Ultimately reason itself, the bedrock on which Kant rests all of his analysis, is for Hamann not the stable Archimedean point Kant supposes it is. Reason is a fluid thing to be studied and learned about, itself inextricably intertwined with our usage and development of it. There is no "self" as such, nor "reason" as such: these too are words and systems of words, created in the way we use them and influenced by one another in their development of meaning. As Hamann summarized the view in a letter to J. G. Herder: "reason is language, *logos*."[13]

Modestly put, Hamann's point is that concepts and words do not have the rigid limits that Kant and the other *philosophes* of the Enlightenment would like them to have. The difficulty begins at the moment when one sets

---

10   J. G. Hamann, *Sämtliche Werke*, ed. Joseph Nadler, 6 vols. (Vienna: Verlag Herder, 1949-1957), here vol. 3, 300-301; Fred Rush, "Irony and Romantic Subjectivity," in *Philosophical Romanticism*, ed. Nikolas Kompridis, vol. 1, part 4 (London: Routledge, 2006), 173-195 at 174-176.

11   Hamann, *Sämtliche Werke*, vol. 3, 284.

12   Hamann, *Socratic Memorabilia: a Translation and Commentary*, trans. J. C. O'Flaherty (Baltimore: Johns Hopkins University Press, 1967), 164.

13   Hamann, *Briefwechsel*, ed. Walther Ziesemer and Arthur Henkel, 6 vols. (Wiesbaden: Insel Verlag, 1955-1979), here vol. 5, 1771.

out their limits in a series of preliminary definitions. Once those words begin to mean anything, which is to say, once they begin to be communicated
between persons, their definitions extend and complicate. Always in use, the
knowledge they are supposed to provide could not possibly have the discreet
form that such definitions presume. The problem is surprisingly familiar to us.
Human beings love to use words in new ways. Indeed, we alter the meaning
of words every time we use them by placing them in new combinations and
situations; we are doing so right here in this book.

For this reason, we cannot use discrete definitions of our concepts or
terms in the hopes of building definite knowledge on the basis of those foundations. Words as language-in-use always change what the speaker claims to
know. Again, more modestly, the argument at least insists that the subject is
never totally isolated from the object, reflection about knowledge is never distinct from knowledge of the thing itself, and the content of language remains
bound to language as a mode of communication.

Irony and Dialectics

Irony's logical contradictions—of being the thing and what it is not—might
sound like Hegelian or Marxist dialectics. Like Hamann, Hegel and Marx
were critics of Kant, but they also perpetuated his faith in historical progress.
What they offered the modern world was a predictive model for how historical
change would take place. At the core of both men's philosophy stood an understanding of the world in which opposites found their limits in one another,
until those oppositions were resolved by the "cunning" of history. For this
reason, we might think that irony is dialectical in structure. As Hegel himself
repeatedly insisted, however, irony and dialectics are false friends.[14]

Dialectics is grounded in definitions that treat concepts as discreet entities. With formulaic precision, dialecticians break apart the ambiguities of selfhood into competing forces as if one thing always finds its limit in another:
for instance, the "subject" and the "object," or "the bourgeoisie" and "the proletariat." With the same mathematical confidence dialecticians then insist that
"sublation" (*Aufhebung*)—a process that negates the negations—transcends
these limits and gives ethical properties to inherently unethical things: that a
class "in itself" will become a class "for itself," that an exploitative state will
"wither away," or that "races" become "fit" through a "struggle for existence"
with one another. The problem lies right here: the deception that the self
finds its limits in others which must then be overcome through the violence

---

14 Hegel, *Werke in Zwanzig Bänden* (Frankfurt: Suhrkamp, 1969-1986), vol. 13, 93-99; Cf.
    Rorty, *Contingency*, ch. 5, esp. 78-79.

of progress.[15] Dialectics is not without its uses, but it appeals to ideologues for the same reason that Kant turned to regulative ideas: because the inherent ambiguity of the self offers no actual assurances of historical progress.

Irony is far more realistic in recognizing the ambiguities of everyday life and much more humble in its approach to its philosophical and ethical goals. In irony, human subjects never completely find their limits, or their freedom, in what they are not. Irony exists only insofar as the ironist inhabits a fluid position both within and without. Dancing back and forth across an inherently porous boundary, the ironist mocks the abstractions of dialectics with the motto of bandits: "We don't need no stinking limits."[16]

Reinhard Oetteling offered a vivid example of irony when he told the story of Adolf Hitler's visit to Hildesheim in October 1934 or 1935.[17] Reinhard referred to him as Germany's "adored Leader," but he also noted the unexpected absence of cheers when he drove through town. His use of the term *heißgeliebter*, which we translated as adored, did not correspond to the dictionary definition of adored, since there were less cheers in town than one would expect for political adoration. Reinhard's use of the term exemplifies another difference between irony and dialectics: where the dialectician defines phenomena in order to study their development, the ironist undermines our confidence in the certainty of definitions.

This anecdote also illustrates the advantages of positioning the self on the edge of things. Reinhard could not recall the precise date when the *Führer* passed through Hildesheim, but he remembered what he did that day.

> It was ordered that a sufficient amount of young people had to stand in an honor guard…When he drove past us…I climbed up a few steps to the pub…and I stood there, up above. I could always see great.

This quasi-Archimedean point up the slope of Moritzberg gave Reinhard a sense of distance from these events, as if he had stood apart from the newly minted Third Reich. Yet he took part in an honor guard for Hitler nonetheless. On the margins, Reinhard positions himself physically and narratively both inside and outside the Nazi movement.

Reinhard did not presume, as many dialecticians do, that the tension inherent in this contradiction would lead to some kind of historical development. He also refused to abstract himself out of everyday life to see more essential historical forces at work. Stuck in the middle of an untenable situation,

---

15   Cf. Spiegel, *Practicing History*, 22-26.
16   Adapting John Huston, *The Treasure of the Sierra Madre* (Warner Brothers, 1948): "Badges? We ain't got no badges. We don't need no badges. I don't have to show you any stinking badges!" S. a. Agamben, *Homo Sacer: Sovereign Power and Bare Life*, trans. Daniel Heller-Roazen (Palo Alto: Stanford University Press, 1998).
17   G134b 10:45.

he had to find a way to satisfy two contradictory pressures: to conform and not to conform. Irony helped him square this circle.

Irony is also paradoxically assertive. When representing the self, ironic statements, situations, or performances leave ambiguous the very thing they insist on: one's "true" identity. Irony clears a space for multiple, even contradictory interpretations. Irony in turn encourages its audience to reflect on established forms without wholly negating them. While claiming it is doing nothing of the sort, irony implicates its audience in an open-ended debate about proper interpretation.

Irony thus stands in stark contrast to the orthodox tradition of German philosophy in all of its political incarnations. It never achieves the degree of alienation necessary for its fictional, and inhuman, abstractions—whether they are Enlightenment or spirit, a dictatorship of the proletariat or of the *Volk*, or even, for that matter, social contracts or an invisible hand. Irony is humane precisely because it is always performed in concrete, particular human situations, fully aware of the limits of abstractions.

For the same reason ironists cannot stomach the protagonist of German Romanticism either—or much of anything for that matter. Self-critical and doubting, ironists look suspiciously at the equally dangerous fictions of the sublime, supernatural, nature, history, and myth. They see in heroism and genius, as conceptualized by Romantics, not an ethical way to cultivate a responsible self but a recipe for hubris. The essential mood of irony is humility. Irony does not focus on what one can know or be, but on what one cannot—though it certainly does believe that it is correct in that self-understanding.

Irony as Criticism

Ironists have a dual loyalty. They insist that they are representing the thing authentically all the while they are scrutinizing it skeptically. This balancing act of prying open forms, so that we can see them for what they are and think critically about them, requires considerable skill—or at least ironists like to think so. They resort to at least three different tactics to that end.

One is to avoid an objective discourse in favor of a discussion about the form of discourse. Hamann did it to Kant by reminding him about the communicative limits of the language that Kant mistook as the substance of our reason. Another is to break the flow of the text to speak directly to the audience, as a way to remind them that theirs—and indeed the artist's—is just one possible interpretation. Theodora did this to us when she asked us to confirm her interpretation, "no?"

Either ironic strategy is shocking because it disrupts the smooth flow of argumentation. It is akin to the surprise induced by the Zen masters when they employ a *Katzu* shout in order to bring their students out of thought and into insight. According to Brecht, the goal of an "alienation effect" like irony is to get the audience to think about what they are seeing on stage instead of just identifying with it. This strategy defines the "epic" quality of Brechtian theater. In describing this aspect of Brecht's work, his friend Walter Benjamin wrote: "The interruption of action constantly counteracts illusion on the part of the audience."[18]

A third tool in irony's toolbox involves linking different human attributes to each layer of meaning—marking them, as it were, for human use. Judith Butler famously argued that a drag queen might encourage us, through her dramatic performance as a woman, to identify emotionally with her feeling that she is "really" a woman in spite of her male biology. Yet by drawing attention to her performance of gender, she simultaneously encourages us to reflect, perhaps also with some humor, about what it means to be a "real woman"—and, for that matter, a "real man."[19]

The distinctions evoked here—between emotion and cognition, identification and reflection, drama and comedy, tacit and articulated; i. e. between apparent opposites that are not nearly so opposite as they appear—do not correspond necessarily or directly to the real and the mask. They could just as well be used in the inverse relationships. The point is that the ironist makes new use of any available circumstances, including cultural distinctions, to pry the signifier from the signified for long enough for her to dance back and forth between them.[20]

The dual loyalty of the ironist is why critical theorists so often laud it as a mature stage in how to make sense of the world. In Hayden White's terms, the final stage of ironic "self-reflexivity" achieves a

> power of thought that is not just conscious but also *self*-conscious, not only critical of the *operations* of the earlier stages of consciousness (metaphorical, metonymic, synecdochic) but critical also of the *structures* of those operations.[21]

Irony shares an essential affinity to any vibrant, on-going intellectual life. Irony, we have been led to believe, keeps our minds open.

---

18 Benjamin, "The Author as Producer," in *Walter Benjamin: Selected Writings*, vol. 2, 778.
19 Butler, *Gender Trouble*.
20 See Hutcheon, *Irony's Edge*, 15.
21 Hayden White, *Tropics of Discourse: Essays in Cultural Criticism* (Baltimore: Johns Hopkins University Press, 1978), 9; s. a. Jean Piaget, *The Child and Reality: Problems of Genetic Psychology*, trans. Arnold Rosin (New York: Grossman, 1973), 24-25.

Liberating Irony

Irony opens a space of relative freedom. It aims not just at negating oppression but at positing liberty, whether that opening leads to more understanding or a wider scope for agency as well. This reading of irony has been revived of late by scholars in different disciplines,[22] but it is as old as Western civilization. Applying Socrates to his disagreement with Kant, Hamann illustrates how irony can be employed to liberate oneself and others from, in this case, the false idols of reason. Hamann's example will serve us here as a model for understanding the use of irony by a modern German playwright, Brecht, to liberate his audience from their bourgeois ideology and similarly by a working-class German, Reinhard, to create some elbowroom in bourgeois society. Our point: irony is ecumenical. No authority is immune from its ability to undermine. No wonder that it is a favorite tool of underdogs as they struggle to clear a space of relative freedom for themselves.

Hamann on Enlightenment

Socrates was the original Western ironist. According to him, it was the only tool that could be used to free oneself from false forms of wisdom. In Plato's *Apology*, Socrates says that his own kind of wisdom is "a human wisdom."[23] He claims to know something about himself: that he does not have knowledge. In the familiar puzzle, his knowledge consists in the recognition of his ignorance.

In part Socrates speaks out against the politicians, poets, and craftsmen in Athens whose claims to have knowledge are trapped in at least two layers of ignorance. First, they are ignorant about what they suppose they know. They are either mistaken in the belief that they know various subject matters; or, if they do know something, they overextend the range of their knowledge into improper domains and thus end up supposing they know what they do not. This ignorance in the first sense leads them into a further ignorance in the second that they suppose they know something about themselves: that they have knowledge. Insofar as the latter is a more intimate kind of failure, it is also a more dangerous ignorance. They are ignorant about themselves.

Socrates uses irony to distance himself from those who profess to know by professing not to know, while he in fact knows something: namely, that he does not know anything else. His irony is enriched by our shared suspicion that Socrates must know something more—and yet he will not say what this is. That something more is, at the very least, that by refusing to claim to know

---

22   Rorty, *Contingency*; Butler, *Gender Trouble*.
23   Plato, *Apology*, 23a, in *Plato: Collected Dialogues*, ed. Edith Hamilton and Huntington Cairns (Princeton: Princeton University Press, 1961).

something he does not, Socrates frees himself from the trap of self-ignorance that holds those who mistakenly claim to know something.

For Socrates to claim that he both knows and knows not puts him in a self-contradictory epistemological situation. He is asserting both *p* ("I know") and *not-p* ("that I do not know"). Yet this contradiction is verified by the Delphic oracle, who recognized Socrates "as the wisest who nevertheless confessed of himself that he knew nothing."[24]

Now forward twenty-two hundred years back to eighteenth-century Germany. The modern attempt to couch the problem of self-knowledge in terms of irony begins with Hamann. Hamann cleverly uses Socrates to place the *philosophes* in precisely the same position as the politicians, poets, and craftsmen of Athens. They are ignorant in what they think they know, which leads them into further ignorance about themselves. They "forget," as he puts it, "for the sake of the *cogito* [reason], the noble *sum* [being]."[25]

Hamann claims that their ignorance stems from their foundationalist approach to knowledge. This approach supposes that adequate knowing proceeds by identifying first principles and then building up knowledge in a deductive or quasi-deductive system. That method both reflects and informs their notion that the self is somehow given, transparent, or immediately known.

Hamann is not attacking reason as such;[26] he is not an irrationalist. His target is Kant's confused idea of what reason is and does. Kant, he argues, understands and analyzes only what Hamann calls *structural reason*—the kind of reason that is good at analyzing the world around us. For Hamann, structural reason is at best half the picture. A better use of reason, he argues, is in the development of self-knowledge. It follows that a more appropriate attitude towards knowledge is one of Socratic humility rather than Enlightenment audacity. That a confession of ignorance can be matched with the determination to continue to inquire is ironic; but self-knowledge is only possible, Hamann believes, from this perspective of self-critical irony.

Brecht on Bourgeois Theater

We do not know if Brecht read Hamann, but he certainly applied a very similar notion of irony to his plays. Like Hamann, Brecht criticized his contemporaries. He disliked what the Marxists called *false consciousness*. Brecht wanted to re-educate the masses. He hoped to encourage the audiences of his plays to break out of their bourgeois prejudices and support socialism, but more gener-

---

24 Hamann, *Socratic Memorabilia*, 157.
25 Hamann, *Sämtliche Werke*, vol. 4, 230; Hamann, *Socratic Memorabilia*.
26 Isaiah Berlin, *The Magus of the North: J. G. Hamann and the Origins of Modern Irrationalism*, ed. Henry Hardy (London: John Murray, 1993), 35.

ally he tried to use theater to encourage ethical responsibility for the victims of history. In some of his early theoretical statements about epic theater,[27] Brecht argued that replicating what he sees as the inconsequentiality of bourgeois society, the emptiness of its pleasures and self-awareness, best communicates social criticism. Like Hamann, Brecht turned to irony as a strategy for liberation.

Brecht frequently encloses his literary works of the 1920s in frames, beginning at least as early as the 1922 play *In the Jungle of Cities*. Here the injunction to readers at the beginning of the play, "direct your attention to the finish," causes misgivings when the play's end reveals a situation virtually the same as that at the beginning. Critics have often regarded these ironic strategies as youthful attempts on the part of Brecht to be provocative primarily for effect. Yet their continuation into Brecht's burgeoning experimentation with epic drama and with politicized poetry suggests that Brecht saw irony as a key element in politically engaged theater.

We can illustrate Brecht's use of irony with the "Salomon Song" from the *Three Penny Opera*, first produced in 1928. Brecht more or less wrote this play on commission, as German theaters sought to cash in on the enormously popular London revival of John Gay's *The Beggar's Opera* from 1728. Although characters and plot are closely related to Gay's play, Brecht takes seriously the opportunity to use contemporary, lowbrow musical forms to satirize highbrow theatrical arts and the patrons that attended them.

These audiences were supposed to recognize the caricature of themselves in the leading roles, particularly in Mack "the Knife." Mack is the successful manager of a gang of criminals. He reaps the spoils of their labor without ever getting his own hands dirty. His inability to resist his carnal appetites overtakes his business acumen, however. Not even his habit of bribing the chief of police can save him from being hanged at the end of the play. Only a *deus ex machina* rescues Mack from the consequences of his bourgeois lifestyle.

How is the audience to read the protagonist? Brecht offers instruction on the matter in the "Salomon Song."[28] (Brecht intentionally misspelled Solomon's name. We use the original spelling to refer to the historical figure and Brecht's to refer to the figure in the "Song.") The first three verses describe a historical figure in terms of an overriding character trait: wisdom for Salomon, beauty for Cleopatra, and boldness for Caesar. Brecht presents these characteristics as both the cause of the person's fame and fortune as well as the cause of his or her downfall. Here is the verse about Salomon:

> You looked at wise Salomon
> You know what became of him.
> Everything was crystal clear to the man

---

27   See Brecht, *GBA*, vol. 24, 68.
28   As it appears in the version of the *Three Penny Opera* in the *GBA*, vol. 2, 293-294.

He cursed the hour of his birth
And saw that everything was vain.
How great and wise was Salomon!
And look, it wasn't even night yet
When the world saw the consequences
Wisdom had brought him to this point;
Enviable, whoever is free of that!

Using the song form, Brecht attaches the same chorus to the end of each verse
to emphasize the surprisingly disadvantageous consequences of each of these
positive personality traits. He simply inserts the new person and their dominant trait. Note the parallel structure in the verse about Cleopatra:

You looked at beautiful Cleopatra
You know what became of her!
Two emperors fell into her clutches
So she whored herself to death
And faded away and turned to dust.
How great and beautiful was Babylon!
And look, it wasn't even night yet
When the world saw the consequences:
Beauty had brought her to this point—
Enviable, whoever is free of that!

In the opening line of each verse, characteristics appear fleetingly as adjectives
describing the person: Salomon is wise, Cleopatra beautiful. These adjectives
gesture toward the end of the verse where the descriptor becomes a noun: wise
becomes wisdom, beautiful becomes beauty. Brecht does the same for Caesar:

You looked at brave Caesar then
You know what became of him!
He sat like a god on an altar
and was murdered, as you learned
just when he was at his greatest.
How he loudly screamed: "Even you, my son!"
And look, it wasn't even night yet
When the world saw the consequences
Bravery had brought him to this point;
Enviable, whoever is free of that!

By the end of each verse, the character trait itself acquires agency. It becomes
the subject of the sentence. "Wisdom brought him to this point." This concluding statement is ambiguous. It allows wisdom to have caused both Salomon's attainments and his debacle. Same for the other historical figures.

Where reason itself is ironic in Hamann's take on Socrates, Brecht creates
an ironic situation surrounding virtues like the wisdom of Salomon. The plot
negates a typically positive attribute. Solomon—the historical figure—became
an esteemed king because of his wisdom, but this same faculty led him to

perceive human undertakings as essentially vain and pointless. According to the constant refrain of *Ecclesiastes*,[29] the biblical book of dark wisdom written in the voice of Solomon, Solomon concludes, "How dieth the wise man? As the fool."[30] This seemingly pessimistic conclusion does not negate the value of pursuing wisdom. The sage has still learned life's lessons and seen things for what they are. Yet Solomon was a man of faith who ultimately trusted that human history was in God's hand. A communist, Brecht did not share this faith that God would make things right in the end; he uses the "Salomon Song" to emphasize instead the paradoxical consequences of presumed strengths.

Brecht leaves the interpretation ambiguous. It is his way of encouraging his audience to think for themselves about the consequences of these character traits. Brecht thus undermines one of the most important generic conventions of the theater: that the audience can anticipate the ending of the play from its narrative development. He uses irony to much the same ends as Hamann: to liberate his audience from their false assumptions about their selfhood.

Reinhard in Bourgeois Society

Irony operates in everyday life in much the same way, even when used by ordinary Germans without any sophisticated theoretical appreciation for its technical definitions or intellectual history. Reinhard Oetteling probably never saw any of Brecht's plays as a young man. A working-class youth growing up in a provincial town, he was an unlikely candidate for attending avant-garde theater. Yet he shared Brecht's interest in irony as a path to liberation. Constrained by the authorities of his bourgeois society, Reinhard used irony in an ordinary, pragmatic way to create elbowroom for himself in everyday life.

In interviews with Drew in 1993, Reinhard described how he lived on the margins of his society. "The world came to an end behind our house," Reinhard explained in his typical dry tone about the building in which he was born in 1922. It stood on the very edge of Moritzberg, a village on the western outskirts of Hildesheim that had been incorporated into the town just a decade earlier. Back then, Reinhard mocked, "fox and hare said goodnight to one another there."[31]

As an infant, Reinhard's family moved to a street where he lived for most of his childhood. The Oettelings inhabited one of the attic apartments in a complex of two buildings constructed for workers. This residence was located near the gardens and wetlands that stood between Hildesheim and Moritz-

---

29   1:17-2:16.
30   2:16.
31   G136b 10:15.

berg.[32] The Innerste River smelled of the pollutants from the plastics factory nearby. The houses themselves were built so close to the level of the river that their basements often flooded in the high water season.[33]

Reinhard grew up among the proletariat. Many Moritzbergers built ovens, made plastics, built agricultural machinery, or refined sugar in one of the four large factories in the area.[34] Reinhard's father was a skilled worker employed at the plastics plant. His father worked long hours but still could not make ends meet. His family could not afford to send Reinhard to school beyond the eighth grade.[35] To help make ends meet, his father left the house after dinner to work in their garden or to tend graves in the cemetery for pay along with Reinhard's grandfather. Reinhard had to wait till his father got home from work between half-past four and five in the evening to have lunch.[36] There was food on the table but it was simple at best and could be rather "shabby." Reinhard recalled some meals with disgust.[37]

Even among the working classes, the Oettelings were marginalized. Foremen from the plant lived in these same apartment buildings, and the wives of the foremen were conscious of their superiority. "They had to be a little better." To be sure, Reinhard described relations with the other families in the two houses as "a good neighborly relationship."[38] The foremen's wives chatted with Reinhard's mother like neighbors do. Yet his father was not a foreman, and these neighbors let it be known what purchases they could "allow" themselves because of their husbands's higher income. "You could not get around that in those houses."

A powerful memory for Reinhard related to the stairwell they shared. The workers living in the upper floors cleaned their own part of the stairs, but of course they also had to use the lower steps to get to the upper apartments, and those steps were cleaned by the foremen's wives. Before entering the building, "when one of them saw that us kids did not clean their shoes, then we got a good one behind the ears." This boxing came not only from the children's own mothers but also from the foremen's wives. "That did not make any difference."[39]

At once in and out of his social group, everything seemed fair game for Reinhard's wit, not the least his family and himself. He boasted that his father was the first to own a radio in the two buildings and that all of his neighbors

---

32   G133a 05:10.
33   G133a 16:48.
34   G133b 04:00.
35   G134a 21:53.
36   G133b 20:08, 21:35.
37   G133a 12:10.
38   G133a 22:25; G135a 27:00 as compared to a romantic view of neighborliness at 22:10.
39   G135a 27:00, 28:24.

met in his apartment to listen to the boxing match between Joe Louis and
Max Schmeling. Yet his father did not acquire this radio through hard work
or because he was clever or innovative, but because he let the radio salesman
convince him to spend money that they did not have. "Yes, because he was
too dumb to throw the salesman out."[40]

Reinhard claimed to be more clever than that. When he committed a
"serious sin," his mother punished him by sending him to bed with no supper.
Anticipating this punishment, Reinhard would sneak out of his room into the
garden beforehand and take some fruit. "I got my nutrition in spite of her."
He even let her know of his resentment. "I remember still," he continued:

> I sat up there in the window sill, and I had stolen some plums in advance, and be-
> cause I sinfully spat out the pits below me, and they lay there the next morning, all
> the pits under my window, she knew what had happened.[41]

Reinhard regularly thumbed his nose at authority and yet avoided punishment
through the appearance of subservience. That is, Reinhard dealt with authority through irony. He parodied obedience in physical ways, looking down on
parental authority from the sill of his window just as he would later do to
political authority from the steps of a pub.

"Every force produces a counter force," he recited.[42] A resentful non-
conformist, Reinhard prided himself on being this Newtonian counterforce to
authority. He used to steal apples and pears with his friends from the garden
that belonged to the sexton of the Church of St. Moritz. One night he went
out with Matthias Berger, whose nickname was *Matjes*, meaning pickled her-
ring. They were stealing some fruit when the sexton came after them with his
big German shepherd. Matjes got caught when he fell in the cow pond. "Oh
well…But the next day we went back anyway."[43] Reinhard and his friends
did not get punished *per se* for this peccadillo. The German term he used,
Kavaliersdelikt, evokes the sense of romantic heroism that Reinhard ascribed
to his adolescent piracy. "Everyone did it. Even if your father had just as big
an orchard, the fruit in the other garden always tasted better."[44] When he
told this part in the story, he made a hand movement like he was snatching
something.

Reinhard was particularly proud of the times when he could even the
score between him and the bourgeoisie. He joined a glider troop in high
school. The one bourgeois boy in the group—his father owned a factory—
believed that he could get special treatment because his father had money.

---

40 G133a 08:20.
41 G133b 02:28.
42 G134a 21:05.
43 G135b 13:15.
44 G136a 25:45.

So Reinhard and the other working-class boys quickly "tamed" him. Twice Reinhard and the other boys conspired to run too slow to launch the wealthy boy's glider. It flew "like this a few times"—Reinhard waved his hand—"and then he was back on the ground."[45] Here Reinhard let Newton's other law—of gravity—serve as the counterforce to elitism on his behalf.

Reinhard claimed that he was "too clever" for middle school. He taught himself using books borrowed from a buddy in the Hitler Youth who attended technical high school. For a year and a half, Reinhard did not participate in classroom instruction at all. "That was cold coffee for me already. I understood it all already." He did not exactly play hooky from school either: he built model gliders in the school's workroom.[46]

Church was no different. Reinhard used to spend Sunday mornings running around in the county or in the forest on the Rottsberg. It was spelled "R-O-T-T-S," he explained, "not like *Rotz* [snot] here in my nose." When he heard the prayer bells ringing, he ran back to church to catch one of his buddies to find out what the pastor had said during his sermon "because I would be asked at home what had gone on." He parodied his own need for haste: "*Pscht-pscht.*" [47] Reinhard lived a life in which nothing, not even the parody of obedience, was sacred.

What makes Reinhard's behavior ironic is that he avoided obeying some rules by obeying others. He went to school but built model gliders. He tamed an arrogant comrade while acting as if he was helping to get his glider off the ground. He informed himself as to the content of the sermon without attending church. He adhered to the letter of adult laws while parodying their spirit.

Obviously Reinhard's ironic strategies of selfhood involved non-conformity and lies. Acting as if he is obeying the rules, while doing precisely the opposite, requires both unruliness and a complex series of deceptions and self-deceptions. In Reinhard we see Sisyphus before his condemnation, when the philosopher thief still believes that he can beat the gods at their own game by manipulating situations to his advantage.

Reinhard knew all too well what he was not. He was not an adult. He was not wealthy. He was not privileged. He was an outsider in bourgeois society. Yet he never let any of his betters get the better of him. He moved fluidly between forms of obedience and disobedience. If Reinhard sounds similar to the characters from our chapter on Non-Conformity, that is our purpose. Whereas we began the last chapter defining non-conformity in terms of oppositional positions, what we discovered, the more we probed non-conformity, was its essentially ironic nature. It is fluid, ambiguous, and fragmentary.

---

45   G135a 19:35.
46   G134a 22:50, 26:00; G135b 18:50.
47   G133a 29:40; G133b 00:00.

What distinguishes irony from non-conformity, and is akin to more responsible forms of self-deception, is the tendency of the ironist to not only
be aware of their irony but to take pride in it. By expressing the self in
circumstances designed to hinder that expression, irony provides a "rush" of
selfhood closely associated with both self-emancipation and self-satisfaction.
Too clever for the authorities, Reinhard's ironic posture afforded him a feeling
of liberation from an oppressive everyday life.

We certainly hope that Hamann's heterodoxy, Brecht's provocations, and
Reinhard's sass finally debunks the myth of an allegedly German tendency
towards conformity and obedience. Quite the contrary: Germans are typical
of many in that they turn to unruliness to create islands of freedom for themselves in oceans of constraint. A "slave's trope," irony is a form of cultural expression best suited to those oppressed by forces beyond their control.[48] Irony
is therefore ideal for modernity. On the one hand, irony is well-suited for
responding to control, oppression, and marginalization. On the other hand,
irony is also useful for adjusting the self to rapidly changing circumstances.
Modernity expects us to cultivate an improved self, often through radical expressions of both authority and rebellion. The ambiguity of irony makes it a
perfect tool for seeking both freedom and domination in these contradictory
conditions.[49]

Ironic Politics

Freedom only takes you so far, however. To return to our initial example from
this chapter, Theodora perhaps wished us to believe that she was acting with
Socratic wisdom with her parody of a Nazi. We have our doubts that her ironic
strategy is worth imitating. Irony here seems to result in an ethical nihilism.
This tendency in irony derives from its very open-endedness. When taken
to the extreme, irony undermines the possibility of any clear interpretation
whatsoever. Consider three examples of the dangers of liberating the self—
from historical interpretation, from aesthetic interpretation, and from political
participation. In each we will show how irony too readily becomes an excuse
for irresponsible behavior. Insofar as irony lands even the ironist in hot water,
one might very well envy a life free from such irony.

---

48 Gates, *Signifying Monkey*.
49 Historians tend to divide the problem of selfhood into ideological pressure from above and
     responses from below. Because it manipulates institutional and normative as well as indi-
     vidual and performative factors, an ironic model of selfhood offers us a way to move beyond
     these artificial divides. See the discussion on this topic in Bergerson, "Forum: Everyday life."

Some Idiot

Like many ordinary Germans, Reinhard faced intense political and social pressure to join the Nazi movement and serve in Hitler's army. Yet Reinhard emphasizes the ironies of these situations, notes the ironic statements made about them at the time, and even recounts them in his own ironic style. His goal was to free himself from the constraints of his fascist society; yet his story leaves us with the distinct sense that he was trying to liberate himself—and us, his audience—from our ability to make a coherent interpretation about his life during the Third Reich.

The way Reinhard talks about his parents tell us much about how he saw himself.[50] His mother "carefully complained" about any regime, fascist or democratic, "if something had gone wrong again." Yet she did the precise opposite when faced with social pressure for her son to join the German army: she encouraged Reinhard to sign up. "You will laugh," Reinhard said to me:

> Before I was drafted into military service, my mother even said, "Why don't you volunteer? Everyone else has already gone." To that I said, "Mama, you probably can't wait long enough for me get a piece of lead in my belly!"

What were his mother's real opinions? What was the right thing to do? The fact that his mother seemed to want to sacrifice his life for the Fatherland is ironic enough; by narrating this ironic situation ironically in the present seems to leave us with no solid perspective from which to judge either of their actions in terms of either historical or ethical responsibility. It fit Reinhard's character that he laughed at these contradictions.

Reinhard dealt similarly with the fact that his father had joined the Party. Reinhard insisted that he did so "only later when it got to be unavoidable." And he did so, Reinhard mocked, "out of clumsy-fuzzy thinking. Out of stupidity."[51] At another point in the interview Reinhard admitted that his father even became the Block Warden. "That is, he had to collect the membership dues. They had to find some idiot to do it." Reinhard made his father out to be an irrational actor.[52] As in the "Salomon Song," however, the ironic repetition of the trope of "stupidity" at the end of these stories suggests the precise opposite: that his father was in fact just as "clever" as his son. Where the son allegedly used his cleverness to resist the authorities, the father did so to profit from them. Yet ironies loaded on top of ironies make it challenging for us to know for sure one way or the other.

Reinhard even seems to insist that he could not know for sure either. Reinhard admitted, for instance, that, where his parents could never afford

---

50   G134a 12:30; G134b 13:00; G136b 26:53.
51   G133b, 27:00.
52   G134a 26:40.

a vacation on their own, his father did take one on the Rhine through the Nazi tourism program "Strength through Joy."[53] In a neighborhood where neighbors used everyday purchases to remind the Oettelings about their poverty, it seems very unlikely that Reinhard's father could have kept the news of this prestigious vacation to himself even if he had wanted to do so. Reinhard showed at other points in the interviews that he was highly sensitive to the ways that his neighbors treated him. Not in this case, however. "But what our neighbors thought of that," Reinhard insisted, "that I do not know."[54] Here Reinhard is making an amazing claim: that he was oblivious to crucial sorts of everyday information that at other times in his autobiography hold the key to his ability to negotiate those same relationships.

Reinhard's multiple layers of irony so undermine the structure of his narrative that we can no longer identify responsible historical agents from his autobiography. Irony forestalls our ability to make clear judgments about the protagonists in his life story on crucial issues like whether or not they were supporters of the Nazi movement. Reinhard used irony to liberate himself from the burden of the Nazi past.

Reinhard was not reinventing the past. In fact, we believe that he was sticking fairly close to the truth as he experienced it. Nonetheless, he was presenting his life story in a strategic way designed to make it difficult to judge the character of his protagonists. Reinhard used irony to wrest control over his life and his life story from those who wished to lock him into politicized categories of selfhood. The cost, however, was great in philosophical and ethical terms. He had to construct a contradictory self whose knowledge and wisdom was so circumstantial that he admitted knowing a thing in one situation which he denied in the next.

Macheath the Generous

Brecht was all too aware of irony's potential for nihilism since he pushed the limits of irony intentionally. We have already seen how, in the *Three Penny Opera*, he created ironic situations in which the ending of a story—for instance, the life of a historical personality like Solomon—undermined audience expectations. There is a substantial difference, however, between an ironic song inserted into a play and the more profound disruption that occurs when a play concludes with an ironic negation. Taken to this extreme, irony backfires as a political strategy.

---

53   G136a 15:50.
54   G134b 10:15.

Let us return to the "Salomon Song," since we are already familiar with it. The final line of each verse never changes. "Enviable, whoever is free of that!" It refers to the highlighted trait of each historical figure. Brecht here seems to be suggesting that persons who are devoid of wisdom, beauty, or bravery are enviable. These are ironic endings because they are contrary to our cultural expectations for the positive value of wisdom, beauty, or bravery.

These endings undermine our positive expectations for the outcome of these particular human stories—Salomon, Cleopatra, Caesar. Irony frames the stories of each figure, drawing the audience's attention to that content, and thus promoting reflection on each story as a story. At one point Salomon understood the entire world as clear as day, Cleopatra had two emperors under her lovely thumb, and Caesar attained god-like power; yet in the end those traits become curses. The original trait was necessary to achieve success at first, but the way things turned out challenge our assumptions. Indeed, the endings are so contrary to expectations that we cannot think of alternative actions and choices for these characters without starting from scratch. In this way, irony can undermine our ability to make sense of human stories.

Making sense of human stories is of course crucial to the very way that plays operate. We are trained to know the ending of stories based on generic signs from the beginning—in the staging, the words, the plot, and the character of the protagonists. Brecht destabilizes those frameworks by creating ironic statements that refer to the situation of the entire play. In this example, the final stanza of the "Salomon Song" treats Macheath, the leading character in the play, in much the same way that he treated Salomon, Cleopatra, and Caesar.

> And now you're looking at Mr. Macheath
> Who is free of any greed
> He continuously showered us with gifts
> And when his hands were empty
> He was sold out and hanged.
> He gave us seven times our pay
> And look, it's not even night yet
> And the world sees the consequences
> Generosity has brought him to this point;
> Enviable, whoever is free of that!

In this stanza, Brecht shifts our attention from historical figures to an ordinary man. This time, however, he inverts the paradigm. Generosity is his asserted trait, yet the audience knows that Macheath is *not* generous. Mackie is in fact a robber who furnishes his hideout with stolen antiques. We never see him give anything away; the only expenditure we hear of is the bribe money he pays the police chief, Brown. So characterizing Mackie as generous is ironic.

At this point, Brecht is using irony not just to challenge the audience to seek out answers to these contradictions but to sow the seed of doubt whether there are any answers at all.[55] In an irony of irony, the final line inverts the values of all the other stanzas. We have translated the German word Brecht uses here, *Verschwendung*, as generosity but its literal meaning is wastefulness or squandering. Notice the way Brecht has just inverted the meanings yet again. In contrast to wisdom, beauty, or courage, wastefulness is usually a personality trait most people would not see as an enviable virtue and would be glad to "be free of it." The verses about Salomon, Cleopatra, and Caesar thus represent paradigms that Mackie does *not* follow. Brecht uses this now familiar verse to set up audience expectations—only to more effectively undermine them using irony.

What is the audience to make of all of these contradictions and inversions? Should they seek a different attribute that compels Mackie's downfall in the play? Or should they understand that his capture has nothing to do with the kinds of character traits portrayed in the song? It is their confusion that is the real lesson. In the larger context of the play, the ironic final stanza does more than inform the audience that Mack is not wasteful or egregiously generous, or that this particular vice cannot be the cause of his misfortunes. It undermines the ability of the audience to select criteria to judge Mackie within the life story of a human being.[56]

We could continue to add more layers of irony,[57] but you get the point. Brecht was hoping that these ironies piled upon ironies would encourage his audience to call into question assumptions about the attributes like wisdom, beauty, and bravery that characterize many a dramatic protagonist. A sincere socialist, he wanted them to recognize that positively connoted characteristics and behaviors can have negative repercussions in particular situations.

In fact, these layers of irony so undermine the structure of meaning in the entire play that the possibility of any communally shared interpretation is called into question. In effect, Brecht removes many of the guidelines that the traditional audience was accustomed to use to make sense of the characters. His extreme use of irony thus seems to "liberate" the audience from their very ability to make sense of the play.[58]

---

55 In "Author as Producer," Benjamin is especially mindful of the songs in Brecht's plays, "which have their chief function in interrupting the action" (p. 778).

56 Hans Mayer, *Erinnerung an Brecht* (Frankfurt: Suhrkamp, 1996), 373-374.

57 E. g., the ironic ending to the play. See Klaus Kocks, *Brechts literarische Evolution: Untersuchungen zum ästhetisch-ideologischen Bruch in den Dreigroschen-Bearbeitungen* (Munich: Fink, 1981), 49-57.

58 See Brecht, *GBA*, vol. 27, 232.

Reinhard the Clever

Precisely because irony seems to liberate us from the abilities of others to judge our actions, it can have widespread political consequences. Reinhard offers us a typical case in point. Around 1937 or 1938, his teacher advised him to join the Hitler Youth along with his other classmates so he too could get an apprenticeship after he left school. "*Na ja*, what did I do? I made the best out of it. I joined the Hitler Youth for Aviators." Reinhard set up an ironic situation: that membership in the Hitler Youth allowed him to avoid the totalitarian pressure to participate in the Nazi revolution.

Reinhard claimed that he had only been pretending to be a Nazi. The other boys in the Hitler Youth had to attend the State Youth Day on Saturdays. Those events were "used for war games of a sort." The Leader of the glider corps, Henry Selle, used to say, "Boys! We don't want to go around collecting for Winter Help," the Nazi-run charity organization. "We will hold flight practice, and then we are excused." Even when the weather was too bad for flying, they went to a pub in the nearby village of Himmelsthür.[59]

Nazi Germany was itself involved in analogous parodies on an international scale. At the end of the First World War, Reinhard explained, the Treaty of Versailles had forbidden the Germans to fly planes with motors. "That's why gliders became so popular."[60] Gliders allowed the Third Reich to act as if it was obeying the Treaty even though it was perfectly obvious to everyone that glider training amounted to just the opposite: preparing for war.

These kinds of policy parodies were long-standing techniques of the Nazis. They won electoral and plebiscite victories as defenders of law and order, while it was the Nazis themselves who were primarily responsible for street violence and undermining the rule of law.[61] Hitler signed treaties— such as the 1933 Reich Concordat between Germany and the Vatican, the 1936 Non-Intervention Agreement concerning the Spanish Civil War, and the 1939 Treaty of Non-Aggression between Germany and the Union of Soviet Socialist Republics—arguably in order to better facilitate breaking them.[62] It was common opinion among Nazi party members that the *Führer* had to remain "two-faced" when it came to public speeches about the Jews. Since he was forced to satisfy international opinion by making conciliatory gestures

---

59   G133b 27:16; G134a 00:00; G135b 21:10.
60   G134a 00:00.
61   Allen, *Nazi Seizure*; Burleigh, *Third Reich*; Hamilton, "The Rise of Nazism: A Case Study and Review of Interpretations – Kiel, 1928-1933" *German Studies Review* 24/1 (2003): 43-62; Pamela Swett, *Neighbors and Enemies: The Culture of Radicalism in Berlin 1929-1933* (Cambridge: Cambridge University Press, 2004); Wildt, *Volksgemeinschaft*.
62   Adapting Klaus Hildebrand, *The Third Reich* (London: George Allen and Unwin, 1984) and Kershaw, *Hitler: 1936-1945, Nemesis* (New York: W. W. Norton, 2000).

that contradicted his real feelings, it was up to loyal Nazis to "act according to the [true] intentions of the *Führer*."[63]

Ironic strategies gave Hitler unprecedented political elbowroom. It made it seem as if the Nazis could "get things done" for Germany in sharp contrast to the domestic political stalemates of the Weimar Republic and the interwar system of international relations designed to punish and constrain Germany. Moreover, irony encouraged Hitler to imagine that he was immune from the long-term consequences of his unruly and violent behavior. Germany's neighbors no longer trusted the Nazis by 1939 in part because they came to suspect that Hitler's ironic posturing recognized no limits.

Reinhard was thus coordinating himself to Hitler's foreign policy in a critical if subtle way. He was probably not thinking specifically of modeling his behavior on the *Führer*'s. More likely, their ironic strategies emerged as a similar response to similar circumstances. Yet Reinhard was perfectly aware of the fact that he was playing war games in the glider troop.[64] During the interviews, he recalled that most of his comrades from the Hitler Youth for Aviators died during the war for which they were preparing. Assigned to the *Luftwaffe*, they were shot down or fell somehow else in battle.[65] Reinhard remembered that fact as a tragedy, but he did not in any way link his preparations for war to their deaths in it. Reinhard even admitted, in other narrative contexts, that he liked the comradeship of this special branch of the Nazi youth organization.[66] Here an ironic posture freed him from having to think too much about the human consequences of his actions.

Reinhard described his own military service in this ironic mode. When Drew asked if he had attended formal dance class, he answered with surprise: "Me!?...Nope. I had to sacrifice my youth for the Fatherland."[67] Reinhard responded to Nazi pressure to participate with a parody. "I had absolutely no interest in it," Reinhard said about the military. "When later I did get called up, it was soon enough, and I made sure to look happy enough."[68] Unclear in both ironic statements is whether he actually bought into the ideology of sacrifice.

While in the military, Reinhard claimed he listened to orders only as much as necessary. "If you were smarter than those who produced the force, then it could work, no? That's all: a little bit more clever."[69] Here again Rein-

---

63 Wildt, *Volksgemeinschaft*, 272-281, quoting a Nazi *Stimmungsbericht* from August 1935 by the Regierungs-Präsident of Wiesbaden. S. a. 297-298.
64 G133b 29:57; G134a 00:00.
65 G135b 20:00.
66 G135a 21:04.
67 G133b 18:40.
68 "*Als ich nachher gezogen wurde, da war es immer noch froh genug und früh genug,*" G134a 13:55.
69 G134a 20:50.

hard reiterated two key tropes of his autobiography: on one hand, his ironic use of Newtonian forces, as if he was the passive instrument of natural forces; and on the other, his proactive cleverness.

Akin to the wisdom of Salomon, Reinhard revisited the trope of "cleverness" throughout his autobiography as the character trait that helped him in each new life situation. As a measure of formal education, his inadequate education was the cause of his outsider status both in civilian and military life. As a measure of his inherent cunning, however, his innate cleverness enabled him to work his way up in society. "The little head was there," he said in self-congratulation.[70]

> When one was in the military, if you were more clever, then you could come through well enough. First you had to let your spirit play it right, but not on the outside. On the outside [just] act a little dumb; you know, slightly touched. But just a bit. Just a bit stupefied, we could say. But still have more in your register than those who plan on whipping you one on the head or tricking you. And that is how I kept it.[71]

A true ironist, Reinhard identified with the cleverness of irony itself. It enabled him to focus on these strategies for surviving the Third Reich and not think about the consequences of his participation in its genocidal war for *Lebensraum*. Irony freed him to act with sovereign impunity.

Figure 8. *Comrades*, Magdeburg, 1940.
Edited for Anonymity. Source: Reinhard Oetteling.

70   G135b 25:52.
71   G135b 24:08.

Reinhard's account is historically accurate in one sense at least: he did live his life in parody. He continued to act like a soldier while keeping a certain distance from the other soldiers. Sometimes he was the only Lower Saxon in his group in the military. In his measurement troop, he was also an eighth grade graduate in a unit full of college prep-school graduates. Reinhard had to prove himself in both cases before he was accepted. Even after he did, he felt that he was still kept at a "distance in spite of [being] a buddy."[72] In many of the photos of Reinhard in the service—or at least in those he chose to keep over the years—he positioned himself at the edge of the group or behind a cloud of cigarette smoke.[73] The historical irony is that Reinhard ended up do-ing the very things he thought he was avoiding. By acting as if he was a Nazi, he became one.

Reinhard's irony need not forestall our historical interpretation; we just need to recognize the historical reality as ambiguous. Reinhard still wanted to be accepted and got himself accepted too. Reinhard may have mocked his role in the Nazi war effort through exaggeration, but he also served. The histori-cal reality included both aspects of this ironic performance: the distance that he kept from Nazi pressure to belong as well as his effective full membership within that organization.

What then were the consequences of his irony? Reinhard preserved a few telling images from his training where he and his comrades explicitly posed in their uniforms, testing out what they would look like as Nazi soldiers.[74] We used one as the figure for this chapter as it seems to epitomize for us the dan-ger when irony is used to mask a claim to sovereign impunity. The point to remember about such parodies is that, throughout the war, Reinhard actually did serve as Hitler's eyes, defending the Nazi regime by targeting its enemies for destruction. He may have thought he was only play acting, but he played the role to the hilt and to the end.

The ironic character of this parody probably reflected his very real doubts at the time. Irony gave his performance as a Nazi soldier a kind of plausible deniability should he face criticism in the future about his behavior. He con-tinued to use irony to negotiate his relationship with the Third Reich through to 1945 and even in the decades thereafter. As a result, Reinhard never felt as if he truly became a Nazi. The irony of the situation is that he became a cog in the Nazi war machine nonetheless, and precisely because of his ironic strategies. Here he was more like his father than he was willing to admit. "I

---

72   G136a 10:09.
73   Drew's Slide Collection, D645, 674, 675, 686.
74   D689, 690-696.

would like to say, out of all the people…in both of these two houses, there was not a single real Nazi—other than my father in the end."[75]

Too Clever

Reinhard seems to share Brecht's sense of the irony of his irony: that the cleverness he so lauded in the end landed him in both mortal danger and an ethical crisis. Liberated from the constraints of everyday life, irony gave him the liberty to act with a sovereign sense of impunity over the people he conquered in Eastern Europe. Reinhard was indeed too clever.

Compare Reinhard's cleverness to Socrates's self-knowledge in this regard. In the place of Socrates's humility about what he could not know, we have Reinhard's pride in the instrumental application of his own cunning. To be sure, Socrates and Hamann used irony in part to criticize Athenians or Enlightenment *philosophes* respectively, but primarily to free themselves from their own false assumptions. Hamann and Socrates did not abandon reason: the main object of their skepticism was their own reason. They directed their skepticism at themselves as the only viable starting point to understanding.

Reinhard employed ironic strategies in everyday life in the converse mode. He acted to create a modicum of liberty for himself in the world by directing his irony at the authorities in his life. In itself, this shift in the focus of disrespect from the self to others is not a problem. Unruliness is part and parcel of modern selfhood. The question is what posture this irony promoted in Reinhard's human relationships.

Unfortunately, the first victim of Reinhard's irony became his ability to know anything worth knowing about his fellow human beings. Reinhard told the story of a comrade who transferred into his unit from Berlin and who was later promoted to an officer. The other officers did not like "peers" who came up through the ranks, so they made him the Nazi Leadership Officer (*Nationalsozialistischer Führungsoffizier*). Equivalent to the Soviet *Kommisars*, this "shit-post" required checking with the men and reporting on them. The Leadership Officer was the local representative of the Nazi party, present in Reinhard's life to ensure ideological conformity—though Reinhard insisted that this particular one was not like that.

Because the Leadership Officer got around from battalion to battalion, he also saw more of the larger picture on the Eastern Front than most of the other soldiers did. Reinhard mentioned the black markets near where they were stationed near Orel-Nekrasovka in Russia.[76] Also because he was a Party

---

75   G134b 10:15.
76   Located between Minsk, Kharkov, and Moscow.

official, this Officer had a clear understanding of the Final Solution to the Jewish Question as well as other war crimes and crimes against humanity.

Reinhard described his relationship with this officer as good. So the Officer told Reinhard some things—"like when people got slaughtered." In other words, this Officer was Reinhard's source for up-to-date information about the genocidal war in which he was participating. "Oh man," the Officer would say, "if you had seen this [or] if you had seen that, then uh oh!" He also said that he hoped that the men of Reinhard's company would be spared seeing what he had seen, at least in this tour of duty. His advice to them: "Just don't think about it at all." Sure enough, these issues remained unspoken in the interviews as well; telling this story, about what Reinhard was told by this Officer *not* to know, was the way that Reinhard answered the question and ended the discussion about his awareness of Nazi crimes against humanity.[77]

The Leadership Officer legitimized Reinhard's desire to stay blissfully innocent all the while that Reinhard seemed to know perfectly well what he was "innocent" of. Here we see a good working definition of *too clever*. Socrates made a similar claim not to know, but he did so in order to search for truth in human experience. Reinhard used irony to the opposite purpose: as a willed ignorance about the human consequences of his collaboration in Hitler's war.

We have learned a lot about the dangers of irony by applying the philosophy of Hamann and the aesthetics of Brecht to an ordinary German during the Third Reich. Reinhard may not have wanted to become a soldier, but he behaved as one; he may also have viewed the image of an Aryan *Übermensch* with the mockery of the ironist, but he performed the role nonetheless. Irony allowed him this flexibility of self so that he could do his part in the violent conquest of a continent but act as if he was not involved in creating any human suffering.

It seems that Reinhard's only concern, beyond surviving the war, was to continue to live his life without qualms. Here is where the ironic strategy of "too clever" came in quite handy. Its self-induced ignorance about the larger systems of violence in which he was operating disclosed a terrifyingly casual disregard for the people he conquered and murdered. Its hubris stands in stark contrast to the humble self-knowledge, astute awareness of context, and deep humanism on the part of Socrates and Hamann.

Reinhard was never alone in his posture of sovereign impunity. The premise of this anecdote was that his self-deceptions depended on co-conspirators. Reading between the lines of his account, it seems evident to us that it only worked as a strategy if the lies he told himself were confirmed by his comrades. From this conspiracy of silence, we cannot avoid the conclusion that

---

77   G136a 06:20.

many ordinary Germans claimed the same right to conquer and kill with sovereign impunity by making skilled use of Reinhard's brand of irony.

The Consequences of Nihilism

Our study thus far has demonstrated that modern selfhood depends on considerable self-deception, non-conformity, and irony to negotiate the contradictory pressures of everyday life. We have also shown how readily these tools of selfhood can be used to excuse our actions as self-cultivators. It is worth pausing here, as we approach the end of our book, to reflect upon how these different strategies of selfhood are related.

Consider Jürgen Ludewig's account of how he came to join the Hitler Youth in Hildesheim.[78] It is designed to explain a typical paradox to a skeptical postwar audience: that Jürgen had been a participant in Nazi organizations and yet felt that he had also been just an "ordinary" German. This example can illustrate how these everyday strategies of self-cultivation worked together to foster a fantasy of sovereign impunity.

Jürgen the Apprentice

Once Jürgen graduated from school, his father began to look for a position for him as an apprentice to a master mechanic. The underlying pressure was economic: "Back then it was pretty difficult to get an apprenticeship. It was still [19]36 after all, and things were not yet so terrific. Many people had to run around a lot" to find a position. We are all familiar with these kinds of situations in everyday life. Constrained by circumstances beyond our control, we often have to make choices we dislike. Jürgen framed this incident as a moral tale about the sacrifices you have to make to get ahead.

Jürgen's father approached the head of the mechanics' guild and was rewarded for his pluck with an informal agreement to hire the boy. When he went down to the shop the next day to introduce himself to his new master, however, Jürgen saw that he was wearing a Stormtrooper uniform under his shop coat, which he conveniently left open. When Jürgen sat down in his office to discuss the position, the master mechanic asked directly whether Jürgen was a member of the Hitler Youth. Jürgen replied that he was not. He replied: "But you will have to join the Hitler Youth now." Jürgen explained to Drew that he was a Catholic and the Catholics

---

78   G103a 10:26.

were somewhat against the Nazis. That's just how it was. Even in school: against the
Nazis. That is, as far as possible voluntarily non-participatory.

Like many other informants in our study, Jürgen cast himself in the role of the
non-conformist in a story whose plot centers on collaboration.

Jürgen was not lying. If the reader takes a close look at his words, then
you will see that he stuck closely to the truth: "as far as possible voluntarily
non-participatory." Yet the essence of his non-conformity was irony. Jürgen assumed a posture of ironic distance to political convictions in order to preserve
his maneuverability in everyday life. This relative freedom enabled Jürgen to
accommodate pressures to participate in Nazi organizations without troubling
his conscience.

Jürgen defined himself in terms of how he saw his actions in relation to
those of his neighbors. He contrasted his non-conformity to the Guild Master
who he depicted as a Nazi by conviction. The Master made clear that Jürgen
should join the Hitler Youth.

> He was a Nazi. He was on that side. [He said that] he found it appropriate, etc., as
> head of the guild, etc...I said, "Yes." He had a Stormtrooper uniform and he stood
> there like that in front of me...What to do now, right? I did want an apprentice-
> ship, after all.

So together with a friend, Jürgen registered for the Hitler Youth. The irony
of the situation was not lost on the local Nazi recruitment officer for the
Hitler Youth. He had a field day. He jumped all over them with comments
like: "*Oho!* Now that you want an apprenticeship, now you come running in!
Before you could not seem to come." Like Theodora, Jürgen depicted this
situation as one of perfect clarity. He claimed that this Nazi was able to see
through his bad attempt to act like a Nazi as nothing other than an instrumental parody. Here the ability of the recruitment officer to see behind his
masks in the 1930s served as evidence in the 1990s of his true nature—as a
non-conformist.

Jürgen goes on to say that he suffered these criticisms with silence, and
was rewarded by being taken into the *Deutsches Jungvolk*, the contingent of
the Hitler Youth for young boys. After all, many other Hildesheimers had
done as he had and waited to join until forced. "In any case, we survived
this," he had noted at an earlier point in the interview. "Well, ok," he concluded emphatically. "So things had to work out with the apprenticeship."
Pretending to be a Nazi allowed him to achieve his instrumental ends of
landing an apprenticeship without having to compromise in his posture of
non-conformity.

Unfortunately for Jürgen, the situation changed again, as often happens
in everyday life. It is here that his protagonist begins, like Reinhard, to acquire
Brechtian characteristics. As we would expect from such a dynamic actor,

Jürgen was able to accommodate himself easily to new conditions—but not without undermining his own justifications for why he was compelled to join the Hitler Youth. What happened simply was that the Guild Master reneged on his oral contract and hired a relative instead of Jürgen. "So there I was, now in the Young Folk, and still in the end I had no apprenticeship." Jürgen faced a classic ironic situation in which the end of the story undermines the premises of the rest of the tale.

Instrumentality was the measure of all things for Jürgen: what he gets for his behavior "in the end." So his father hit the streets again and organized another position for him. In this case, the story gets reversed. His potential new master did not ask him about his politics. This man was already in his mid-sixties and was "an old Hildesheimer" by which Jürgen meant that he was "completely apolitical. He did not make a single noise about it. It interested him not at all." This situation worked out for both of them. Jürgen was this man's last apprentice and he was an excellent master. Jürgen concluded his anecdote with the irony of a *deus ex machina*. "So this is how I was dragged into the Hitler Youth."

The problem with this conclusion is that it undermines our earlier assumptions about Jürgen's protagonist—himself. The surprise ending reveals that it was within the scope of his power to find a master who would not have forced him to join a Nazi organization. So he was deceiving himself as much as us when he insisted that economic necessity had compelled him to join the Hitler Youth; or at least, Jürgen could have left the Hitler Youth after he lost his spot in the first shop, as Theodora did, for instance. He told this story in an ironic mode to paper over precisely those unsavory ambiguities in the story.

Jürgen the Hitler Youth

The reality is that Jürgen stayed in the Hitler Youth for other reasons. Here is his response to the question of whether he had fun in the Hitler Youth:

> Of course I had fun. That's understandable, isn't it? It was very nice. One cannot say it was "inspiring," but because *everyone did it*, and the more it went on in this direction, *those who were not in it* were gradually outsiders in town.

The words we italicized here are typical of ironic narrative in that they are mutual contradictory statements. They suggest to us not that every boy in Hildesheim joined the Hitler Youth but that Jürgen felt tremendous pressure to conform. We can certainly appreciate this circumstance. Many ordinary Germans flocked to Nazi organizations for this reason. His ironic description of his situation also suggests to us that, in this context of political mobilization, he struggled to maintain his non-conformist posture to political convictions.

> What young boy wanted to be an outsider…called a coward, or a wimp, or a weakling, as it was in those days?…Who would have wanted to endure something like that? So, in this way a lot of people got into it and then it was good. I made my way into the Hitler Youth.

What should we make of this conclusion: that "it was good" once "a lot of people got into" the Hitler Youth in this same way that Jürgen did? Again we should read it as ironic, for this surprise ending allowed a non-conformist like Jürgen to conform to the totalitarian demands of the Nazi regime without feeling like he had sold his soul to the Devil.

All this irony leaves us wondering which Jürgen is the real Jürgen. Yet Jürgen was no fool. Recounting these ironic situations and his ironic responses raised the same questions in his own mind of how to fit together these seemingly inconsistent fragments of his own life into a coherent story of his self. Without prompting he addressed this tacit query. He directly insisted that, in spite of his membership in the Hitler Youth, he remained Jürgen the non-conformist.

> They did practically nothing to us, and the political instruction, well it really was not as bad as all that. Most of all this political garbage was told to us in vocational school, but not directly in the Hitler Youth, not at all so directly in the Hitler Youth. There wasn't a lot of importance put on it.

> You just had to appear once a week in the evening, yes, and then also for special events, the First of May; or when Hitler had his birthday, there was an event at the Steingrube. So we had to appear and then we marched there and then we stood there and a Group Leader gave a speech and then we stood there and we had to march back. So, it practically did not affect us [at all, at least] not directly in this way.

Jürgen again measured the meaning of his behavior in purely instrumental terms: whether it affected his attitudes, his experience, or his future. Herein lies another irony in his story. All the politics which seemed so very important to the Nazis turned out not to mean very much at all—at least not to him.

The problem with Jürgen's use of irony is that it creates contradictions that even he cannot resolve to his satisfaction. If his apprenticeship was not really tied to membership in the Nazi youth organization, then why did he join after all? If the Hitler Youth was not very political after all, then why did he resist joining for so long? His account relies on a witness for its veracity, reminding us of the crucial role played by the audience in the performance of a parody. In 1993 he used the sarcastic response of the Nazi recruitment officer, who allegedly saw through his mask to the real Jürgen, to verify that he had in fact been a non-conformist. In 1938, however, Jürgen had used his parody of a Nazi to communicate the exact opposite about himself: that he had done his duty as an Aryan boy, joined the Hitler Youth, and followed where the *Führer* led. It is worth remembering that, regardless what the recruitment officer thought, Jürgen was still rewarded for acting as if he was a

Nazi with actual membership in the Hitler Youth. Jürgen seems to be asking us to believe him in the present that he was not believable in the past.

Jürgen the Mechanic

Jürgen's problems did not begin in the Hitler Youth. There seemed to have been enough dupes in the Hitler Youth who were willing to accept his lies to smooth his way through the organization. He did not even have many problems during the war. Even though his later career building airplanes for the *Luftwaffe* was hardly that of a non-conformist, he admitted to Drew that, so long as Germany was winning the war, he had cheered the victories of the Fatherland. "Young people…were enthusiastic. That is clear. National pride. That is logical, no?"[79] The fact that Jürgen oversaw the construction of long-range bombers was a source of pride for him, not embarrassment. To a significant degree, Jürgen must have believed the lies that Hitler told him about Aryans and their superiority to other human beings, since he was more than happy to see their homes get bombed and their cities flattened using the bombers that he helped to build. Or at least, he ignored his role in his own self-deceptions so that he did not have to think much about these matters at all.

Like Theodora, Jürgen's participation in Nazi youth organizations smoothed his way into a successful career that was intimately tied to the success of the Third Reich. He welcomed the conquest of a German empire in Europe without concern for the human costs of this genocidal war. To iron out the contradictions in his biography, he continued to turn to irony. As late as 1944 he worked in the Heinkel Factory in Oranienburg. There he spoke with concentration-camp inmates from Sachsenhausen on a daily basis because it was his responsibility to verify that they were installing the engines correctly. Jürgen depicts himself as a non-conformist, recounting how a Polish forced laborer shared with him the latest radio reports of the advancing Soviet army.[80] His ironic posture enabled him to assume the role of Aryan master over Polish slaves with an easy conscience. At each stage in his life, an ironic posture, informed by the lies he told himself about being a non-conformist, seemed to give Jürgen the freedom to pursue his career within the Nazi war economy with a sense of sovereign impunity.

Jürgen and Sarah

Finally, Jürgen justified his participation in the Hitler Youth by noting that this organization succeeded in creating a sense of community where there

79 G107a 03:20.
80 G105b 14:20.

had once been Catholics and Protestants. He ignored the fact that this sense of integration was made possible in large part by excluding and attacking his Jewish neighbors.[81] This point is reinforced when we view Jürgen's behavior from the perspective of his victims.

Sarah Meyer vividly recalled hearing Nazis march by her house on the southeastern edge of town singing "When Jewish Blood Squirts from my Knife."[82] She remembered it "because it was very—[the memory] won't go away." It was early in the morning, maybe 7 o'clock. "And it was always these terrible songs." She was very young at the time, so it is appropriate that she was a little unclear who these people were precisely. At different times in the interviews, she referred to them as soldiers, Stormtroopers, or some other group. "Who knows what they were. They were Nazis!"

After reading the testimony of so many ordinary Germans in this book, Sarah's blanket statement may seem somehow unfair. Like many, Jürgen supported some parts of the Nazi program while trying to avoid participating in others. He made all sorts of careful distinctions as a non-conformist and ironist *vis-à-vis* the Third Reich, and he altered these positions according to the needs of the situation. Yet non-conformity is not what Sarah saw from her window.

> And they came by with their flags and their singing, and they marched, and there were a lot of them. And they marched, and you hear[d] them, goose-stepping, coming. And they would sing these songs. And just imag[in]e a little person, a child hearing this, and you know you are a Jew, and you can already picture it.

She could picture them using their knives on her, that is. To Sarah, these Nazis were wholly sincere. There was nothing ironic about this threat—except perhaps that she was the daughter of an army officer who had served the Second German Empire patriotically during the Great War, only to be ostracized, expropriated, and threatened with murder in the Third.[83]

Certainly it is true that children often do not understand the intricacies of an adult strategy like irony. Sarah understood as an adult that her memories were conditioned by her age. Explaining that young children take the world at face value, Sarah thought that her neighbors meant what they were saying: that they would attack them "today, now, this minute." Not knowing otherwise, she presumed that "they would come upstairs and do just that." As Sarah wrote in her unpublished autobiography:

> Even small children, who are generally protected by their parents and families feel the tension…Children are so perceptive, that no amount of protection can save them from these terrible happenings.

---

81   G103a 16:16; Wildt, *Volksgemeinschaft.*
82   G177a 11:35; G177b 27:40; Meyer, "Memoires," ch. 3.
83   G177a 23:10.

We should not dismiss this account because of her age. It is useful to us precisely because of the innocence of a child, which sees through the lies of adults to state the obvious: that even *pretending* to be a Nazi communicated a clear message of violence. Jürgen is our case in point. Depicting himself as a skilled ironist, he claimed that he only acted *as if* he was a Nazi.

> One had to "howl with the wolves," as it is said in German. If commanded to march on the First of May or for the *Führer*'s birthday, then you had to march along with everyone else. And when everyone sang, then you at least had to move your mouth. That was what we did for the most part. Like this.

Jürgen then demonstrated how to mouth the words without singing them.[84] Yet when Sarah woke each morning to the noise of singing Stormtroopers marching below her window, it did not matter if some of them only mouthed the words. "These words are very clear and most understandable, even to the mind of a small child. I had a constant feeling of not being able to breathe deeply, because the inherent fears continually loomed in my mind."[85] Sarah's fear was entirely realistic: the only reason why her family did not become Nazi victims was that they fled Germany in the nick of time.

Our point is that Jürgen's parody of a Nazi helped him collaborate in fascist terror by assuaging his guilty conscience. He went on to build bombers as part of the Nazi war for *Lebensraum* with the same attitude of nonchalance. Irony enabled him to participate as much as he wanted or needed in Nazi violence with a sense of sovereign impunity for those who suffered on his account.

In Jürgen we see once again Sisyphus before his condemnation—so convinced by his self-deceptions, so confident in the righteousness of his nonconformity, so impressed with the cleverness of his irony, that he fancies himself free to act with sovereign impunity. The difference is that the German Sisyphus was no myth. If parodic displays of Nazi principles were enough for ordinary Germans to have fun in Nazi organizations and enjoy successful careers within the larger framework of the Nazi war for *Lebensraum*, then they were also enough to make their Jewish neighbors fear for their lives.

We conclude from this analysis that ordinary Germans provided an invaluable service to the Nazi regime: some because they were sincere Nazis, but others precisely because of their ambiguity towards the Third Reich. Our scholarly explanations of the Third Reich are not exhausted by demonstrating how many ordinary Germans agreed with how much of the Nazi ideology. Initially it was ardent Nazis who spread an atmosphere of terror for socialists, Jews, and other vulnerable minorities on the Nazi hit list. Yet if principled

---

84 G057b 07:25; see Theodora's earlier description of singing similar songs.
85 Martha Paul tells a similar story. See G097a 23:20; G98a 26:40, 28:15.

non-conformists, supported by a terrorist regime, were a necessary condition for Sarah's fear, they were also an insufficient one. The atmosphere of terror and system of genocide depended on the vast majority of ordinary Germans going along with them regardless of how they might have felt about them.

Our point is that ordinary Germans made themselves into better engineers, leaders, teachers, colonists, and conquerors for the Third Reich by adopting an ironic posture *vis-à-vis* the Third Reich. Parodic performances of Nazi support were actually more significant than sincere ones precisely because it was the response of choice among ordinary Germans who had mixed feelings about the Third Reich. Taken together, the ironic posture of uncommitted Germans combined with the principled behavior of ardent Nazis to create no-win situations for vulnerable minorities in which every choice led to exile or death. This system was insidious because it was so easy to take the first small steps toward violence. They seemed so ordinary a part of selfhood. And most stuck to them to the end.

Committing Irony

These many examples from the Third Reich are extreme, but not so very different from the ones we make in our own lives. One purpose of revisiting these extraordinary times of fascist terror and racist genocide was to demonstrate just how ordinary they were in fact. Irony produces ambiguity. Ambiguity provides us with the liberty to act, even in constraining and violent conditions. The outcome turns on how we use that freedom.

We began this investigation in order to interrogate this terrible tendency within the way we modern individuals construct our selfhood historically and biographically. All too often, we use the freedom available to us through irony to excuse the worst kinds of violence against our neighbors and then disguise it behind an attitude of sovereign impunity. This kind of abuse is why many scholars believe that irony is an amoral trope in form and immoral in its consequences.

Yet our hope in writing this book lies in another possibility. We believe that we can use the powerful ambiguity of irony towards humane ends. We conclude this chapter with that investigation. Returning to Hamann, we draw the readers attention to a subtext of many of the anecdotes and analyses that you have read so far: that our selfhood depends on other people. In *Mother Courage and Her Children*, Brecht's 1939 play about ordinary people in violent times, he provides us with a model for how an ironic self, cultivated through relationships with others, in everyday situations, can commit irony to ethical purposes. And from Simone de Beauvoir we learn the value of maneuvering in the ambiguity and doubt of irony when working towards responsible selfhood.

Hamann on Intersubjectivity

Like other ironists, Hamann's attack on the *philosophes* seems to leave us with a radical and unappetizing skepticism, or as he puts it in characterizing Socrates, with nothing more than "human ignorance and curiosity."[86] Hamann agrees with both the *philosophes* and Socrates that the self is the natural place to look for the origins of conceptual knowledge. Yet Hamann disagrees with the fantasy that we have some "inner faculty" or "inner sense" that allows us to sense ourselves from within: not even an inner moral sense, a "still, small voice" of conscience. Without any way to touch, hear, taste, or "sense" ourselves, we cannot ever truly know ourselves. If there is a set of inner states that we ourselves know, those traits are inaccessible to us. "If our frame is hidden from us, because we are made in secret, because we are wrought in the depths of the earth, how much more are our concepts evolved in secret."[87] Hamann does not merely say that our self is a secret, but that its nature, origin, and evolution are also secrets.

This argument has significant implications for the historical analysis of ordinary Germans during the Third Reich. For many decades, scholars have tried to determine the degree to which they were "really" antisemitic or fascist. This approach to the self is precisely what Hamann is criticizing. We cannot ever truly know our own inner states, including racism or fascism. Historians have no easy basis—especially in retrospect—to measure the same. We are certainly able to evaluate past persons on the basis of their actions; however, we cannot claim exhaustive, transparent insight into a past person's selfhood on the presumption of mastery over a coherent, identifiable subjectivity. Moreover, Hamann insists that the self is not stable; how then can historians reconstruct it? The evolution of other people's concepts are secrets hidden from their own empirical sensibility no less than ours sixty years later.

This debate in hindsight only replicates a common and very serious problem for ordinary Germans on all sides of the political spectrum during the Nazi era itself: trying to figure out if your interlocutor was a Nazi of convenience or conviction. Jürgen wished to convince us that the Nazi recruitment officer could see through his parody, but only because he wanted to convince us in retrospect that he was a non-conformist. The purpose of his parody in 1938 was the precise opposite: to be utterly convincing in his parody. In fact, the recruitment officer could not know for certain if Jürgen was sincere in his National Socialism. The more that Jürgen even thought about it, the more his motives for joining became clouded by multiple and inscrutable intentions.

---

86 Hamann, *Socratic Memorabilia*, 139.
87 Hamann, *Socratic Memorabilia*, 153.

Hamann's insight into the self does not leave historians powerless to know past persons. He just insists that our truth claims about ourselves or others cannot be the result of some putatively privileged access to our or their inner states. The only things we can verify about the world, including ourselves, is what we say of it based upon our shared experience.[88] This claim suggests, at the least, that our self-knowledge is necessarily *intersubjective*.[89] Jürgen made sense of himself by observing the reactions of others to his performance of self. This book has been filled with examples of ordinary Germans becoming themselves in the process of interacting with others. Here is the point that Hamann is driving at: our claims about ourselves can only be discovered in the words we use to describe our self and our self-development. We extend Hamann's argument to suggest that we can know ourselves and others best through the act of telling our story and presenting ourselves to others.

Autobiographical statements have something akin to the anticipatory memory of Walter Benjamin. Every act of making a claim about the self in discourse is a moment of self-cultivation in which the autobiographical needs of a future self—to retrospectively narrate that self-becoming—are anticipated. Identity and integrity remain temporally open, and the authenticity of the self cannot be reduced to any objective measure.[90] As scholars we must capture this anticipatory process of self-cultivation by looking at those acts.

Written sources have traditionally served scholars well for reconstructing those acts, since writing presents the self to others or others to the self. Self-cultivation takes place even when those narratives are written as a diary, for instance,[91] or in the classic historical source of the eye-witness account. Narrative interviews are particularly well suited for these purposes, since the interviewee and interviewer replicate that intersubjective process during the research itself. We will get closer to this open-ended process of self-cultivation as scholars if our methods, theories, and explanations take seriously the ambiguous dimensions of the self. We need to discover selfhood where it is cultivated: between past and future, self and other.

Because we must cultivate our identities intersubjectively, Hamann sees an ironic shuffle happening within selfhood. We move between an unknowable interior that we nevertheless must appeal to for authenticity, "the real me," and a projected exterior that we can know but that is not entirely what we

---

88   See Arendt, *Human Condition*, 50-58 on "publicity" and reality.

89   Butler, *Gender Trouble*; J. E. Malpas, *Place and Experience: A Philosophical Topography* (Cambridge: Cambridge University Press, 1999); Steege, Bergerson, Healy, and Swett, "A Second Chapter."

90   See Gerhard Richter, *Walter Benjamin and the Corpus of Autobiography* (Detroit: Wayne State University Press, 2000).

91   Miriam Gebhardt, *Das Familiengedächtnis: Erinnerung im deutsch-jüdischen Bürgertum 1890 bis 1932* (Stuttgart: Franz Steiner Verlag, 1999).

are after when we are thinking about the self.[92] Socrates takes this position.[93] What we can know of ourselves is that we do not "really" know, so we go on curiously looking for it: that is, we go on creating these intersubjective selves that nevertheless make appeal to this unknown inner self.

The ironic posture might sound untenable if it were not so familiar to all of us. In a very ordinary way we are all constantly aware, Hamann thinks, of the oscillation between seeming to be what we are and insisting that there is something more to ourselves than that seeming—or else we would be nothing but a façade.[94] It is within this ironic arena of oscillation that the possibility of moral responsibility may arise. We are able to see this process so well under the Third Reich because totalitarianism politicized a strategy that we usually all agree to ignore so that we can go on employing it.

We uncover a self in cultivation. We have arrived back at one of the fundamental claims of this book: that the self is best understood not as a state but as a process. What Hamann demands of us is to recognize that this process is impossible without others.

In order to understand myself as a subject, I must make myself understood as a subject to another. Yet I cannot merely insist that what I am is what I am between the two of us in conversation or interaction. If I were *just* my performance, then I would be nothing more than my façade. Both I and the other person have to believe that there is more to me than whatever I am at that particular moment. We have to share that faith in order to believe in our larger human potential.

The suspicion arises that I change who I am depending on my interlocutors. Akin to our doubts about our ordinary German informants as to which role was the parody, one imagines the fair yet unfriendly question: "But are you a different person with everyone you meet?" In fact, our close inspection of their testimony reveals that, in many cases, they did change their roles according to the situation, as indeed we all do. What we take from Hamann, then, is that there is no coherent, consistent, or even discreet self outside of its performance. The very act of being ourselves is fraught with doubt and danger.

A happy consequence of Hamann's account of self-knowledge is that it invites an attitude of humility toward the difficulty of the project of knowing who we are. Humility tends to lead us away from the dangerous certitudes that result from a commitment to an ideology. We cannot judge or condemn others, because we see them in the same difficult, ironic state of flux that is oscillating within ourselves; we can never attack, because we are never really

---

92   Hamann, *Briefwechsel*, vol. 5, 6.
93   S. a. Butler, *Gender Trouble*.
94   Hamann, *Sämtliche Werke*, vol. 2, 164.

in position to defend. *We become tolerant.* For us, responsibility begins by recognizing our dependence on others. A responsible self involves cultivating those relationships and incorporating interdependence into our selfhood.

How do we do it? How does one become oneself through others? Hamann's answer is that we make comparisons. "Analogy constituted the soul of [Socrates's] reasoning, and he gave it irony for a body."[95] The same could be said of the self in general: its immediately evident exterior is ironic, while we can gain access to its core only through analogy. These comparisons are not trivial. We define ourselves from our infancy by recognizing what is not like us and by what we resemble.[96]

Multiple examples from our study illustrate this point. In almost every everyday situation we have described, ordinary Germans were defining themselves through their interactions with others: Gerhard and Hartmut, Theodora and Hannah, Hans and Heinrich. We used this ordinary logic of selfhood to reconstruct the past—like when we compared Jürgen and Sarah. We had no evidence that they personally interacted and yet the postures they assumed in everyday life presumed one another: Aryans and Jews, *Übermensch* and *Untermensch*. Brecht made similar comparisons available, or unavailable, to the audience in the form of Galy Gay and the Soldiers as well as Salomon, Cleopatra, Caesar, and Macheath. Scholarly criticism is grounded in the same everyday principles. We can understand Hamann only in terms of how he cultivated his selfhood in relation to Socrates and Kant. Knowing oneself not only requires but also implicates knowing others and being known by them.

By this point in our study, the reader can now appreciate more fully why we are so skeptical about modern notions of individuality. The hubris that we are autonomous selves ironically leaves us imposing ourselves on others, often without much consideration for the impact it has on their lives; we reject those other human beings, especially in their suffering, because they seem to impose on our freedom of selfhood. The ironical self, by contrast, is not an imposition. It cannot liberate itself from relationships. It solicits collaboration in the cultivation of selves. At least as a form of interaction, it means that we have to respond to others rather than control them. We draw this lesson from our analysis thus far: *by self-consciously performing the self ironically, we remind ourselves of our responsibility and our ability to respond.*

---

95   Hamann, *Socratic Memorabilia*, 143.
96   See Gary Handwerk, *Irony, Ethics and Narrative: From Schlegel to Lacan* (New Haven: Yale University Press, 1995), 138-171.

Brecht's Mother Courage

Another concrete example might help, but this time we turn to a play rather than an interview precisely because of the way art can help us to see things otherwise buried in everyday life. Brecht understood the political problem with irony quite clearly. One of his dramatic responses to it was *Mother Courage and her Children.*

It is an obvious choice for this study. In a more traditional sense than *A Man's A Man, Mother Courage* is a station play where the characters move from situation to situation like ordinary people; it is up to the audience to figure out how these different fragments in a life fit together. Brecht reuses the "Salomon Song" in a fascinating way in *Mother Courage* that allows him to explore new uses of irony. It is also an appropriate choice for this study because of its setting. Written in the late 1930s and published in 1939, it anticipates the Nazi war for *Lebensraum* by setting the protagonists in the horribly violent Thirty Years War that devastated Central Europe in the seventeenth century. In *Mother Courage*, we find a model for how to use irony intersubjectively to promote responsibility even in a historical setting conditioned by systematic violence.

Brecht begins his fictional play in the same position as Reinhard's factual autobiography: with the experiences of an entirely indeterminate person. In contrast to the explicit literariness and timeless everyday of the *Three Penny Opera*, Anna Fierling maneuvers her vending cart through a specific historical context. That grander framework raises political and social issues that dominated contemporary public interest in the late 1930s and 1940s: the ravages of war as well as the links between market economics and war production. It allowed Brecht to reiterate, in stark terms, a central concept of the *Three Penny Opera*: "First comes food, then morality."

Always concerned for his next meal, Reinhard would certainly have agreed with that principle. Speaking about his training in Magdeburg and Lippstedt, he commented: "The main thing was that the food was still good, and the food was still good at that time. There you could still digest it. That was important: the food."[97] Like a Macheath, however, he told his life story without reference to the historical context in which he was operating. Brecht staged his story of ordinary Germans in a particularly traumatic historical context to the opposite end: to draw our attention to that human suffering.

Yet there is nothing that the protagonist can do, ironic or otherwise, that will change this situation. Anna is trapped in a system of violence beyond her control. Brecht reminds us of this helplessness in the way that he sets up the scenes. Each station stands on its own. Each reflects Anna's actions and

---

97   G136a 03:42; s. a. G135b 30:00; G136b 20:35, 26:53; D270.

decisions on an immediate level, in response to the circumstances with which she is confronted. These individual scenes are not tied together into a classic plot; rather the scenes are linked together by the fact that they describe an on-going condition that Anna's family must suffer and survive. Disempowered as historical subjects, the protagonists can never hope to influence the outcome of the play.

Appropriately, the songs in *Mother Courage* pertain almost exclusively to the scene in which they appear. Most of these songs come at the end of the scene and act like a coda in which the characters comment on the dramatic events. The Cook and Anna reprise the "Salomon Song" in the middle of one scene, but it still comments solely on the situation in which they find themselves. It is an unfortunate one. The Cook and Anna come upon a burned out village with a darkened parsonage. The Cook notes that the state of the village makes it unlikely that the Pastor will have any soup available to share with them. Indeed, the Cook doubts that the Pastor will be generous even if there is soup to be had. Regardless, they choose to sing the "Song" in the hopes of just that.

These songs are akin to the classic Greek chorus. Although they address other characters on stage, the singers speak directly to the audience about the events of the play, commenting on them while also drawing attention to the play as a play. As a performance within the performance, the songs are intentional strategies on the part of the characters to specific ends. In the case of the "Salomon Song," the Cook and Anna want to convince the Pastor to give them soup against his inclination. Before they sing the "Song" however, the Cook frames their performance for both of their audiences, on-stage and in the theater, so that the listeners understand his purpose:

> *He calls.* Worthy gentleman and members of the household! We shall now sing the Song of Salomon, Julius Caesar, and other great men, whose greatness didn't help them any. Just to show you that we're God-fearing people ourselves, which makes it hard for us, especially in the winter.

Only after explaining their goals to the audience do Anna and the Cook actually sing the first stanza. Before going on to the next verse, the Cook again explains the meaning of the "Song" to the audience:

> Our beautiful song proves that virtues are dangerous things, better steer clear of them, enjoy life, eat a good breakfast, a bowl of hot soup, for instance.[98]

As we have seen, the "Song" undermines our confidence in great leaders by showing that their strengths of character are also the cause for their downfall. It thus serves as a warning: to the authorities to check their hubris, and to the audience to rethink their assumptions about protagonists. In the commentary,

---

98   *GBA*, vol. 5, 197-198, trans. Baker.

the Cook casts the Pastor as one of the "great men" who have the power and responsibility to help the poor, like with a bowl of hot soup. The Cook contrasts these powerful elites with "God-fearing people" like himself and Anna who have no control over their own fate. Here is what we mean when we say that this song is a strategy: the Cook is using it to manipulate the authorities to get what he wants and needs from them. His is a doubly ironic strategy insofar as the poor are reminding their religious leaders of their ethical obligations.

Figure 9. Bertolt Brecht, *Mother Courage*, "Singing at the Church," 1939.
Source: Akademie der Künste, Berlin, Bertolt-Brecht-Archiv, BBA-FA 053/091.

The Cook's annotation of the "Song" for both the on-stage and theater audience marks a significant departure for Brecht from the way he used this same "Song" in the *Three Penny Opera*. The Cook has absolutely no intention of allowing the Pastor or his audience the freedom to interpret his irony in any way other than the way he wants. The "Song," as we know, is itself ironic; and a Cook who cannot cook for himself but must sing for his soup is even more ironic. Still, the Cook provides a commentary on its meaning for his audience in order that they will understand the message of the irony *as he intends it*. It can hardly work as a strategy to get some food from the Pastor otherwise. It would be too great a leap for the Pastor to interpret a song about Solomon, Cleopatra, and Caesar as a message about feeding the poor without the Cook's explanation.

The Cook uses the final verse of the "Song" to drive home his point. In a parallel construction to the poem from the *Three Penny Opera*, the last verse shifts from historical persons to the characters in the play. Typical of a skilled ironist, the commentary and the content have become one:

> You're looking here at ordinary people
> Keeping the Ten Commandments.
> It hasn't done us any good so far.
> You who sit by the warm stove
> Help ease our great need!
> How truly brave we've been so far!
> And look, it wasn't even night yet
> When the world saw the consequences:
> Fear of God has brought us to this point!
> Enviable, whoever is free of that! [99]

This time, the explicit iterations of the "message" were effective. At its conclusion, a disembodied voice from the parsonage invites the Cook and Anna up for soup. An ironic strategy finally succeeded in convincing someone to behave ethically—and ironically, that person was a Pastor.

In the *Three Penny Opera*, Brecht layered so many ironies on top of one another without explanatory comments that the audience had unlimited scope for interpretation. As a work of art this strategy was provocative, but this interpretive latitude did not satisfy Brecht's political goals of encouraging responsibility in everyday life. In *Mother Courage*, he combined irony with explicit instructions on how to interpret that irony in order to direct the audience towards his ethical message. One reason why this strategy is so successful has to do with the fact that it is staged ironically: the message for the theater audience about how to interpret this scene in *Mother Courage* is embedded in an on-stage performance of interpretation. The other lies in the way that Brecht speaks to the audience through the Cook to make sure they understand the meaning of the irony. Taken together, this scene offers us one model for how we might use irony to promote responsibility.

Anna's Choices

That said, Brecht does not want us to walk away from *Mother Courage* with a false sense of confidence. This point can be made by looking at Anna's choices in the larger context of the play. The distinctiveness of this scene cautions us to remember that responsible selfhood is an ongoing challenge.

In a typical drama, the protagonist's actions have consequences for himself and often for the world around him that are revealed by the end of the

---

play; the endings tell the audience how to think about the choices made by the characters. In *Mother Courage*, by contrast, each scene has its own ending and they are not related to the larger situation in which Anna finds herself: the Thirty Years War. We might be inclined to believe that, by isolating these scenes from a larger interpretive framework, Brecht is encouraging irresponsibility on the part of the protagonists. After all, nothing that they do in these stations will influence the war. In the actual situation in which Anna and the Cook find themselves, however, they are able to use irony not only to get the food they need but to remind others of their obligations to their fellow man.

Just before they start to sing, the Cook makes Anna an appealing offer: to open up a pub together in Utrecht. Away from the war and implying a romantic relationship, this business opportunity would provide them both with financial and personal stability as well as safety and security. The only catch: the Cook insists that she would have to abandon her ugly, mute daughter, Kattrin. Anna is thus confronted with a stark choice between a selfish and a selfless act. In our terms, either choice would end up perpetuating the very violence that she has been experiencing around her by sacrificing either herself or her daughter to save the other.

In its tight focus on a particular situation, Brecht encourages us to think about what we can do here and now for human beings in the often untenable situations in which we find ourselves. Extrapolating from Brecht, we can neither rely on external grounds for determining what responsibility means nor can we measure our actions in the present based on utopian hopes for the future. Our aspirations are far more humble. Yet it is precisely in the untenable situation in which the Cook and Anna find themselves that they discover their ability to respond to their situation. Thanks to irony, they can manipulate the "Song" to goad the Parson to ethical action.

Yet Brecht does not want us to be confident about our newfound ethical wisdom, as if the specific response modeled by the "Song" is some new kind of prescription for responsible selfhood. Brecht's point about irony is far more sophisticated. In *A Man's A Man*, Galy Gay fully inhabited the role of soldier and killed 700 innocent people in the end, but we took heart in the notion that this choice was only one among many options for our protagonist. Brecht wanted us to imagine the possibility that the same protagonist in other situations might make more responsible choices. Again using irony, Brecht kept that play's conclusion open rather than closed in order to teach us about role-playing *per se* rather than just about the choices of one person in a specific situation.

Brecht chooses a different strategy in *Mother Courage*, one that corresponds to the restriction of interpretation modeled by the Cook. Instead of an open-ended range of possible futures, the Cook presents Anna, and thus the audience, with an "either-or" choice for how to respond to the problem of hunger. On the one hand, he succeeds in using irony to pressure the Pastor into giving him soup. On the other, the Cook pressures Anna to abandon her daughter so that she can come with him to Utrecht. In this case, the Cook's aims are wholly selfish, and he manipulates Anna's desperation to compel her to do what he wants. Here Brecht is reminding us that the same person who can commit irony to help the poor can create circumstances to exploit them too.

In a sense, the entire play turns on how Anna then chooses to respond. She decides to ditch the Cook and remain both with her daughter and economically independent, and yet isolated and vulnerable to the on-going war. Ironically, her choice influences the outcome not only of this scene but the play as a whole. For the first and only time, Anna altruistically puts the welfare of one of her children before her own. By setting up this explicit contrast between the Cook's selfishness and Anna's sacrifice, Brecht seems to be saying that this choice, in this situation, was responsible. Yet her actions in this moment contrast with her selfish choices at the end of every other scene in the play and thus seem ironic when viewed in light of the rest of her life. At least in this moment, then, in front of the parsonage, someone who has consistently made poor choices has demonstrated that she can also make responsible choices—ironically.

One particular anecdote cannot provide us with a universal model for ethical action in all of the circumstances of our lives. Brecht refuses to give us any pat answers about what it means to be a responsible person. In the scenes after she leaves the Cook, Mother Courage again makes the selfish choice to go into the beleaguered city of Halle in order to buy cheap goods. Kattrin, left alone, decides to warn the city of an impending night attack—and she is killed by soldiers. When Anna returns, she feels sincere sorrow at the death of her daughter; nevertheless the play ends with Anna heading onward with her cart to the next situation. Anna has proven that she is able to act responsibly; she also proves that every new situation tests the resolve of each person to be responsible.

Irony's ambiguity opens up the space of freedom that allows for responsible agency. Our problem is how to develop our capacity for judgment in the context of irony's unrelenting criticism. Such ironic praxis entails an ironic form of commitment. As the example of the Cook and Anna suggests, standards of responsibility and hope are like the self: the products of commitments that a person has the courage to make in each new intersubjective context. There is no one single prescription; *responsible selfhood depends on what we do with the situations we are given.*

Larmore on Committing Ourselves

We have seen that the ironist is both committed and not committed. She is of two minds. The ironist has the sense that, especially when it comes to knowledge of oneself, no commitment is an absolute commitment. This tentative, provisional nature of the ironist's commitments has been the subject of many of the attacks against irony. Peter Szondi reiterated a classic one:

> Whatever irony encounters it measures against infinity and thus destroys it. Acceptance of his own incapacity prevents the ironist from respecting what has nevertheless been accomplished—therein lies its danger for him.[100]

Ironists recognize they cannot achieve wholeness or completeness, what Szondi describes here as "infinity." This seeming failure can lead to a kind of despair in which nothing worthwhile is accomplished because everything cannot be. Anna seems on the verge of this kind of despair when she sticks to her wagon in the end despite the fact that the "higher" purpose of her venture—providing for her family—is no longer a factor. Actively resisting the Third Reich no doubt seemed a similarly awesome task to ordinary Germans, and the stakes of this decision were made intentionally high by the terror policies of a police state. It is the despair of nihilism.

It was just this sort of all-or-nothing thinking that Hamann rejected in the name of irony. To despair of reaching completeness or infinity only makes sense where infinity, and the control it promises, is a theoretical possibility and therefore the standard for knowing. That control is what the committed ironist rejects. The ironist says: "I accept this belief, indeed, I endorse it; but I am not unequivocally advocating it, because there is more to be thought on the subject." In this way the ironist's commitment reflects the same pairing of ignorance and curiosity that inform self-knowledge. Accordingly, the ironic stance might in fact express a more serious kind of commitment.

Charles Larmore argues that all "mature minds" must be ironical in their approach to commitment, belief, and self-knowledge. These ways of thinking involve the assertion of what one is not entirely entitled to assert and knows one is not entirely entitled to assert. As Larmore writes, irony expresses

> the essential nonidentity between the commitments we have and *our ability to commit ourselves*. Even our deepest commitments...would not be ours if we had not bound ourselves to them.[101]

For Larmore the ironic understanding of self-knowledge is motivated by a tolerance for restlessness and resistance within the self, and by the suspicion

---

100 Peter Szondi, *On Textual Understanding and Other Essays*, trans. Harvey Mendelsohn (Minneapolis: The University of Minnesota Press, 1986), 68.
101 Charles Larmore, *The Romantic Legacy* (New York: Columbia University Press 1996), 82-83, our emphasis.

that a project like "wholeheartedness" is misguided or impossible. Irony is the appropriate response to totalitarianism in everyday life precisely because irony challenges the certainties on which totalitarianism is based. The Cook and Anna have this kind of "courage." They are not afraid of placing themselves at risk to demand responsibility from others and themselves. They move on the moment this situation is over; yet in the moment itself, they commit themselves, and they are even aware of their ability to commit.

Beauvoir on Maneuvering in Doubt

Taking responsibility for proximate human ends does not remove ambiguity; on the contrary, commitment—and humanity—thrives in ambiguity. It is the condition of ambiguity that calls for our commitments, for it is only through our ability to commit that we can provide meaning within the ambiguity of life.

What is needed is what Simone de Beauvoir called an "ethics of ambiguity." Beauvoir accused philosophy of masking the tragic quality of human existence. Instead she accepted the task of realizing the ambiguity that comes with human freedom. "Every man is originally free, in the sense that he spontaneously casts himself into the world."[102] Freedom is not just the means but the goal of human action. As such, freedom sets the standard by which actions may be ethically evaluated. "The goal toward which I surpass myself must appear to me as a point of departure toward a new act of surpassing."[103]

Beauvoir suggests in part why ethics remains ambiguous: it is never "done," and there is no rest. She approaches Arendt's notion of natality. The human condition is defined by creative freedom. This openness is particularly important to remember when we feel constrained by circumstances beyond our control or when our participation is being solicited for systems of terror or genocide. Our capacity to do something new means we act and hope, but without guarantees. Beauvoir further defines ethics as "the triumph of freedom over facticity." She means that "morality resides in the painfulness of an indefinite questioning." It means as well that "ethics does not furnish recipes."[104]

Beauvoir's existentialism does not allow for a retreat into an abstract notion of the self as a source for ethical standards. We must recognize that our freedom is defined concretely by the existence of other people. "To be free," she writes,

---

102 Simone de Beauvoir, *The Ethics of Ambiguity*, trans. Bernard Frechtman (New York: Citadel, 1976), 25.
103 Beauvoir, *Ambiguity*, 27. S. a. 48-49 and 70.
104 Beauvoir, *Ambiguity*, 44, 97, 133, 134.

is not to have the power to do anything you like; it is to be able to surpass the given toward an open future; the existence of others as a freedom defines my situation and is even the condition of my own freedom.[105]

We must act under conditions in which "our hold on the future is limited." Ironically, "we must decide upon the opportuneness of an act and attempt to measure its effectiveness without knowing all the factors that are present." This uncertainty means that, "at each particular moment we must…maneuver in a state of doubt."[106] Is it any wonder we might be tempted by what she describes as "the flight from the anguish of freedom"?[107] Yet it is a temptation we must resist if we are to act responsibly.

Irony can be used as a strategy to avoid commitment to a future together and to insulate the self from responsibility for its past. The Reinhards of the world are guilty of just this "flight from freedom," and they use irony to do so. Our Reinhard would be a good example of what Beauvoir labels a *nihilist*. "The nihilist is right in thinking that the world *possesses* no justification and that he himself *is* nothing. But he forgets that it is up to him to justify the world and to make himself exist validly."[108] Irony can thus be a tool for striving towards the kind of existential freedom Beauvoir endorses. The crucial step for the committed ironist lies in recognizing the degree to which even the ironic selves we cultivate are inherently bound to others.

At this point in the book, we feel the reader's expectation to finally offer either a definition for what it means to be responsible or to explain why we cannot. In good ironic fashion we will do both, and neither. We reject the inclination to turn to the past to learn its lessons and then move on as if we can ever put history in its place. In our experience, that boulder will not stay where we put it. We always encounter something more and other in the past than we expect. Ironically, these unexpected acts are what we *should* expect given the human capacity for natality. Remember the anonymous Hitler Youth who came to the assistance of the Jewish girl Ruth as an example of this human capacity for the surprising. Still, we wonder if this young man was able to come to the aid of other Jews, and what he did with the rest of his time during the Third Reich. His ability to surprise us with his response to this situation only leads to more questions about his responsibility in other situations.

The same can be said of our own stories as well. We all have what Benjamin and Metz have helped us identify as dangerous memories that disrupt the

---

105 Beauvoir, *Ambiguity*, 91. It is true that there is a residual Cartesianism in Beauvoir's thinking that would seem to indicate a confidence in subjectivity as foundational of values, but she undermines this confidence repeatedly. See 17, 62, 63, 72.

106 Beauvoir, *Ambiguity*, 119, 123.

107 Beauvoir, *Ambiguity*, 119.

108 See Beauvoir, *Ambiguity*, 57.

smooth progress of our memory work as well as our history. As we commit ourselves today, we need to keep in mind that those selves are as dependent on the dead from the past as the living in the present. Perhaps what we hope for is the courage to confront our pasts and let them change our presents, even belatedly as we saw with Metz and with Hans. What this study shows is the wide variety of ways that people have responded and continue to respond to their situation, thanks to such vehicles for selfhood as myth, lies, non-conformity, and irony.

What we take from Sisyphus is the simple fact that, when it comes to responsible selfhood, there can be no certainty—or rest. Our rock will always be waiting for us. Larmore and Beauvoir tell us we face the necessity and risk of commitment to others by our fragmentary selves. Committing irony involves more than recognizing our responsibility for others whose lives are directly or indirectly affected by our becoming. It involves more than just taking care that our irony helps in the present or heals the past rather than harms.[109] The responsible self recognizes that there is no self without irony, which means that there is no self outside human relationships. We are not masters, and our responsibility is not a matter of prescriptions or control. *We are our ability to respond.* How we do so is up to us.

---

109 Cf. Camus, *The Plague*, trans. Stuart Gilbert (New York: Modern Library, 1948).

The Finish

The last thing I should promise would be to "improve" mankind...The good
have always been the beginning of the end.
– Friedrich Nietzsche, *Ecce Homo*, 1908

Figure 10. Andrew Bergerson, *Reinhard with Caricature*, 1993.

Outside Himmelsthür

There is a road extending down from Himmelsthür. People are busy going up and down.[1]

Theodora is on this road. She moved to a modern apartment on Moritzberg in 1963. Now we find her making her way from there up the hill to Himmelsthür. She pushes an empty grocery cart.

Reinhard is on this road as well. He remains a *Bergenzer* at heart—the name Moritzbergers give to themselves.[2] He often said that he would always live and die there. But he had to move on in 2006.

Now we find him outside a pub. The historicist facade of this castle-like edifice seems completely out of place next to the modern architecture of postwar Germany. A wrought-iron gate surrounds its front courtyard, with a wide opening that looks large enough for all. A large basin stands within, full of clean running water.

But a waiter stands at the closed Gothic doors. He looks strangely formal in his apron and black attire. He is wrapped in a fur jacket to stay warm. Someone asks if they would be allowed in anytime soon. "It's possible," he says matter-of-factly, "but not now."

Reinhard stands on the sidewalk with some drinking buddies. They wait for the owner to open for business.

"I don't think we can leave it at that."

Scott, Clancy, and Steve look at Drew. We walk in the recently developed spaces between town and village. They technically belong to Hildesheim but feel like a world apart.[3]

We stop across the street from the pub. After writing, we are thirsty and hungry. We hope to get some food there.

"Surely we have written enough already."

"We offered a reasonable interpretation."

"And provided ample evidence in support of it."

Another group arrives. After what seems like a lifetime of labor, they too are in need of something to drink and eat; they want to get into the pub.

"Something is bothering him again," Steve teases.

"That's evident."

In the spotlights of the streetlights, the courtyard looks like a stage, the gate its proscenium edge, the sidewalk its apron. New actors enter but do not exit.

"It's the conclusion, isn't it," Scott guesses.

---

1   *Genesis* 28:12.
2   G133b 04:00.
3   G133b 04:00.

Drew nods. The door to the pub remains closed. Everyone stands around shuffling feet in the cold.

Reinhard chats with the other members of his *Stammtisch* on the sidewalk. He leans on the far side of a traffic sign, between him and them, that reads "no standing."

They talked about *Gott und die Welt*—anything and everything. Like *Bergenzer* did in the days of his youth,[4] however, they do not spend too long on most topics and avoid others as if on purpose.

"Perhaps I am too concerned about endings."

"No need to apologize," Steve puts his hand on Drew's shoulder. "It's a real problem: how to bring criticism to a close without closing it off from criticism. I'm surprised you didn't think of it before."

"We should have anticipated the problem."

"Yes, from the start."

Clancy thinks about this. "Histories end in human outcomes. Plays end in human fates. Historians and literary critics are naturally sensitive to endings."

"But if we are," Drew counters, "it's thanks to theologians. The Western tradition of eschatology attaches an inordinate degree of meaning to the endings of our stories and histories."

Steve scowls. "That's the problem. We get eschatology all wrong. It's *not* about the flow of time. It's about *disruption*. The messiah *breaks* time. Only if we draw our attention away from a utopian end of time can we open ourselves to the possibilities of disruptions within our daily lives."

"Disruptions can be dangerous—"

"True, but they are preferable to beginnings and endings! Those are the times of the gods. They're no place for human beings. We need to rediscover rupture as a condition of our being in the *middle* of the story."

"While the story can still be changed," Scott adds.

Reinhard sees the four of us. He waves. Drew waves back. Drew suddenly recalls an incident from their interviews, and an image.

"You know, when I asked Reinhard if I could take his picture, he seemed shy about his size. It took me a while to get him to consent. And when he did, he positioned his body behind a caricature of himself from the war. It was a charcoal drawing of him on the back of a Soviet propaganda poster."

"I love the metaphor," Scott says. "A caricature of an ordinary German on the one side, a caricature of Stalin on the other."

"When I took the image, it seemed to me that he wanted to use this image to prove a point: that even his comrades on the Eastern Front had seen him as more interested in the food than the fight."

---

4   G135a 10:10, 22:10; G136a 23:10.

"But had they been right?" Scott asks. "I mean, during the war, had he been an eating machine or a killing machine?"

"He wore so many different masks over the course of his lifetime it's hard to tell."

Reinhard has grown fantastically fat. It suddenly seems to them that his body is positing an argument.

"By now, at the end of his life," Drew suggests, "Reinhard wears his bulk the way a drag queen wears her dress, as if his external form validates his internal experience of who he is."

"As a man more interested in supping than soldiering."

"As a dupe who has always only been the antifascist he became after 1945 and never the fascist he had also been before."

"As coherent."

Zarathustra can be heard from afar, always returning without regret.

"Funny," Scott says. "His caricature killed him in the end."

"This reading of disruption reminds me a little of Nietzsche's notion of eternal recurrence," Clancy says. "It's not a model for responsible selfhood, but at least Nietzsche's trying to rethink historical responsibility in nonlinear terms."

"The Czech novelist Milan Kundera refers to it at the beginning of *The Unbearable Lightness of Being*," Scott mentions. Milan appears on the sidewalk across the street. The author reads out loud from his book.

"The myth of eternal return states that a life which disappears once and for all, which does not return, is like a shadow, without weight, dead in advance, and whether it was horrible, beautiful, or sublime, its horror, sublimity, and beauty mean nothing."[5]

Steve nods his head. "This is what I think of when I hear Benjamin or Metz demand justice for the dead—we can never reach the end of this demand or succeed in meeting it. We can't change the past, so we should stop acting as if we can control it."

Drew: "I'm willing to admit that historians have a disciplinary tendency to try to reduce the ambiguities of everyday life. In our conclusions, we write endings that frame the past in coherent, reductive analyses to give ourselves and our readers a false sense of certainty. But how can history be written any other way?"

"The alternative," Steve thinks out loud, "would be to try to write histories that preserve the *ethical* orientation that comes with an awareness of consequences, but stay with our historical agents in the *middle* of everyday life where the situation is still ambiguous and their selfhood fragmentary."

---

5   Milan Kundera, *The Unbearable Lightness of Being*, trans. Michael Henry Heim (New York: Harper, 1991), 3.

Zarathustra and Milan are caught up in conversation about books, inn-keepers, and food. Nearby, Walter scrutinizes the pub which is still dark and shuttered.

"The point here would be to emphasize the situatedness of the self and how the self negotiates these situations." Clancy steps in circles as he speaks. "The philosophical reasons for doing so is that it draws our attention to the obvious fact that we can and often do act surprisingly in the world. That should give us hope."

"While the historical reasons for doing so," Drew talks at the moving target, "are that it makes for better explanations for events. The ambiguous insights afforded by staying within everyday life help historians explain the origin of both violence and courage."

"For literary critics," Scott jumps in, "the point relates to the very nature of performance. Of course there are endings to our stories, and often very nasty ones. But things can and do end not only in *this* way; they could also very well end in *that* way. We cannot control the actual ending to our own stories. But it's still up to us to decide what role we wish to perform."

"So how do we get our readers to see this crucial point: that the roles we choose for ourselves lay in the hands of the performer? The moment we finish the book in any one way, the danger arises that our readers will draw the false conclusion that our *one* answer is *the* answer to the questions of the book."

"Or more dangerously, that responsible selfhood involves discovering authoritative answers."

The owner is not yet come. The courtyard fills, the crowd spilling out onto the sidewalk. Bertolt enters from left. He stands close to Walter and writes poetry, but he looks directly at us now and again, which makes us feel out of place.

"It's a real problem, isn't it? What can we possibly do as scholars to influence our readers to stand in solidarity with the victims of history?"

An Agitator appears. He is well fed but appears famished. From his uniform, we can tell that he is a decorated veteran of the First World War.

He approaches the pub from far to the right—or maybe from the left, it's hard to tell sometimes. In an overwrought provincial accent, he begins to preach about the need to build a new pub, a better pub, a pub that will provide for all of its clientele. It will be a more exclusive pub for the right kind of people. His kind of people.

"Aren't we expressing solidarity just by writing this book?"

"Certainly this much is true: we may or may not have gotten it right in what we said about responsibility, but we did *respond*—with irony, nonconformity and," Clancy laughs, "probably a healthy dose of self-deception. Our response matters. It reminds us of our ability *to* respond. That might just encourage us to do so again in everyday life, where it matters most."

The historian rubs his brow with closed eyes. The Agitator gets more and more frenetic as he speaks. He begins to sweat profusely with an almost sensual ecstasy. He calls for the removal of those who do not fit the future. No food for the living who are unworthy of life! It's an ugly kind of enthusiasm that would be comical if it were not so deadly earnest.

Most of the customers ignore him. We cannot.

"Something's still wrong with the conclusion."

More people join Zarathustra. Karl takes out a chess set and plays against him.

Clancy makes the first move. "Is it the problem of *historicity*? This is a common criticism of Leftists who are so convinced that the revolution is about to happen that they do nothing to make it happen. Our faith in history inclines us to rely on supra-human forces to bring about change rather than to act ethically ourselves."

"No, that's not it."

Zarathustra lost his first pawn. Karl asserts his pieces with mechanical precision.

"Maybe you are looking for more positive examples," Steve suggests. "History is often written as hagiography, presenting the reader with heroic narratives from the past as models for ethical action."

Another group of paying customers approaches the gate from the left. Simone arrives with her French boyfriend. Hannah searches the crowd for her German one. But they do not stay put. They reposition themselves *vis-à-vis* this popular Leader in a volatile situation.

Bertolt sips something out of a flask. He sings bawdy songs at the windows of the pub. The Leader just raises the volume of his own speech.

"Like survival during the Holocaust. It was not predicated on one universal strategy but was more often a result of dumb luck and complicated ethical compromises made in response to particular situations. Survival itself often required participating in the very systems of violence that were threatening you."

Scott folds the lapel of his jacket up. "We certainly identify with those courageous few who stood up to the Nazis either directly or by coming to the aid of their victims. It would be relatively easy to put stories of so-called *righteous gentiles* in our study, for instance. They often acted for complicated reasons ensnared in the kinds of contradictions we analyze in the book, and yet they acted nonetheless."

"But the danger is that our readers might draw from those examples the false assumption that they now know *for sure* what they need to do in their own lives when faced with fascism or racism. Responsibility ends when certainty begins."

"First food, then responsibility!" Bertolt interrupts.

"Our responsibility," the Agitator shouts back, "is to feed our own people first!"

"That's what's important," Reinhard looks directly at us. "The food."

"Nonetheless, we want our readers to be able to apply what we have learned from the past to the present," Drew reminds them. "What we have learned from our book is that we can act responsibly because we have the ability to respond; we have it within our power to respond on behalf of the victims of history simply because we are always already responding to others. How can we possibly communicate that message without some kind of synthetic, explanatory conclusion?"

Theodora stops a block away. From the way she is standing there, leaning on the traffic sign, the four authors are suddenly reminded that she is mostly blind. She suffers from macular degeneration—a progressive disease that is robbing her of her ability to see fine details starting from the center of her field of vision. Now she can only make out strong lights and colors on the periphery.

But she is otherwise fit, thanks to a life of physical activity. She insists on living independently. She pushes her own cart up the hill to the grocery store. Even simple things like crossing streets or staying on the sidewalk can be treacherous if you cannot see too clearly ahead of you. So she takes her time. She stands at a sign to get her bearings. She assesses each situation as she comes to it. Then she moves on to the next.

Looking at her, Scott smiles.

"You figured it out," Clancy guesses.

"Tell us the answer."

"I will ask you a question instead. Why isn't Hans waiting here with us?"

In unison: "*Who?!*"

"Hans. The man who deceived himself that he could not act. The ordinary German from the chapter on Lies."

Drew looks shocked, alienated. He turns to the others. "How could Hans possibly be here with us? He died years ago."

Scott risks a sidelong glance across the street. But Hans does not appear. He smiles and shrugs.

"I am one theologian who does not believe in resurrection," Steve quips. "At least not that kind."

Clancy answers. "No, Scott's referring to *metanarrativity*: how authors or playwrights draw attention to the constructed nature of narrative."

"Please explain."

"Scott set up an ironic situation. Hans cannot be both alive and dead, just as he cannot be inside and outside the narrative at the same time."

"A paradox."

"And not just any one—it is the paradox of how to end the book. For what we are struggling with is how to translate wisdom discovered within a text to the world of everyday life outside of it."

"The classic problem of theory and practice."

"An impossible contradiction."

"And yet," Scott counters, "here we are."

"I don't understand: where are we precisely?"

"We are caught up in everyday life."

"I see," Steve says to Scott.

"You want us to think about our place in our own narrative. Hans was both an object of study and a living person. We are academics who can think about everyday life objectively from the outside as well as protagonists of our own stories, able to act in our daily lives."

"Yes, the more we think about ourselves as the authors of our own biographies, the easier it is to imagine our ability to respond to the situations with which we are confronted."

"What else do we have to do with our time? We are, after all, still waiting."

"But what are we actually doing?" Drew provokes. "We are still just talking, just debating. Typical academics."

"As useful as irony may seem in freeing us from conventions and even to think for ourselves," Steve suggests, "it does not tell us what we should do with this newfound freedom. The question is not how to finish this book, but how to do so responsibly."

"Yes, that's it!" Drew cries out. "What bothers me about the book is the contradiction between what we wrote and the way we wrote it. It makes no sense to me to conclude our book with a typical academic conclusion that abstracts ourselves away from the problem of violence."

Dark and shuttered, no sign of life comes from the windows of the pub. The crowd starts getting loud.

"We are hungry!"

"And thirsty!"

"It's insufferable."

"The nerve!"

They debate how to respond. Some want to throw stones, others demand civil disobedience. There are calls for hunger strikes and for ridding the world of its excess mouths. Frustration mounts as the pub provides nothing concrete on which they can vent their rage.

"We are deceiving ourselves if we think we have succeeded in writing a good book about historical responsibility if we contradict ourselves in the end just to get our book published and promote our careers."

"The beginning of responsible selfhood is to look critically at our own behavior."

"We should practice what we preach."

"But how?" Clancy asks. "What kind of conclusion does not conclude? What kind of ending does not end?"

"We need to finish the book from the same point of departure that we employ in each of the chapters," Steve concludes. "The perspective from within everyday life, from the middle."

"Sisyphus half-way up the mountain."

"In the midst of the jungle."

"Yes, yes," Drew waves his hand in frustration, "from within the Hildesheimer Forest. That is all very well, but completely impractical. Please tell me *pragmatically* how we go about doing it. What form should the finish take? What content should fill our final words?"

"I get your point. We cannot communicate our insights to the reader from a posture of objectivity, abstraction, and control if we have warned in the rest of the book about the dangers inherent in that approach to selfhood."

Scott inhales the cold air deeply.

"We are in a sense confronted with the problem of our contradictory responsibilities as teachers and scholars."

He steps up on the stoop and places his hands on either side of a wooden rostrum. We are his pupils. J. G. is with us on this side of the street. He holds his chin in his hand, observing the observers.

"As scholars we engage in a skeptical dialogue about the truth. We challenge our sources and they challenge our assumptions. The purpose of this mutual interrogation, we believe, is to get at some kinds of *strong* truth, but we never reach that degree of confidence. Nor would we want to. As investigators, we know that we are best suited at proving things wrong than proving them right."

"Check," Karl called out. Zarathustra leans forward, intent on the game. Others are watching, like Søren and Ludwig.

"The problem for us as scholars is that we often assume the very opposite role as teachers and authors. As experts in our field, our students and readers expect us to already know all of the answers that as researchers we know we are always only searching for. This is an untenable position to maintain for any one person—at least not without considerable self-deception."

Zarathustra smiles. "But not mate."

"I see what you mean. As teachers we force our students to learn truths that we cannot really believe in ourselves as researchers. Even if we ultimately wish to free our students to think for themselves, forcing them to do so with the authority of an instructor seems to demand an irresponsible degree of authoritarian didacticism."

"So liberation pedagogy can be an oxymoron," Steve says. "Is that it?"

Scott nods from the makeshift podium. "At least insofar as we dupe our-

selves into believing the lies we tell ourselves about our authority as instruc-
tors."

He steps down. Steve takes his place at the rostrum.

"We have identified strategies people use to create a little more elbow
room for themselves in everyday life, and we even think we have identified
what we can do to keep those strategies ethical. And yet we write it in an
academic essay as if we are ourselves masters of everyday life, professing truths
as *profess-ors*. Who are we to tell our students or our readers what to do?"

Clancy moans. "What a scam! We like to think that we are different,
that academic freedom means we can allow ourselves the hubris of principled
non-conformity. But we are only using the rostrum to validate our vanity."

J. G. smiles. He leans close to a man in a toga and whispers something in
his ear. The two walk back to the other side of the street in deep conversation.

Drew is relieved. He knows that he needed the others to figure out this
conundrum. He holds a book in his hand. It's about a man, a mountain, and
a boulder. Drew steps up onto the podium and taps the book on the rostrum
in cadence with his words like a preacher.

"Just imagine how annoyed our readers will be! They buy our book and
patiently read what amounts to a long-winded, technical, didactic sermon.
They then expect to know how to use myths, non-conformity, lies, and irony
ethically in everyday life. As if people learn how to live from instruction
manuals!"[6]

Drew tosses the book on the pavement.

Ludwig feels confident enough to try it out for himself. He challenges
Søren to a game.

"In effect you are saying that we are making the same mistake that most
every post-Enlightenment political movement has made from modern dicta-
tors to postmodern missionaries of democracy." It is Clancy speaking. "We
are trying to compel others to be free."

Jean-Jacques is nowhere to be seen. He detests cities, crowds, and above
all, polite philosophical conversation.

"Yes. Teaching people how to use irony responsibly can become, ironically, rather irresponsible."

And in the pub nothing stirs.

---

6   Ludwig Wittgenstein, *Philosophical Investigations*, trans. G. E. M. Anscombe, P. M. S.
     Hacket and Joachim Schulte, 4th ed. (Oxford: John Wiley and Son, 2009), §31.

Epic Scholarship

Theodora hears but cannot see what is happening. She pushes her cart from the traffic sign towards the street light. She wants to cross the street safely but she also wants to avoid the crowd. It's on the verge of a brawl.

Reinhard is closer to the commotion. He postures as if he will fight with his comrades if it comes to blows, but all he talks about is the food.

We are still watching the scene from across the street. It seems too familiar a tragedy whose end has been foreshadowed from the beginning.

"You know, Brecht tried to write plays that bridged this gap between theory and politics." Scott picks up the book as if seeing it for the first time. "We have seen how he tried to use irony to break the attachment of his audience to bourgeois ideology."

"Did he succeed?" Drew's curiosity is piqued.

Scott weighs the book in his hands. "In the case of *Three Penny Opera*, not to his satisfaction. Brecht's audience did pick up on his critique of organized religion and of the social repercussions of poverty. But Brecht worried that his ironic endings so undermined the audience's ability to interpret that they prevented his audience from finding any overarching meanings to the play, no less an ethical politics. It seemed to Brecht that irony actually prevented his audience from recognizing the imperative to act responsibly in everyday life."

Clancy crosses his arms. "Our choice to treat the problem of the Third Reich ironically may very well prevent actual responsible action as well, if our readers misinterpret our irony as nihilism."

It's getting hard for us to hear one another. Bertolt is singing at the top of his lungs about virtuous innkeepers who dispense spirits to the thirsty for free. His song seems to be directed at the dark and shuttered windows, without noticeable effect. The Austrian Lance Corporal has long since forgotten about the pub. He is enthralled by the hungry crowd. They begin to take sides, each with their own champion.

Simone looks at Hannah with a worried expression. She does not understand what Hannah sees in her German boyfriend. Now wearing academic robes, he throws himself behind the speaker's podium.

Walter is caught far from the gate in a corner of the courtyard. He looks at the crowd, and then back down the street, with a worried expression. He grips his books tightly.

"The problem with *Three Penny Opera*," Scott explains, "lay in Brecht's assumption that irony *in and of itself* would bridge the gap into politics.[7] He

---

7   See Mayer, *Erinnerung*, 105.

220 The Finish

saw irony as preparing an empty space to be filled by the audience's construction of a synthesis. But irony neither compels nor models a constructive response."

"How did his audience respond in fact?" Steve asks.

"Brecht's general audiences were entertained,[8] but many audience members did not recognize his political agenda. It was a disappointment for him."

"Still he had to do something," Clancy looks at the growing number of fists in the crowd. "He could not just sit back and watch in the face of human tragedy."

Some of the people flee. Others brace for the inevitable. Hannah finally leaves her boyfriend behind, but she keeps watching him. She is not done with him just yet. Walter records every event in a notebook and almost loses his glasses while trying to avoid a scuffle.

"Brecht came to believe that, in the absence of a socialist revolution, the habits of bourgeois entertainment would persist. The *Three Penny Opera* would be nothing more than pleasurable absurdities and paradoxes."[9]

"So Brecht ended up having to assume the very thing he was striving to produce. He decided that the play needed to be performed within a revolutionary context in order for people to understand its revolutionary message."

Drew laughs.

Steve: "He lost faith."

Clancy: "He lost hope."

Scott: "His courage wavered."

The waiter waits. He wants neither to go to work nor to lose his wages. He is indifferent.

A full-fledged riot unfolds. We watch from the other side of the street as if these events were on television and we could change the channel once it gets too close or too ugly. We check our pockets, but none of us have the remote control.

"So what did he do?" Drew asks.

Scott smiles, handing the book back to Drew. "He changed genre."

It takes a moment for this new irony to sink in.

"He wrote essays!"

Drew shakes his head. "*Terrific.*"

"Brecht began by attaching an elaborate explanatory apparatus to the first publication of the *Three Penny Opera* in 1931.[10] This introduction begins

---

8 Brecht, *Grosse kommentierte Berliner und Frankfurter Ausgabe* (Frankfurt: Suhrkamp, 1988-2000), here vol. 24 (1991), 437-443.

9 S. a. Max Horkheimer and Theodor W. Adorno, *Dialectic of Enlightenment: Philosophical Fragments*, ed. Gunzelin Schmid Noerr, trans. Edmund Jephcott (Palo Alto: Stanford University Press, 2002), 94-136.

10 Brecht, *GBA*, vol. 24, 57-68

with a disclaimer about the insufficiency of theater to accurately present the true meaning of the work."

"This has all the markings of tragedy."

"Then he wrote a series of pieces on epic theater that explained precisely how to stage the play in order to highlight his political message."

"For instance?"

"Well, he instructed directors and actors on how to make it clearer to the audience that Mackie belonged to the bourgeoisie. He also explained a bunch of other technical innovations that were not immediately obvious if you read the dramatic text—things like the function of the gest, the Marxist analytical conception of the base and superstructure, as well as the plurality and mutability of individual identity. He writes these essays in a playful tone but almost entirely avoiding irony."

"Brecht was a communist. It should not surprise us that he got didactic and doctrinaire."

"What an irony! When his irony fails to ensure responsibility, as it inevitably must, Brecht writes an instruction manual on how to disambiguate his own irony."

"Precisely."

Drew steps up and down on the low stoop to someone's house. "Brecht was probably right. The 1930s were full of utopian political movements, each grounded in dialectic thinking and yet diametrically opposed to one another. There was no guarantee that his audience would view his irony as he wanted."

"But there are *never* any guarantees." Steve moves to the middle of the street. He motions with open arms to the crowd on the other side. "Imagine if you filled a theater with ordinary people, each with their own fragmentary selves and contradictory strategies. Think of all the opportunities Macheath makes available to them for *avoiding* political and historical responsibility. There's no certainty here."

No one is winning the chess match between Ludwig and Søren. But they play anyway. Karl makes decisive moves. Zarathustra is down to his last man.

"I think the problem with epic theater lies in *direction*," Clancy suggests. "Brecht was not only the *director* of the play; he also seemed to want to *direct* people's attention to a particular kind of political response."

"Brecht's experience with the *Three Penny Opera* was that, without some form of political meaning imposed from *outside* the theater, in the historical situation, his layers of irony felt empty."

Steve: "Or worse than empty. Irony afforded his audience the chance to play in the fields of ambiguity without recognizing any need for action. It led not to responsible selfhood but sovereign impunity."

"There was one other option," Scott adds. "Brecht also imagined that he could restore an ethical content to his irony by constructing a *negation of negation*—a dialectical operation that saves irony from itself. Of course, this *un*ambiguous structure of meaning undermines the whole point of irony—which is ambiguity. Either way, he gives up on irony."[11]

Steve laughs. "The two Brechts contradicted one another. Where the playwright understood that only we can give meaning to the roles we play, the political activist abandoned irony as a tool for responsibility and found some external ground to give meaning to his plays."

Bertolt is hoarse from all his singing and shouting. He staggers around. Walter tries to finish writing before the crowd overwhelms him. Ludwig pays scant attention. He loses himself in the rules of the game. Karl asserts his pieces, but Zarathustra does not give up.

"Well, Brecht leaves us in quite a quandary," Drew says. "It's a catch-word of the postmodern that there is no real revolutionary context in the twenty-first century. Alternative postures are fashion statements or terrorist cults, not responsible politics."

Clancy: "Nor is dialectical historicism a reasonable option for us. Putting our faith in abstractions has justified some of the most horrendous violence."

Scott: "Our problem is that the didactic essay with which we, as academics, are most comfortable is also not appropriate. We cannot profess strong truth as talking heads and remain skeptical at the same time about ourselves and our wisdom."

Bertolt has made his way to safety, but Walter refuses to leave his books. Simone takes the flask from Bertolt and offers it to Walter through bars of the wrought-iron fence. He looks at it as if it were poison.

Walter considers for a moment, and then passes his notebook to Simone so he can hold the flask in his one free hand. As soon as he drinks, he is engulfed in the crowd.

Simone escapes, but is visibly shaken. The man in a toga points up the hill into the darkness. They take Walter's notebook, open it, and begin reading.

"But then we are no closer to a responsible finish than before," Clancy concludes. "We have just conceded to nihilism."

Reinhard shifts his weight uncomfortably from side to side. He leans on the wrought-iron fence which groans under his tremendous bulk. He looks up briefly at the pub and then turns away.

"His weight's a burden for him."

---

11   Cf. Reinhold Grimm, "Vom Novum Organum zum Kleinen Organon: Gedanken zur Verfremdung," in *Das Ärgernis Brecht*, ed. Willy Jäggi and Hans Oesch (Basel: Basilius, 1961), 51-70, esp. 70.

"What he needs is some kind of cane."

"Someone should build a bench here."

"Yes, someone."

They look at the waiter but he takes no notice. He is on his feet all day. He does not see why everyone else should not suffer as he does.

Theodora reaches the corner. She pauses to orient herself but there is no place to rest. She starts to cross the street.

"What we need," Drew thinks out loud, "is an example of scholarship that refuses such strong truths more consistently than Brecht."

Clancy takes the book from Drew and takes its measure. "Socrates might offer a nice contrast to Brecht for our readers."

Clancy points the book towards the man in the toga. "Here was someone who was so little concerned with what others thought of him that nonconformity was a non-issue. He spent his whole life rigorously interrogating himself as a way to acknowledge the roles he played and avoid self-deception. Who could be a better model of an open self, acting responsibly?"

Steve: "It certainly could draw our reader's attention to the problem of how to finish things. Socrates ended his life a condemned man, executed by the Athenian state for refusing to recognize the gods and corrupting youth."[12]

Scott: "And Socrates was such a Brechtian figure. He was in effect accused of the very thing that made him great: of the content and style of his teaching. His condemnation undermines our cultural expectations for what happens to very wise people."

Clancy flips through the pages. "There are also interesting comparisons to be made to Sisyphus. Socrates could have escaped his execution. His friend and supporter Crito presented him with the opportunity, even the demand, that he escape and go into exile. But Socrates refused on the basis of respect for the very laws that condemned him."[13]

Drew: "I like the fact that he was as much a teacher as a scholar. It allows us to think through this problem of how best to share our insights with others. But I worry that, if we chose Socrates as a model, we would be suggesting that self-sacrifice is the ultimate form of responsibility. It strikes me as just another justification for violence—this time against the self."

Steve raises his hand. "Not at all. Socrates was neither playing roles to avoid responsibility nor trying to destroy himself. His questioning was intended to keep the subject open to others, to history, to existence. His questions were truly 'the piety of thinking.'"[14]

---

12 Plato, *Apology*, 38c.

13 Plato, *Crito*, 45-46.

14 Heidegger, "The Question Concerning Technology," in *Martin Heidegger: Basic Writings*, ed. David Farrell Krell (San Francisco: Harper, 1993), 341, translation altered.

Scott: "I love the sarcasm of Socrates during the punishment phase of his trial.[15] Having been judged guilty of capital crimes and facing the possibility of execution, he has the courage to shock his jurors with the suggestion that rather than be punished he should be rewarded with the same kind of pension received by famous athletes and others who served the glory of the state."

Clancy turns the book over. "But the people closest to him still did not understand him even in the end. D'you remember his amusement when Crito asked him how he would like to be buried?[16] Crito missed the whole point. Socrates didn't fear death. He knew it was of absolutely no significance what one did with the corpse after the soul had left it."

"So what is the point? Why did Socrates choose death?" Drew asks.

"He did not want to die; but neither did he want to abandon his ironic understanding of wisdom even if it meant that it would be the last thing that he did. Plato tells us in the *Phaedo* that Socrates died with such equanimity that even the executioner who brought him the cup of hemlock broke down in tears at his leaving."[17]

Drew: "It seems rather senseless to me."

Steve: "His death remains senseless only if we think of Socrates as a pawn of circumstances beyond his control. What Socrates understood was that he and only he could give meaning to his life even in the end. He chose to give his life meaning by using a condemnation imposed on him as a way to continue to teach about responsible selfhood—to the end."

Scott: "But this also means that Socrates needs *us* to understand his death as ironic; only when we recognize the ironic way he undermined his own condemnation does his death become a model for how to live responsibly in the world."

Hannah joins Simone's conversation with the man in the toga. He instructs them by asking them questions. Then he winks, as if he knows something more but will never tell.

"Unlike Brecht, Socrates was willing to trust his students that they will be able to read his irony responsibly."

"It's hard to escape the conclusion that it is up to us to somehow make sense of this irony."

"And to do something with it!"

Clancy hands the book back to Drew.

"It seems to be the only way to finish."

---

15   Plato, *Apology*, 36e.
16   Plato, *Phaedo*, 115c.
17   Plato, *Phaedo*, 118.

Macular Degeneration

Theodora finally crosses the street but seems a little disoriented from all the commotion.

Drew hands the book to Steve so he can take her arm. "Here I am."[18]

"Who is that?" she asks, leaning on him. "What is your name?"

"*Andreas Bergerson—der Amerikaner.*"

"Oh, *Herr Bergerson!*" She smiles, putting her hand in his. "How nice! I am sorry. I did not see you. You know how it is. My condition is getting worse."

"It's no matter."

"Are you back in Hildesheim for a while?"

"Not really."

"Oh, too bad. But you can come by for *Kaffee und Kuchen?*"

"I would love to get together again."

"Me too," she added. "How is your research going?"

"The new book is almost done."

"I would love to hear what you have learned. I cannot read for myself anymore."

"I would be happy to tell you all about it."

"*Toll!* I'll look forward to it."

The grocery store was up a bit further up the hill.

"Do you need any help?"

"No, I'll be fine."

Theodora takes up her cart and makes her careful way to the next sign.

"So that was Theodora?" Steve asks once she moves out of hearing range.

"Yes, I try to visit her when I come back to Hildesheim."

"What's that like?" Clancy inquires. "Does she know that you are Jewish?"

"Now that is an interesting story."

"I never really knew how you conducted your interviews. Our readers may want to know more about them."

"And how you wrestled with your relationship with your interview partners. We should put it in the book."

Scott turns to the crowd before the pub. *He calls.* "Worthy gentleman and members of the household! We shall now tell you the story of a historian whose skills as an interviewer did not help him any. Just to show you that we're humble people ourselves, which makes it hard for us, especially in the winter."

---

18 *Genesis* 22:1, 32:25-28.

Few listen. The pub remains dark and silent. Here is Drew's story:

I was able to establish a foundation of trust with most of my interview partners. I was surprised when they revealed personal experiences that they had not even shared with their children. There were exceptions of course, but most chatted away glibly once they realized that I was sincerely interested in hearing the stories of their lives. Many failed to deal with their Nazi past in a *critical* sense, but most of them struggled to make sense of their life stories in light of the Third Reich.

I often felt compelled to reciprocate this trust, but there were limits to what I was willing to share with them. At the beginning of the interviews, I had promised each of them that, after the four interviews were complete, they could pose questions about me, and I would respond truthfully. Obviously they could tell that I was American, a man, and a member of a younger generation—about the age of one of their grandchildren. But they did not know that I was Jewish. It was the white elephant in the room. I fully expected to be confronted about it.

Scott: "Does this include Hans or just the Hildesheimers?"
Drew: "Just the Hildesheimers. Hans had worked with my mother for many years so he knew that we were Jewish."
Steve: "But you are not *just* a Jew—and not even a very observant one."

True, but the other aspects of my identity were less salient. Sometimes my vegetarianism came up in these exit interviews. But this was not that strange anymore in 1992. I didn't expect the members of this generation to ask me about more private matters, like my sexual orientation. They did ask me if I was married, to which I answered that I had been, but was at the time recently divorced.

Clancy: "You dodged that one nicely."
Steve: "But what about the Jewish question? Did they ask you about that?"

Never directly—not once. They often asked about my family and my parents, especially what my parents did for a living and where I grew up. I responded that my parents are New Yorkers; that I grew up in a suburb on Long Island; and that my father is a Certified Public Accountant and my mother a science teacher. They asked me what brought me to Hildesheim, which to them seemed an unlikely place for an American to conduct his research. I explained that I had sought a mid-sized provincial town statistically representative of interwar Germany in 1925, and Hildesheim was the best fit.

Many asked if I had some kind of family connection to Hildesheim—a loaded question, I realize in retrospect. Even more pointed was the first question some of them asked—some variation on: "*Bergerson, Bergerson*, what kind of a name is *Bergerson*?" To German ears, *Bergerson* sounds Scandinavian. Both of these questions were code for race.

I did not lie to them, but I also did not clarify the ambiguity. I didn't say, for instance, that my paternal great-grandfather had been a *Bergersohn*—a name that sounds obviously Jewish to a German ear—and that they changed it to *Bergerson*, perhaps to efface their Jewishness. I did not mention any of the names of my other great-grandparents who had fled Europe before the Great War: *Berkowitz, Hymen, Numeratz, Oshinsky, Staragursky*. I am only half certain of the spellings myself.

I certainly didn't say that my grandparents were still in contact with their many cousins in the old country until the Germans exterminated them all. Apparently the last survivor died in his own bed in Slovakia but from malnutrition a few months after liberation from Auschwitz. I didn't offer this information and they didn't ask.

Clancy: "Who is the liar and who is the dupe?"

It was mutual. It makes perfect sense that they wanted to figure out where I stood in the sociology of World War Two so they could adjust their answers to their audience. But I wasn't being any more responsible. I certainly felt uncomfortable outing myself as a Jew to my elderly German interview partners, some of whom had been and still were supporters of the Nazi party. But my motive was far more devious. I wanted to know them without having to let them know me.

Scott: "You wanted to preserve your sovereign impunity."

I assumed the role of an objective social scientist, responding to any subtle question about my Jewishness with the authority of the expert. I said, simply, that my family came from Eastern Europe: "The old Russian and Habsburg Empires—*K-und-K*."[19] Of course I recognized the irony: this pedantically factual answer about my ethnic origins was in fact the deceptive one. But I got away with it—or at least that is what I thought. The result was that I always wondered if my interview partners suspected, and I often felt guilty that I was hiding something from them.

Steve: "What happened after the interviews?"

I tried to stay in touch through letters and visits. I informed my interview partners about publications, career moves, and the latest in my life. They sometimes shared new stories from their lives as well. In a letter to me dated 18 December 1997, Theodora admitted that she "belonged to the silent collaborators." She read one of my essays, however, and corrected me, saying that the interviews had not been the first time that she had asked herself the question *what should I have done?* Still, the interviews had made the question "tremendously pressing." Speaking of those who experienced "this time," she insisted that "we will never be free from" this question. But she conceded that another question was just as pressing: *what can I do now for the future?*

The next time we saw each other in Hildesheim, she told me some new stories. She explained that she developed an interest in the history and culture of German Jewry which she investigated together with her daughter. She also told me how she got together with her old classmates for their reunion. They chatted animatedly about old times. But they never spoke about the Jewish girl, Hannah Mendelsohn, the classmate who emigrated to Palestine to escape the Third Reich. Theodora spontaneously decided to ask: "Why don't we ever talk about Hannah?" They decided to start.

I worried to some degree that she was telling me these stories to prove to me that she had successfully come to terms with her Nazi past. But I couldn't ignore the fact that she had taken action where she could have remained silent. She changed her present

---

19   This German abbreviation refers to the Dual "Empire" (*Kaiserreich*) of Austria and "King-dom" (*Königreich*) of Hungary.

in light of her past, in solidarity with the dead. This time, at least, she insisted on standing on the side of the victims. What she did seemed more important than the possible ambiguities in why she did it.

More interestingly, it seemed to me that it was not enough for her. She seemed to want to continue the kinds of critical self-reflection not only with an outsider like me but with both her peers and her family. Overstating the case, I hypothesized that our interviews had evoked a shift in her attitude towards the Nazi past. I even wrote one of my first articles on this subject. I used her to illustrate how oral history might work in some cases to "narrate enlightenment."[20]

Clancy: "She appealed to your vanity as a scholar. You wanted to believe what she was saying *about herself* because you wanted to believe what that said *about you*."

Drew: "You may be right. It's hard for me to tell."

Steve: "What I find interesting is that you were still so much of a Kantian back then."

Drew: "I was—but I knew that she was an exception to the rule. Most of my interview partners used the interview process as a way to further justify their irresponsibility."

Meanwhile I was still sincerely believing the lies I told myself about my role as a distanced observer of scientific phenomena—that the really strong truths that I could find in the interviews lay in what I could discover about how they had behaved. My mistake was to believe that I could measure historical responsibility in terms of what my German informants did rather than what I do.

Scott: "How do we balance our responsibilities as academics to 'get it right' with our historical responsibilities as human beings? We are back, once again, at the problem of how to finish."

Steve: "If we got any part of historical responsibility correct in this book, then it's that we have no business using even the Germans and their long struggle to deal with the Nazi past as an excuse for our own irresponsibility."

Clancy: "Quite right. It would be rather hypocritical of us to tell others how to be responsible if that posture is designed, at any level, to preserve our sovereign impunity. Treating our German informants as a means to our scientific ends lands us precariously close to Mengele's laboratory."

OK, so this is right where the story gets interesting. In 2006, I returned to Hildesheim to teach a course at the University and do more research. By this time, you will recall, we had already begun work on this book. My children, Kyle and Skye, joined me for most of the time: I brought them to day care on Moritzberg before sitting down in the archives. My wife, JJ, came during the summer.

---

20 See Bergerson, "Narrating Enlightenment," 49-52; and *idem*, "Aufklärung durch Erzäh-lung," 242-248.

When I called Theodora, she did something that surprised me: she asked to meet my family. During our first visit, we took a walk in the Magdalene Garden—a wonderful playground and garden hidden behind the historic walls of town. We ate lunch in a restaurant on a small island in the Innerste River. In spite of her macular degeneration, she was still able to see that my wife was African-American and our children biracial. She made a point of telling me several times that she found them to be beautiful and charming children.

The second time, we met in Caféonion in a historic half-timbered house for the best hot chocolate in Hildesheim. As my kids ran around the patio hyped on sugar and cocoa, the three adults talked about many things. Without really thinking twice about it, I mentioned something about *Rosh Hashanah* or *Yom Kippur*, the Jewish High Holy Days. Here is how I remember the dialogue that ensued:

Theodora said, "You know, Mr. Bergerson, this is the first time that you admitted to me that you are Jewish."

I immediately felt a wave of panic. "You knew all along?"

She smiled. "I am not dumb. Why else does a young American come to a place like Hildesheim to do research about the Third Reich?"

We both laughed. Then she said, "May I ask *you* a question now?" I agreed. "What is it like for you to have built up a friendly relationship—*freundschaftliche Beziehung*—with me?"

At first I considered sticking to my old habits of deception, but then I changed my mind.

Steve: "Why?"
Drew: "Because she deserved an honest answer from me."
Clancy: "What did you say?"

I said, "Sometimes, when I look at you, I think, 'Why is she alive and yet all of my relatives are dead?' Other times I think about our relationship, and what we have been able to share together, and I cherish it."

I will never forget Theodora's response: "I think that sounds about right."

Of course, this being Germany, we could not avoid being confronted immediately thereafter with the challenge of historical responsibility. We decided to walk to Ernst Ehrlicher Park where there was a playground for the kids. It was only a few hundred steps from the Café. But to get there, we had to walk past no less than three different local places of memory, each of which were deeply embedded in radically different narratives of violence, suffering, and responsibility.

First we passed some of the few remaining half-timbered houses of historic Hildesheim—*Alt-Hildesheim*. The vast majority of these buildings had been destroyed in the massive Allied bombardment of March 1945, together with thousands of people, a few short weeks before the end of the war. Next to these historic homes lay the foundations of the destroyed synagogue on Lappenberg; it was destroyed during *Kristallnacht*. A monument stands there now that disturbingly sets these two acts of destruction in parallel. Just beyond lay the earthen embankments that comprised the historic town walls. Theodora showed us where she and her daughter had found refuge in a bunker in those walls during the March air raid.

Steve: "There is no rest."

As Theodora recounted this story about the air raid, we both seemed to fall back into the old pattern of me listening to her autobiography. I grew angry that she assumed the role of the victim as my interview partners had sometimes done in the past. But for the first time, my Jewishness was part of that conversation; and it seemed to me that placing all of these pasts into discourse gave a new set of meanings to each those memories.

Scott: "I think that's true of all narrative texts. I certainly find new things every time I read the books and plays that make up my work."
Steve: "What did you discover this time?"

Something quite unexpected.

I found myself retelling this story, about this encounter between Theodora and me in 2006, in many different kinds of settings: to students in courses, to members of my family, and even in public lectures. It seemed to capture something essential about how we might respond to the Nazi past, though I was not able to say precisely what it was that this story expressed. I thought about it often, but surprisingly, given my almost compulsive inclination to analyze everything, I did not try to dissect it further. The story stood as a kind of placeholder where analytic thinking stops and experience begins, and I liked it that way.

Now, after writing this book with the three of you, I suspect that what I like about the story is the priority it gives to ambiguity as a necessary component of what it means to cultivate a historically responsible self in memory of the Third Reich. It reminds me that the work is never done; just when you think that you have accomplished something, you find yourself back at the foot of the mountain again, facing the boulder.

Steve: "There is no parole from the responsibility of becoming human."
Clancy: "It also seems to matter that you learned this lesson about responsibility together with Theodora."
Drew: "Yes, Much of what I have learned about these issues came through my relationships with Germans. I think I learned the most when my interview partners talked back, challenging my assumptions. When they were unruly."
Scott: "So is that the last time you saw Theodora?"

No, I saw her again last summer in 2009.

I went to do more research and to teach at the University again. This time I did not bring the family because I was there for only a short time. Of course I called Theodora again. She was the only member of my original interview cohort in Hildesheim who was still alive and mentally fit, and with whom I could still establish contact.

As I walked up the stairs to her apartment, I found myself thinking that it's entirely likely that this would be the last time that I would see her, and by extension my last contact with the last of my interview partners. I suddenly realized that I was not sure what I was going to say to her.

I knew that, if I walked in her door, I would feel an overwhelming desire to tell her *this* story: to remind her of all that had passed between us during the interviews, and after, and through our letters over the years, and then over hot chocolate; and then to explain to her how this story, a story of our friendship, had come to play such an important role in my life, though even as I walked up the stairs to her apartment, I still could not yet find the words to explain precisely what that role had been.

But I also felt a strong, even overwhelming, compulsion to resist saying anything of the sort to her. I did not want her to think that I was somehow letting her off the Nazi hook. I did not want her to use me to verify her completion of the course in *Vergangenheitsbewältigung* 101 with a passing grade.

I thought of my responsibility to the dead. Before my eyes, as I walked up the stairs, I could literally see the images of death-camp inmates and gassed Jews making their claims on me in the present. And they were not just anonymous Jews; they were also my family. I worried that I would betray them, and myself, if I was honest with her.

Clancy: "So what did you do?"

I rang the bell. We greeted each other. She took my jacket and I sat down on her couch in her living room. I waited until she got the tea and cookies organized. I poured for us because she had gotten so blind in the meantime that we both feared that she would miss the cup and pour hot water all over the table. Then, as I stirred sugar into my tea, but before I took any of the cookies, I told her a story: a story about the two of us, about our relationship, and our work together to make sense of historical responsibility in the shadow of terror and genocide.

What decided the matter for me at that moment was the fact that we were back again in her living room for yet another conversation. It reminded me of the obvious: that, by 2009, we had known each other for seventeen years, and for all of these seventeen years, she had tried to confront her responsibility for the Nazi past. And here she was trying to work on it some more. *She was not done.*

She listened and she thought and she acted. I realized that I could trust that she would not abuse this information about me, and us, to act as if she had somehow mastered her Nazi past. But I also came to understand that this was a bit of an excuse. In that moment, I realized that there were certain things about myself that I could figure out only with her. I needed her help at that moment to make sense of what I had experienced during our many years of interaction. She taught me that about responsible selfhood.

Steve: "So what precisely did you say to her?"

I said that her recognition of my ambiguous feelings towards her in 2006 meant more to me than I realized at the time. I told her about how I retold this story many time in the intervening years. And I told her that, as a result, the Holocaust does not hang around my neck quite so heavily as it did before.

Theodora responded: "That makes me so very happy."

She then thanked me for sharing this with her, and she turned the conversation to contemporary racism, and the need to be vigilant—as if she was as aware as I of the danger that either of us might seek closure on the Nazi past. We agreed on the need to respond—there can be no rest. I then told her about this book and summarized its contents, since she cannot read English and struggles to read at all, given her failing eyesight. We had not yet put her into the book; but as always, she wanted to know the latest from my research. Then we went on to discuss our families and our lives. *Gott und die Welt.*

Steve gestures at Drew with the book. "I wonder if she is not a bit of a role model for him."

"I think it's all rather ironic," Scott replies. "The very talents which enabled Drew to conduct such interesting interviews—his research skills—also prevented him for so long from learning the meaning of responsible selfhood for himself."

"In Theodora," Clancy adds, "it sounds like Drew found a willing collaborator."

Open Models

In the silence Steve marks the time, tapping the book in his hand.

Out of the blue Reinhard smiles and winks. Drew feels a pang of guilt and uncertainty.

"You came to understand Reinhard," Steve observes. "You enjoyed being with him just as you liked Theodora."

"Yes," Drew admits. "I liked talking with him. His irony was very amusing. But it always left me feeling unsure as to what he really believed."

"So he was a *skilled* ironist."

"Yes. It made me feel totally uncomfortable that I had befriended this man who I knew hid his collusion with the Nazi regime behind that same irony."

"His irony attracted and repulsed. It reminds you of the fragmentary nature of your own self, of the many masks that you also wear, and of the ways you deceive yourself and others."

"I just did not like the way that I identified with him. I felt that he had somehow tricked me into liking him."

"He did!" Clancy laughs. "The ironist always solicits interpretation and identification from his audience."[21]

"You feel betrayed because Reinhard used irony to solicit your collaboration in whitewashing his Nazi past."

---

21 Hutcheon, *Irony's Edge*, 121.

"So how is that interpretive collaboration done ethically?"

"More to the point, how do we solicit collaboration, both for responsibility and in a responsible way, from our readers and students? We should not leave the most effective strategies to the fascists."[22]

By now, the riot is in full swing. Blood shows on the pavement and on the hands and faces of the rioters. Bodies accumulate.

Scott once again played the theater critic. "Brecht talks about something close to this point. He thought his ideal audience member would take advantage of the opening provided by the play to explore their own beliefs about responsible action in that context. But he also believed that his audience member could do so on the basis of recognized interests, or *erkannte Interessen*.[23] The audience member must bring to bear the fragmentary experience of their own everyday life in similar situations in order to make sense of these performances."

"It is similar to the way myth operates." Steve falls back into his role as a political theologian. "It's up to the reader of a myth to recognize those human situations as similar to the situations that he faces in everyday life. But myth leaves open the possibility of reinterpretation: either performing or writing new myths."

"Mate," Zarathustra announces. He takes Karl's last pawn. It was a surprise move.

"In other words, we do not have to give up on irony." Steve speaks with his hands; the book serves as an extension of his arm.

"We can trust that our readers will recognize its value even for as sensitive a topic as the Nazi past. We can hope that they will make their own associations between the stories we have told and analogous situations in their own lives or their own research."

The riot escalates. Some of the combatants try to run away. Baptist, for one, does not. He steps back, watches, and begins to question. A few join him in conversation.

Steve looks at the young soldier. "We all have faced this challenge in everyday life: when we know intuitively that we are collaborating in violence; and yet up to this point, we did not fully appreciate our options for how we can act differently. Thanks to our book, we have some viable tools at our disposal."

He opens the book. "We understand the importance of interrogating our self-deceptions so that we do not let them master us. We see the value of doing the unexpected act and maneuvering in doubt. We know that responsible

---

22 Bauman, *Modernity*; Koslov, *Gewalt*.
23 Brecht, "Thesen über die Aufgabe der Einfühlung in den theatralischen Künsten," *GBA*, vol. 22.1, 175-176.

selfhood emerges only within our ambiguous relationships with other human beings. We appreciate our potential to commit irony on behalf of the victims of history."

"And now," Steve turns to us, "through this dialogue, we have rediscovered that responsibility also involves modeling responsible selfhood for ourselves and others. It is up to us, to them, to all of us, to figure out how to do so in particular situations."

Hannah is safely away from the chaos but she cannot stop looking at it either. She speaks: "There is something I learned."

We look for her instructor but he is long gone.

"The reason why you should not kill, even if no one can see you, is that you cannot possibly want to be together with a murderer. By committing murder, you deliver yourself to the company of a murderer for as long as you live."[24]

Walter's glasses lie broken on the pavement. The young soldier picks them up. He stands on the edge of darkness, in the middle of the street, half way up the hill, looking backwards towards the riot, unwilling to take his eyes away from the destruction.

He carefully begins to clean the blood from the spectacles with his shirt.

The theologian closes the book. "It seems that we missed the most obvious and perhaps most crucial aspect of responsible selfhood: its unruly method of transmission."

Unexpectedly, he crosses the street. He enters the courtyard and digs through the seething crowd until he finds Reinhard. We follow.

"Excuse me, Reinhard," he says. "I've heard many of the humorous stories from your life during the Third Reich from Drew. I wonder if I could ask you some questions too."

"Sure."

"How did you learn to be an ironist?"

"First and foremost," Reinhard insists, "I was a non-conformist. I inherited my seemingly oppositional spirit from my mother and she from her father."[25]

"But what about *your* father? Didn't you learn how to be 'too clever' from him?"

"No, he was that *other* kind of clever—called *dumb*. He deceived himself into thinking otherwise. I only played the idiot. He really was one."

"Did you ever consider that maybe he was playing the idiot too?"

Reinhard shrugs. "That would have been clever of him."

---

24 Adapted from Arendt, *The Promise of Politics*, ed. Jerome Kohn (New York: Schocken Books, 2005), 22.

25 G134a 20:50.

"Did you have any other role models?"

"Well, when I used to play hooky by hiding in the school's workroom, my teacher in *Hauptschule* came once in a while to check up on me. He ended up staying to help me build my model gliders."[26]

He thinks for a moment. "And then there was Henry Selle. Though he was the Leader of the Glider Corps, Selle was only a nominal member of the Nazi Aviation Corps. He only had his uniform and his badges, but inside he was different. Only on the outside was he a Nazi, not on the inside. Just like my class teacher. Exactly the same."[27]

"Anyone else?"

"In the military, I had the Leadership Officer. He would come to visit his old unit to see if everyone was there. But as soon as the door was closed and he was alone again with us ordinary soldiers, then it all started. 'Who knows the latest joke?' Instead of lecturing his old comrades about 'Final Victory' or some other Party slogan as he was supposed to do, we gossiped and laughed. I felt like I was back with Selle in the glider troop."[28]

"You can meet them if you would like," Reinhard continues. "They are all here with me." He points to his four drinking buddies. "We have a *Stammtisch*."

For a moment, the circle of friends seems to insulate Reinhard artificially from the war taking place around him.

"No thank you. But we sincerely appreciate your candor, and your willingness to share your stories."

We look around us. There is no way to fight our way back out. We are caught in the midst of the violence. We have to shout to be heard.

The theologian speaks first: "I don't think that we have to look much further to understand how to promote responsible selfhood than those human relationships that stand at the core of our lives. Teaching is a good example but it's just one of them. Our responsibilities lie here, in the kinds of people we are with others."

The philosopher follows: "Listening to Reinhard, I cannot help but think of the positive alternative that Nietzsche posits in *Ecce Homo*.[29] Nietzsche wrote this book at the very end of his life. As he reflected back on his intellectual life from its finish, he summarized his critical agenda simply as expecting more from human beings than they normally wish to give. His *Übermensch* was a self-deceptive, ironic non-conformist who is not estranged or removed from reality but exemplifies all of its ambiguities and contradictions."

---

26 G134a 22:50, 26:00.
27 G133b 30:20; G134a 00:00; G135b 21:13.
28 G135a 17:00.
29 Nietzsche, "Why I am a Fatality," in *Ecce Homo*, 326-335.

The literary critic: "Nietzsche was imagining a new kind of human being who's strong enough, courageous enough, and above all skeptical enough to challenge his conventional neighbors to socially and intellectually responsible action."

Finally the historian: "Nietzsche 'became' Zarathustra in his own mythologizing prose because he recognized that the best way to promote this kind of responsible selfhood is by modeling it for himself and others."

The theologian taps the book in his hand. The wounded and dead accumulate at their feet.

"So, here we are."

"This door will never open—at least not for us."

"We must do something."

The literary critic rubs his hands. "Something surprising."

"But what?" the philosopher asks. "Do we simply participate in the violence and hope for the best?"

"There are no good choices here."

"Then at least we are aware of our own tragic condition."

"And yet," the historian says hopefully, "here we are doing things—lots of things."

"We are already responding," the literary critic suggests.

The theologian nods. "Why not try to act responsibly?"

They get to work.

One strikes with blows carefully and intentionally placed. The book is weighty enough to serve as a bludgeon.

One flashes news of the battle across the globe with chilling prose and simultaneous audiovisual. Laid on its side and turned length-wise, the book proves useful as a platform for new media.

One uses the body as a human shield, insisting on non-violence. The book deflects at least one blow to the heart. Lucky it was hardcover.

One pulls the wounded into the safety of the street for care—elevating a lacerated leg with this and several other thick books—and lays out the dead in meticulous rows.

Each of us must do what we can in the situation given to us. You may choose to make impassioned pleas for intervention. You may offer to help both sides find ways back to peace. You may admonish, threaten, beg, bribe, steal, or even fight. You try not to make matters worse than they already are.

But there are no assurances.

One Way To Imagine It

There is a pub on Himmelsthürstraße. Its windows are dark and shuttered. Inside nothing stirs.

The basin in its courtyard is filled with clean running water; its pavement covered in blood. Some wash their hands after their work, some to begin it.

"The matter is hardly settled."

The theologian sits on the curb. Blood runs from his forehead. The historian tends to him. The violence continues.

"But we have done all that we can for now."

The literary critic sighs. He is dirty and tired. "We were not very surprising in the end."

The philosopher picks up the book. It is in a bad state. "At least we tried."

The theologian's stomach growls loudly. They laugh, and suddenly recall where they started that evening: in the search for sustenance.

The historian smiles.

"What?"

"That reminds me of something I just read in *Ethics of the Fathers*."

"What's that?"

"A collection of aphorisms: part of the commentaries on the *Torah* originally used by Jewish judges as a training manual."

"A book of ethics?"

"Not exactly a book. It had been an oral tradition for many centuries, handed down from teacher to student generation after generation. It was recorded only in the third century of the common era."

Two Rabbis stand at the wrought-iron fence. One speaks while the other transcribes.

"Where there is no meal, there is no teaching; where there is no teaching, there is no meal."[30]

"I think it is time we prepare a meal for ourselves."

So they head up the hill to the grocery store. Theodora is gone with her cart. Perhaps they will see her again. They hope so.

Then they head down the hill. They look back one last time at the pub. They see Baptist with some students, immobile in the middle of the street, transfixed by the mass of bodies on the pavement and trying to figure out what to do next. He is wearing Walter's glasses.

They reach a rented apartment in town but take no rest. They wash, chop, mix, season, fry, and bake. They convert the raw into the cooked.

---

30 Adapted from *Chapters of the Fathers*, comm. Rabbi Pinhas Kehati, trans. Rabbi Abraham J. Ehrlich and Avner Tomaschoff (Jerusalem: World Zionist Organization, 1986), 3:17.

"The German spirit is an indigestion," Zarathustra recites in a single spotlight from a lifeless stage. "It does not finish with anything."[31] But they do not notice him, and the scenery changes for the next act.

"There is no way to ensure that readers will respond as we wish."

"No, that is the irony."

They put the book down to free their hands for their new project. In a single large bowl they combine a pound of whole-grain human needs with a heaping tablespoon of finely milled self-deception, a carefully measured cup of hope, and a dash of myth. They stir the dry ingredients and add just enough of the unexpected to make a thick batter. They wait—in the silence that follows both labor and death—until their collaboration starts to show bubbles.

"But that uncertainty is far better than compelling our readers to be free."

They fall into the rhythm of the familiar. There is always another meal to prepare, for there always will be hunger to contend with, just as there will always be violence. Still we must imagine them happy.

"Just so I am clear about it: are we actually considering using fictionalized performances of irony to finish an academic monograph?"

"That is one way to finish it but by no means the only way. By choosing one, we are not excluding the possibility that we might choose another in a different situation."

"Or that there is more that needs to be said and asked."

"Or that we got it wrong."

Drew shakes his head. "This book is really going to undermine our credentials. People are going to think we are not taking the issue of the Nazi past seriously."

"Or they will see that we are utterly serious about grounding our ability to respond ethically to terror and genocide in the only kind of self we actually have."

They pour the batter into a pan lined with parchment paper and liberally sprinkle the top with the capacity, every day perpetually, to renew the work of creation.[32] They put it in the oven and set the timer.

They pause to reflect on what they have made, but the next task is already at hand.

"No one would publish it."

"It would take a lot of courage."

They raise their drinks in anticipation of the meal and the continuing conversation it will foster about human beings in the world.

"One might very well envy a life free from such courage?"

---

31 Nietzsche, *Ecce Homo*, 238.

32 Cf. Rabbi Nosson Scherman and Rabbi Maier Zlotowitz, *The Complete Artscroll Siddur* (Brooklyn: Mesorah Publications, 1990), 84-85.

Bibliography

Interview Collections

Andrew Stuart Bergerson. Interview with Hans F. One narrative interview on a single 90-minute tape cassette conducted in English in his home in Locust Valley, New York, on 28 December 1989. Miscellaneous Interview Collection. M001.

——————. "Geselligkeit in Hildesheim zwischen den Kriegen." 126 audio, 13 written interviews on 198 (mostly) 60-minute cassettes conducted mostly in German in Hildesheim, Germany; Tel Aviv and Haifa, Israel; Chicago, Washington, and New York, USA from 1991 to 1994. Stadtarchiv Hildesheim Bestand 904-2.

Books etc.

Abel, Theodore. *Why Hitler Came into Power*. Cambridge, MA: Harvard University Press, 1938.

Agamben, Giorgio. *Homo Sacer: Sovereign Power and Bare Life*. Trans. Daniel Heller-Roazen. Palo Alto: Stanford University Press, 1998.

——————. *The Time that Remains: A Commentary on the Letter to the Romans*. Trans. Patricia Dailey. Palo Alto: Stanford University Press, 2005.

"Algeria: Truth and Justice Obscured by the Shadow of Impunity." *Amnesty International*, 8 November 2000. >http://wwww.amnesty.org/en/library/info/MDE28/014/2000/2n>. Downloaded November 2008.

Allen, William Sheridan. *The Nazi Seizure of Power: The Experience of a Single German Town, 1922-1945*. New York: Franklin Watts, 1965.

Andersen, Hans Christian. "The Emperor's New Clothes." 1837. Trans. H. P. Paull, 1872. Downloaded from *Hans Christian Anderson: Fairy Tales and Stories* http://hca.gilead.org.il/emperor.html, October 2008.

Appleby, Joyce. Lynn Hunt, and Margaret Jacob. *Telling the Truth about History*. New York: W. W. Norton, 1995.

Arendt, Hannah. *Eichmann in Jerusalem: A Report on the Banality of Evil*. New York: Penguin Books, 2006.

——————. *Essays in Understanding 1930-1954: Formation, Exile, and Totalitarianism*. Ed. Jerome Kohn. New York: Schocken, 1994.

——————. *The Human Condition*. 2nd Ed. Chicago: University of Chicago Press, 1998.

——————. *The Origins of Totalitarianism*. New York: Harcourt, Brace, 1951.

——————. *The Promise of Politics*. Ed. Jerome Kohn. New York: Schocken Books, 2005.

——————. "Reflections on Little Rock." *Responsibility and Judgment*. Ed. Jerome Kohn, 193-213. New York: Schocken, 2003.

Aristotle, *Nicomachean Ethics*. Trans. David Ross. Oxford: Oxford University Press, 1998.

Barbin, Herculine. *Being the Recently Discovered Memoirs of a Nineteenth Century French Hermaphrodite*. Intro. Michel Foucault. Trans. Richard McDougall. New York: Pantheon, 1980.

Bauman, Zygmunt. *Modernity and The Holocaust*. Ithaca: Cornell University Press, 1989.

Beauvoir, Simone de. *The Ethics of Ambiguity*. Trans. Bernard Frechtman. New York: Citadel, 1976.

Benjamin, Walter. *Walter Benjamin: Selected Writings*. Trans. Edmund Jephcott and others. Ed. Howard Eiland and Michael W. Jennings. 4 vols. Cambridge, MA: Belknap Press of Harvard University Press, 1996-2003.

Bergen, Doris L. *War and Genocide: A Concise History of the Holocaust*. New York: Rowman & Littlefeld, 2003.

Berger, Stefan. *The Search for Normality: National Identity and Historical Consciousness in Germany since 1800*. New York: Berghahn, 2007.

Bergerson, Andrew Stuart. "Aufklärung durch Erzählung: mündliche Geschichte und bürgerliche Gesellschaft nach Hitler." In *Inspecting Germany: Internationale Deutschland-Ethnographie der Gegenwart*. Ed. Bernd Jürgen Warneken and Thomas Hauschild, 222-249. Berlin: Lit Verlag, 2002.

—————. "A History of Neighborliness in Alt-Hildesheim, 1900-50: Custom, Transformation, Memory." Doctoral Dissertation. History Department. University of Chicago, 1998.

—————. "Eigensinn, Ethik, und die nationalsozialistische *Refomatio vitae*," *Sehnsucht nach Nähe: Interpersonale Kommunkation in Deutschland seit dem 19. Jahrhundert*, 127-56. Ed. Moritz Föllmer. Stuttgart: Franz Steiner Verlag, 2004.

—————. "Forum: Everyday Life in Nazi Germany." *German History* 27/4 (October): 560-579.

—————. "Narrating Enlightenment: oral history and civil society after Hitler," *Issues in Integrative Studies* 16 (1998): 31-55.

—————. *Ordinary Germans in Extraordinary Times: The Nazi Revolution in Hildesheim*. Bloomington: Indiana University Press, 2004.

Berghaus, Günter. *Theatre, Performance, and the Historical Avant-Garde*. New York: Palgrave Macmillan, 2005.

Berlin, Isaiah. *The Magus of the North: J. G. Hamann and the Origins of Modern Irrationalism*. Ed. Henry Hardy. London: John Murray, 1993.

Blackbourn, David and Geoff Eley. *The Peculiarities of German History: Bourgeois Society and Politics in 19th century Germany*. Oxford: Oxford University Press, 1984.

Bloch, Ernst. *Heritage of Our Times*. Trans. Neville and Stephen Plaice. Berkeley: University of California Press, 1990.

Blumenfeld, Ralph. *Henry Kissinger: The Private and Public Story*. New York: Signet, 1974.

Booth, W. James. *Communities of Memory: On Witness, Identity, and Justice*. Ithaca: Cornell University Press, 2006.

Brecht, Bertolt. *A Man's A Man*. Trans. Eric Bentley. *Seven Plays by Bertolt Brecht*. Ed. Bentley, 69-147. New York: Grove Press, 1961.

—————. *Mann ist Mann*. Berlin: Suhrkamp Verlag, 1953.

—————. *Grosse kommentierte Berliner und Frankfurter Ausgabe*. 30 vols. Frankfurt: Suhrkamp, 1988-2000.

—————. "To Those Born Later." *German 20th Century Poetry*. Ed. R. Grimm and I. E. Hunt. Trans. Joh Willet, 84-89. New York: Continuum Books, 2001.

Broszat, Martin and Elke Fröhlich, eds. *Bayern in der NS-Zeit*, 6 vols. Munich: Oldenbourg, 1977-1983.

Browning, Christopher R. *Nazi Policy, Jewish Workers, German Killers*. Cambridge: Cambridge University Press, 2000.

—————. *The Origins of the Final Solution: The Evolution of Nazi Jewish Policy, September 1939-March 1942*. Lincoln: University of Nebraska Press, 2004.

Brustein, William. *The Logic of Evil: The Social Origins of the Nazi Party, 1925-1933*. New Haven: Yale University Press, 1996.

Buber, Martin. *I and Thou*. Trans. Walter Kaufmann. New York: Charles Scribner's Sons, 1970.

Burleigh, Michael. *The Third Reich: A New History*. New York: Hill and Wang, 2000.

Burrow. J. W. *The Crisis of Reason: European Thought, 1848-1914*. New Haven: Yale University Press, 2000.

Butler, Judith. *Gender Trouble: Feminism and the Subversion of Identity*. London: Routledge, 1990.

Camus, Albert. "The Myth of Sisyphus." *The Myth of Sisyphus and Other Essays*, 88-91. New York: Vintage International Edition, 1991.

—————. *The Plague*. Trans. Stuart Gilbert. New York: Modern Library, 1948.

Caruth, Cathy, ed. *Trauma: Explorations in Memory*. Baltimore: Johns Hopkins University Press, 1995.

Celan, Paul. *Todesfuge*. Komm. Theo Buck. 2. Auflage. Aachen: Rimbaud, 2002.

Chakrabarty, Dipesh. *Provincializing Europe: Postcolonial Thought and Historical Difference*. Princeton: Princeton University Press, 2000.

Chapters of the Fathers. Comm. Rabbi Pinhas Kehati. Trans. Rabbi Abraham J. Ehrlich and Avner Tomaschoff. Jerusalem: World Zionist Organization, 1986.

Childers, Thomas. *The Nazi Voter: The Social Foundations of Fascism in Germany, 1919-1933*. Chapel Hill: The University of North Carolina Press, 1983.

Connerton, Paul. *How Societies Remember*. Cambridge: Cambridge University Press, 1989.

Culler, Jonathan. *Structuralist Poetics: Structuralism, Linguistics, and the Study of Literature*. Ithaca: Cornell University Press, 1975.

Derrida, Jacques. *Of Grammatology*. Trans. Gayatri C. Spivak. Baltimore: John Hopkins University Press, 1976.

—————. "Violence and Metaphysics." *Writing and Difference*. Trans. Allen Bass, 79-153. Chicago: University of Chicago Press, 1978.

Descartes, Rene. *Discourse on Method and Meditations on First Philosophy*. Trans. Donald A. Cress. 4th edition. Indianapolis: Hackett, 1998.

Durst, David. *Weimar Modernism: Philosophy, Politics, and Culture in Germany 1918-1933*. Lanham: Lexington, 2004.

Elon, Amos. "The Excommunication of Hannah Arendt." Arendt, *Eichmann in Jerusalem*, vii-xxiii.

Ettinger, Elzbieta. *Hannah Arendt/Martin Heidegger*. New Haven: Yale University Press, 1995.

Falk, Richard, "Revisting Westphalia, Discovering Post-Westphalia." *The Journal of Ethics* 6/4 (2002): 311-352.

Felman, Shoshana, and Dori Laub. *Testimony: Crises of Witnessing in Literature, Psychoanalysis, and History*. New York: Routledge, 1992.

Felstiner, John. "Paul Celan's 'Todesfuge'," *Holocaust and Genocide Studies* 1/2 (1986): 249-264.

Feuerbach, Ludwig. *The Essence of Christianity*. Trans. George Eliot. New York: Harper, 1957.

Fischer, Fritz. *Germany's Aims in the First World War*. Trans. James Joll. London: Chatto & Windus, 1967.

Fischer-Lichte, Erica. *Semiotics of the Theater*. Trans. J. Gaines and D. Jones. Bloomington: Indiana University Press, 1992.

Foucault, Michel. *The Care of the Self: The History of Sexuality*. Vol. 3. New York: Vintage, 1986.
—————. *Discipline and Punish: The Birth of the Prison*. Trans. Alan Sheridan. New York: Vintage, 1977.
—————. *Madness and Civilization: A History of Insanity in the Age of Reason*. New York: Vintage, 1988.
Freud, Sigmund. *The Future of an Illusion*. Trans. and ed. James Strachey. New York: W. W. Norton, 1989.
Friedlander, Saul. *Probing the Limits of Representation: Nazism and the "Final Solution."* Cambridge, MA: Harvard University Press, 1992.
Fritzsche, Peter. *Life and Death in the Third Reich*. Cambridge, MA: Harvard University Press, 2008.
—————. "Nazi Modern." *Modernism/Modernity* 3/1 (1996), 1-22.
Gates Jr., Henry Louis. *The Signifying Monkey: A Theory of Afro-American Literary Criticism*. Oxford: Oxford University Press, 1988.
Gebhardt, Miriam. *Das Familiengedächtnis: Erinnerung im deutsch-jüdischen Bürgertum 1890 bis 1932*. Stuttgart: Franz Steiner Verlag, 1999.
Gellateley, Robert. *Backing Hitler: Coercion and Consent in Nazi Germany*. Oxford: Oxford University Press, 2001.
—————. *The Gestapo and German Society: Enforcing Racial Policy, 1933-1945*. Oxford: Clarendon Press, 1990.
Geiss, Immanuel. *July 1914: The Outbreak of the First World War: Selected Documents*. New York: Scribner, 1968.
Geoghegan, Vincent. "Remembering the Future." *Not Yet: Reconsidering Ernst Bloch*. Ed. Jamie David Owen and Tom Moylan, 15-32. London: Verso, 1997.
Goethe, Johann Wolfgang von. *Wilhelm Meister's Apprenticeship*. Trans. Thomas Carlyle. New York: Heritage Press, 1959.
Goffman, Erving. *The Presentation of Self in Everyday Life*. New York: Doubleday, 1959.
Goldhagen, Daniel Jonah. *Hitler's Willing Executioners: Ordinary Germans and the Holocaust*. New York: Alfred A. Knopf, 1996.
Graves, Robert. *Greek Mythology*, vol. 1. New York: Penguin, 1960.
Grimm, Reinhold. "Vom Novum Organum zum Kleinen Organon: Gedanken zur Verfremdung." *Das Ärgernis Brecht*. Ed. Willy Jäggi and Hans Oesch, 51-70. Basel: Basilius, 1961.
Habermas, Jürgen. *A Berlin Republic: Writings on Germany*. Trans. Steven Rendall. Lincoln: University of Nebraska Press, 1997.
—————. *The New Conservatism: Cultural Criticism and the Historians' Debate*. Trans. Shierry Weber Nicholsen. Cambridge, MA: The MIT Press, 1989.
Hamann, Johann Georg. *Briefwechsel*. Ed. Walther Ziesemer and Arthur Henkel. 6 vols. Wiesbaden: Insel Verlag, 1955-1979.
—————. *Sämtliche Werke*. Ed. Joseph Nadler. 6 vols. Vienna: Verlag Herder, 1949-1957.
—————. *Socratic Memorabilia: a Translation and Commentary*. Trans. J. C. O'Flaherty. Baltimore: Johns Hopkins University Press, 1967.
Hamilton, Richard F. "The Rise of Nazism: A Case Study and Review of Interpretations – Kiel, 1928-1933." *German Studies Review* 24/1 (2003): 43-62.
—————. *Who Voted for Hitler?* Princeton: Princeton University Press, 1982.
Handwerk, Gary. *Irony, Ethics and Narrative: From Schlegel to Lacan*. New Haven: Yale University Press, 1995.
Harootunian, Harry. *History's Disquiet: Modernity, Cultural Practice, and the Question of Everyday Life*. New York: Columbia University Press, 2002.

Harvey, Elizabeth. *Women and the Nazi East: Agents and Witnesses of Germanization*. New Haven: Yale University Press, 2003.

Hasenclever, Walter. *Der Sohn*. Munich: K. Wolff, 1917.

Heidegger, Martin. "The Question Concerning Technology." *Martin Heidegger: Basic Writings*. Ed. David Farrell Krell. San Francisco: Harper, 1993.

Hegel, G. W. F. *Elements of a Philosophy of Right*. Ed. Allen W. Wood. Trans. H. B. Nisbet. Cambridge: Cambridge University Press, 1991.

—————. *Phenomenology of Spirit*. Trans. A. V. Miller. Oxford: Oxford University Press, 1977.

—————. *Werke in Zwanzig Bänden*. 20 vols. Frankfurt: Suhrkamp, 1969-1986.

Herwig, Holger H. *The First World War: Germany and Austria-Hungary, 1914-1918*. London: Arnold, 1997.

Hilberg, Raul. *Perpetrators, Victims, Bystanders: The Jewish Catastrophe, 1933-1945*. New York: Aaron Asher, 1992.

Hildebrand, Klaus. *The Third Reich*. London: George Allen and Unwin, 1984.

Hobbes, Thomas. *Leviathan*. Introd. Herbert W. Schneider. Indianapolis: The Liberal Arts Press, 1958.

Horace. *Odes and Epodes*. Ed. by Paul Shorey. The University of Michigan Digital General Collection. January 2006. Http://name.umdl.umich.edu/1808630.0001.001.

Horkheimer, Max and Theodor W. Adorno. *Dialectic of Enlightenment: Philosophical Fragments*. Ed. Gunzelin Schmid Noerr. Trans. Edmund Jephcott. Palo Alto: Stanford University Press, 2002.

Hull, Isabel V. *Absolute Destruction: Military Culture and the Practices of War in Imperial Germany*. Ithaca: Cornell University Press, 2005.

Huston, John. *The Treasure of the Sierra Madre*. Warner Brothers, 1948.

Hutcheon, Linda. *Irony's Edge: The Theory and Politics of Irony*. London: Routledge, 1995.

Isaacson, Walter. *Kissinger: A Biography*. New York: Simon and Schuster, 1992.

Jarausch, Konrad H. and Michael Geyer. *Shattered Past: Reconstructing German Histories*. Princeton: Princeton University Press, 2002.

Kalb, Marvin and Bernard Kalb. *Kissinger*. Boston: Little, Brown and Co, 1974.

Kant, Immanuel. "An Answer to the Question: What is Enlightenment." In *What is Enlightenment? Eighteenth-Century Answers and Twentieth-Century Questions*. Ed. and Trans. James Schmidt, 58-64. Berkeley: University of California Press, 1996.

—————. *Critique of Pure Reason*. Trans. Paul Guyer and Allen Wood. Cambridge: Cambridge University Press, 1999.

—————. *Fundamental Principles of Metaphysics of Morals*. Trans. T. K. Abbot. New York: Prometheus, 1987.

—————. *Prolegomena to Any Future Metaphysics*. Introd. Lewis White Beck. Upper Saddle River: Prentice Hall, 1950.

Kater, Michael. *Hitler Youth*. Cambridge, MA: Harvard University Press, 2004.

Keil, Lars-Broder and Sven Felix Kellerhoff. *Deutsche Legenden: Vom "Dolchstoß" und anderen Mythen der Geschichte*. Berlin: Ch. Links, 2002.

Kershaw, Ian. *The 'Hitler Myth': Image and Reality in the Third Reich*. Oxford: Oxford University Press, 1989.

—————. *Hitler: 1936-1945, Nemesis*. New York: W. W. Norton, 2000.

Kierkegaard, Søren. *The Concept of Irony*. Trans. Howard V. Hong and Edna H. Hong. Princeton: Princeton University Press, 1989.

—————. *Concluding Unscientific Postscript to Philosophical Fragments*. Vol. 1. Trans. and ed. Howard V. Hong and Edna H. Hong. Kierkegaard Writings. Vol. XII. Princeton: Princeton University Press, 1992.

Kocka, Jürgen. "Asymmetrical Historical Comparison: The Case of the German Sonderweg." *History and Theory* 38/1 (1999): 40-50.

Kocks, Klaus. *Brechts literarische Evolution: Untersuchungen zum ästhetisch-ideologischen Bruch in den Dreigroschen-Bearbeitungen.* Munich: Fink, 1981.

Koslov, Elissa Mailänder. *Gewalt im Dienstalltag: Die SS-Aufseherinnen des Konzentrations- und Vernichtungslagers Majdanek 1942-1944.* Hamburg: Hamburger Edition, 2009.

Kundera, Milan. *The Unbearable Lightness of Being.* Trans. Michael Henry Heim. New York: Harper, 1991.

KZ-Gedenk- und Begegnungsstätte Ladelund, <http://www.kz-gedenkstaette-ladelund.de/>, downloaded September 2007.

LaCapra, Dominic. "Revisiting the Historians' Debate: Mourning and Genocide." *History and Memory after Auschwitz,* 43-72. Ithaca: Cornell University Press, 1998.

Landsman, Mark. *Dictatorship and Demand: The Politics of Consumerism in East Germany.* Cambridge MA: Harvard University Press, 2005.

Langer, Lawrence L. *Versions of Survival: The Holocaust and the Human Spirit.* Albany: State University of New York Press, 1982.

Larmore, Charles. *The Romantic Legacy.* New York: Columbia University Press, 1996.

Lethen, Helmut. "The Subject in the Danger Zone." *Telos* 144 (2008): 75-81.

Levi, Primo. *The Drowned and the Saved.* Trans. Raymond Rosenthal. New York: Vintage International, 1989.

Lilla, Mark. "Martin Heidegger—Hannah Arendt—Karl Jaspers." *The Reckless Mind: Intellectuals in Politics,* 1-46. New York: New York Review Books, 2006.

Liulevicius, Vejas Gabriel. *War Land on the Eastern Front: Culture, National Identity and German Occupation in World War I.* Cambridge: Cambridge University Press, 2004.

Locke, John. *Second Treatise of Government.* Ed. C. B. Macpherson. Indianapolis: Hackett, 1980.

Löwith, Karl. *Meaning in History.* Chicago: University of Chicago Press, 1949.

Lukacs, Georg. *The Theory of the Novel: A Historico-Philosophical Essay on the Forms of the Great Epic Literature.* Trans. Anne Bostock. Cambridge: MIT Press, 1977.

Maier, Charles. *The Unmasterable Past: History, Holocaust and German National Identity.* Cambridge: Harvard University Press, 1988.

Malpas, J. E. *Place and Experience: A Philosophical Topography.* Cambridge: Cambridge University Press, 1999.

Marrus, Michael. *The Nuremberg War Crimes Trial, 1945-1946: A Documentary History.* Boston: St. Martin's Press, 1997.

Martin, Clancy. "Nietzsche." *The History of Western Philosophy of Religion.* Ed. Graham Robert Oppy and Nick Trakakis. New York: Oxford University Press, 2009.

Marx, Karl. *The Marx-Engels Reader.* 2nd ed. Ed. Robert C. Tucker. Princeton: Princeton University Press, 1978.

——————, and Friedrich Engels. *The Communist Manifesto.* Ed. John E. Toews. London: St. Martin, 1999.

Mayer, Don. "Sovereign Immunity and the Moral Community." *Business Ethics Quarterly* 2/4 (October, 1992): 411-434.

Mayer, Hans. *Erinnerung an Brecht.* Frankfurt: Suhrkamp, 1996.

Meinecke, Friedrich. *The German Catastrophe: Reflections and Recollections.* Trans. Sidney B. Fay. Cambridge, MA: Harvard University Press, 1950.

Metz, Johann Baptist. "Anamnestic Reason: A Theologian's Remarks on the Crisis in the Geisteswissenschaften." *Cultural-Political Interventions in the Unfinished Project of the Enlightenment.* Ed. Axel Honneth. Thomas McCarthy, Claus Offe, and Albrecht Wellmer. Cambridge: MIT Press, 1992.

—————. "Communicating a Dangerous Memory." *Love's Strategy: The Political Theology of Johann Baptist Metz*. Ed. John K. Downey. Harrisburg: Trinity Press International, 1999.

—————. "The Future Seen from the Memory of Suffering: On the Dialectic of Progress." *Faith in History and Society*. Trans. J. Matthew Ashley, 97-113. New York: Herder and Herder, 2007.

—————. *Hope Against Hope: Johann Baptist Metz and Elie Wiesel Speak Out on the Holocaust*. Ed. Ekkehard Schuster and Reinhold Borschert-Kimmig. Trans. J. Matthew Ashley. New York: Paulist Press, 1999.

Meyer, Sarah [pseudonym]. "Memoires" [altered title], unpublished manuscript.

Mosse, George. *The Nationalization of the Masses: Political Symbolism and Mass Movements in Germany from the Napoleonic Wars through the Third Reich*. New York: Fertig, 1975.

Nietzsche, Friedrich. *On the Genealogy of Morals and Ecce Homo*. Trans. Walter Kaufmann and R. J. Hollingdale. Ed. Kaufmann. New York: Vintage, 1989.

—————. *Daybreak*. Trans. Walter Kaufmann. New York: Viking, 1972.

—————. *Human, all-too-Human*. Trans. Walter Kaufmann. New York: Viking, 1967.

—————. *Thus Spoke Zarathustra*. Trans. Clancy Martin. New York: Barnes and Noble, 2005.

—————. *The Portable Nietzsche*. Ed and Trans. Walter Kaufman. New York: Penguin, 1954.

Nossack, Hans Erich. *The End: Hamburg 1943*. Chicago: University of Chicago Press, 2004.

Nussbaum, Martha. *The Fragility of Goodness: Luck and Ethics in Greek Tragedy and Philosophy*. Updated Ed. Cambridge: Cambridge University Press, 2001.

Orwell, George. *Nineteen Eighty-Four: A Novel*. New York: Harcourt, Brace, 1949.

Ostovich, Steven T. "Carl Schmitt, Political Theology, and Eschatology." *KronoScope: Journal for the Study of Time* 7 (2007): 49-66.

—————. "Dangerous Memories and Reason in History," *KronoScope* 5/1 (2005): 41-57.

—————. "Epilogue: Dangerous Memories." *The Work of Memory: New Directions in the Study of German Society and Culture*. Ed. Alon Confino and Peter Fritzsche, 239-256. Urbana: University of Illinois Press, 2002.

—————. "Melancholy History." *Missing God? Cultural Amnesia and Political Theology*. Ed. John K. Downey, Jürgen Manemann, and Steve Ostovich, 93-101. Berlin: LIT Verlag, 2006.

Otto, Rudolf. *The Idea of the Holy*. Trans. John W. Harvey. 2nd ed. London: Oxford University Press, 1950.

Overesch, Manfred. *Von Hildesheim in die USA: Christ und Jude im Dialog über den Wiederaufbau des Weltkulturerbes St. Michael, 1946-1949*. Hildesheim: Olms, 2004.

Owen, Wilfred. "Dolce et Decorum Est." In *Poems*. Whitefish: Kessinger, 2004.

Peukert, Detlev. *The Weimar Republic: the Crisis of Classical Modernity*. New York: Hill and Wang, 1992.

Piaget, Jean. *The Child and Reality: Problems of Genetic Psychology*. Trans. Arnold Rosin. New York: Grossman, 1973.

Plato. *Collected Dialogues*. Ed. E. Hamilton and H. Cairns. Princeton: Princeton University Press, 1961.

Postone, Moishe. "Antisemitism and National Socialism." *Germans and Jews since the Holocaust*. Ed. Anson Rabinbach and Jack Zipes, 302-315. New York: Holmes and Meier, 1986.

Richter, Gerhard. *Walter Benjamin and the Corpus of Autobiography*. Detroit: Wayne State University Press, 2000.

Rorty, Richard. *Contingency, Irony and Solidarity*. Cambridge: Cambridge University Press, 1989.

Rosenfeld, Gavriel D. *The World Hitler Never Made: Alternate History and the Memory of Nazism*. Cambridge: Cambridge University Press, 2005.

Rousseau, Jean-Jacques. *The Social Contract*. Trans. Maurice Cranston. London: Penguin, 1968.

Saussure, Ferdinand de. *Course in General Linguistics*. Ed. Charles Bally and Albert Sechehaye in coll. with Albert Riedlinger. Trans. Wade Baskin. New York: McGraw-Hill, 1959.

Scherman, Rabbi Nosson, and Rabbi Maier Zlotowitz. *The Complete Artscroll Siddur*. Brooklyn: Mesorah Publications, 1990.

Schleiermacher, Friedrich. *On Religion: Speeches to Its Cultured Despisers*. Trans. John Oman. New York: Harper Press, 1989.

Schlaffer, Heinz. *The Bourgeois as Hero*. Trans. James Lynn. Lanham: Rowman & Littlefield, 1990.

Schlegel, Friedrich. *Philosophical Fragments*. Trans. Peter Firchow. Minneapolis: The University of Minnesota Press, 1991.

Schmitt, Carl. *Political Theology: Four Chapters on the Concept of Sovereignty*. Trans. George Schwab. Chicago: University of Chicago Press, 2005.

—————. *Political Theology II: The Myth of the Closure of Any Political Theology*. Trans. Michael Hoelzel and Graham Wind. Cambridge: Polity Press, 2008.

Schneewind, J. B. "Autonomy, Obligation, and Virtue: An Overview of Kant's Moral Philosophy." *The Cambridge Companion to Kant*. Ed. Paul Guyer. Cambridge: Cambridge University Press, 1992.

Schreyer, Lothar. "Das Bühnenkunstwerk." *Der Sturm* 7 (August 1916).

—————. "Das Bühnenkunstwerk: Die Wirklichkeit des Geistes." *Der Sturm* 8 (May 1917).

Schoenbaum, David. *Hitler's Social Revolution: Class and Status in Nazi Germany, 1933-1939*. New York: W. W. Norton, 1980.

Sedgwick, Eve Kosofsky. *Epistemology of the Closet*. Berkeley: University of California Press, 1990.

Siemens, Daniel. *Horst Wessel: Tod und Verklärung eines Nationalsozialisten*. Munich: Siedler, 2009.

Smith, Helmut Walser. *The Butcher's Tale: Murder and Antisemitism in a German Town*. New York: Norton, 2002.

Spiegel, Gabrielle M. "Introduction." *Practicing History: New Directions in Historical Writing after the Linguistic Turn*. Ed. Spiegel, 1-31. London: Routledge, 2005.

Stedman, Stephen John. "Spoiler Problems in Peace Processes." *International Security* 22/2 (1997): 5-53.

Steege, Paul. *Black Market, Cold War: Everyday Life in Berlin, 1946-1949*. Cambridge: Cambridge University Press, 2007.

—————, Andrew Stuart Bergerson, Maureen Healy, and Pamela Swett. "The History of Everyday Life: A Second Chapter." *Journal of Modern History* 80 (June 2007): 358-378.

Swett, Pamela. *Neighbors and Enemies: The Culture of Radicalism in Berlin 1929-1933*. Cambridge: Cambridge University Press, 2004.

Szondi, Peter. *On Textual Understanding and Other Essays*. Trans. Harvey Mendelsohn. Minneapolis: The University of Minnesota Press, 1986.

Taylor, Richard. "The Meaning of Life," *Good and Evil*, 256-68. Buffalo: Prometheus, 1984.

Theweleit, Klaus. *Male Fantasies*. Minneapolis: University of Minnesota Press, 1987.

Villa, Dana R. *Arendt and Heidegger: The Fate of the Political*. Princeton: Princeton University Press, 1996.

Vlastos, Gregory. *Socrates: Ironist and Moral Philosopher.* Ithaca: Cornell University Press, 1995.

Weber, Max. *Theory of Social and Economic Organization.* Trans. A. M. Henderson and Talcott Parsons. New York: Free Press, 1947.

White, Hayden. *Tropics of Discourse: Essays in Cultural Criticism.* Baltimore: Johns Hopkins University Press, 1978.

Whyte, William H. "Groupthink." *Fortune* (March 1952): 114-117, 142, 146.

Wildt, Michael. *Volksgemeinschaft als Selbstermächtigung: Gewalt gegen Juden in der deutschen Provinz 1919 bis 1939.* Hamburg: Hamburger Edition, 2007.

Williams, Simon. *German Actors of the Eighteenth and Nineteenth Centuries: Idealism, Romanticism, and Realism.* Contributions in Drama and Theatre Studies 12. Westport: Greenwood Press, 1985.

Wittgenstein, Ludwig. *Philosophical Investigations.* Trans. G. E. M. Anscombe, P. M. S. Hacket and Joachim Schulte. 4th Ed. Oxford: John Wiley and Son, 2009.

Wolin, Richard. "Carl Schmitt: The Conservative Revolution and the Aesthetics of Horror." *Labyrinths: Explorations in the Critical History of Ideas*, 103-122. Amherst, MA: University of Massachusetts Press, 1995.

—————. "Carl Schmitt, Political Existentialism and the Total State." *The Terms of Cultural Criticism: The Frankfurt School, Existentialism, Poststructuralism*, 83-104. New York: Columbia University Press, 1992.

Young-Bruehl, Elisabeth. *Hannah Arendt: For Love of the World.* New Haven: Yale University Press, 1982.

www.ingramcontent.com/pod-product-compliance
Lightning Source LLC
Chambersburg PA
CBHW070027100426
42740CB00013B/2613

* 9 7 8 3 1 1 0 4 8 5 9 7 4 *